D0312380

# NEW FOUNDATIONS THEOLOGICAL LIBRARY

*General Editor*

PETER TOON, MA, M.TH, D.PHIL

*Consultant Editor*

RALPH P. MARTIN, MA, PH.D

# NEW FOUNDATIONS THEOLOGICAL LIBRARY

OLD TESTAMENT THEOLOGY:
A FRESH APPROACH
*by R. E. Clements*

EVANGELICAL THEOLOGY 1833–1856:
A RESPONSE TO TRACTARIANISM
*by Peter Toon*

NEW TESTAMENT PROPHECY
*by David Hill*

*Other volumes in preparation*

# OLD
# TESTAMENT
# THEOLOGY

*A Fresh Approach*

RONALD E. CLEMENTS
Fitzwilliam College, Cambridge

JOHN KNOX PRESS

ATLANTA

Copyright © Ronald E. Clements 1978

**Library of Congress Cataloging in Publication Data**

Clements, Ronald Ernest, 1929–
  Old Testament theology.

  (New foundations theological library)
  Bibliography: p. 207
  Includes indexes.
    1. Bible. O.T.—Theology. I. Title. II. Series.
BS1192.5.04 1979      221.6      79–16704
ISBN 0–8042–3701–8


Co-published by Marshall, Morgan & Scott in Great Britain in 1978 (in
Marshalls Theological Library) and John Knox Press in the United
States of America in 1979.


John Knox Press
Atlanta, Georgia


Printed in Great Britain by
St. Edmundsbury Press Limited, Haverhill, Suffolk

TO THE STUDENTS OF
SPURGEON'S COLLEGE
PAST, PRESENT, AND TO COME

# CONTENTS

PREFACE     ix

1. THE PROBLEM OF OLD TESTAMENT THEOLOGY    1
   1. The Origins of Old Testament Theology    4
   2. Historical Criticism and Theological Method    11
   3. The Old Testament as Canon    15
   4. The Old Testament and the Bible    19

2. DIMENSIONS OF FAITH IN THE OLD TESTAMENT    26
   1. The Literary Dimension of Faith    27
   2. The Historical Dimension of Faith    33
   3. The Cultic Dimension of Faith    40
   4. The Intellectual Dimension of Faith    46

3. THE GOD OF ISRAEL    53
   1. The Being of God    58
   2. The Names of God    62
   3. The Presence of God    66
   4. The Uniqueness of God    72

4. THE PEOPLE OF GOD    79
   1. People and Nation    82
   2. The Theology of Election    87
   3. The Theology of Covenant    96

5. THE OLD TESTAMENT AS LAW    104
   1. The Meaning of *tôrâh*    106
   2. The Pentateuch as *tôrâh*    110
   3. The *tôrâh* and the Prophets    120
   4. From *tôrâh* to Law    127

6. THE OLD TESTAMENT AS PROMISE    131
   1. Prophecy and the Judgment of Israel    137
   2. Prophecy and Hope    140
   3. The Forms of Prophetic Hope    144
   4. The Promise in the Law and the Writings    149

7. THE OLD TESTAMENT AND THE HISTORY
    OF RELIGION                                          155
    1. The Old Testament and the Religions of the
       Ancient East                                      157
    2. Religious Polemic in the Old Testament            165
    3. Authority in Israelite Religion                   170
    4. The Old Testament in Religion                     174

8. THE OLD TESTAMENT AND THE STUDY OF
    THEOLOGY                                             179
    1. The Old Testament and Biblical Study              182
    2. The Old Testament and the Study of Theology       186
    3. The Old Testament and the Study of Religion       191
    4. The Old Testament and Mankind                     196

NOTES                                                    201

SELECT BIBLIOGRAPHY                                      207

GENERAL INDEX                                            210

INDEX OF AUTHORS                                         211

INDEX OF BIBLICAL REFERENCES                             212

# PREFACE

The lectures set out here are based upon a course given under the Louisa Curtis Foundation at Spurgeon's College, London, on 21–23 January, 1975. I have taken the opportunity provided by a period of sabbatical leave, and prompted by numerous suggestions of colleagues, to develop the original arguments into the form here presented. That they still represent only a tentative essay in a well-trodden field will be obvious to all Old Testament scholars.

Already there are a number of 'Theologies of the Old Testament' in current publication, as well as many volumes of history and critique of the subject. Rumour indicates that even more volumes of a similar kind are in course of preparation. I am genuinely reluctant to add to them, however disingenuous such a remark must appear in a preface of this nature. The original lectures were intended primarily as a critique of the theologies of the Old Testament which are at present available, with some suggestions about the way in which the discipline might be carried further. To have published them in this form, however, would quite properly have been subject to the criticism that they simply exploited the difficulties which others have sought to overcome. I have therefore endeavoured to carry the arguments of the original lectures further in the direction of suggesting how a theology of the Old Testament might look.

It will become clear to the person who reads this book that much of the argument hinges upon the question of the essential nature of theological thinking. That theology is the handmaid of religion, and not necessarily its crowning achievement, is a conviction that underlies this work. Writing from a Christian context, I find myself, in the company of most Christians, committed to the Old Testament as a consequence of the history and genesis of my own faith. To pretend that this is not so, and that some better reasons for studying the Old Testament might be found, would not be intellectually honest. There is a need therefore for seeking to understand the Old Testament theologically from this perspective. I am also made very profoundly aware that the Old Testament is a Jewish book, and that the pattern of study of Old Testament theology, as it has developed, offers little by way of understanding and explanation of this relevance of the Old Testament to Judaism. The failure here seems particularly lamentable, especially in its consequences for Christian theological education.

A third factor has also impinged upon the arguments laid out in the following pages. At the present time the study of theology in an academic context is being seriously, and quite properly, challenged by the need for a fuller attention to the problems of the historical and comparative study of religion. No more readily available text exists for beginning this than the Old Testament, since it occupies a central place in the sacred texts of Judaism and Christianity and has profoundly affected a third religion, Islam. Furthermore, the study of the Old Testament raises many far-reaching issues about the nature of religion and the role of theology and rational thought within it. Not least also the Old Testament continues to affect very profoundly the attitudes adopted towards other religions by Christians, Jews and Muslims. In all of these ways, therefore, a renewed interest in the theological impact of the Old Testament would appear to be highly desirable. To add yet another volume, therefore, to an already overcrowded library of volumes on this subject can at least be defended.

R. E. CLEMENTS

*October 1977*

# CHAPTER ONE

# THE PROBLEM OF OLD TESTAMENT THEOLOGY

The large and varied number of theological works which are currently available bearing the title of 'Old Testament Theology' would lead us to suppose that we know clearly what such a subject is. Yet there is a considerable diversity of content in such volumes, and increasingly it has become commonplace for them to devote a good deal of time and attention to a relatively extended treatment of matters of introduction explaining what the discipline is. If we may judge by the progress of scholarly discussion in the past thirty years, we may feel entirely justified in drawing the conclusion that the most interesting and controversial aspects of the subject are to be found in these 'introductions'. Once we know how a particular scholar intends to treat the subject, it is usually not difficult to plot with a reasonable predictability what he will actually have to say about the theological significance of the Old Testament. In other words, the resolution of certain basic issues concerning the nature and proper methodology of the subject tends to exercise a dominant effect upon what the Old Testament is actually believed to offer by way of a 'theology'.

Two other relevant points may be made here. The first is that this pursuit of an Old Testament theology has been an exclusively Christian undertaking. It is hard to find more than a very few tentative essays in this field from the pens of Jewish scholars.

Secondly, and this may be felt to be even more surprising, these presentations of Old Testament theology bear very little relationship either to the way in which the New Testament interprets the Old, or to the ways in which Christian theologians of all periods have actually made theological use of the Old Testament.

In fact, alongside the production of specialised Old Testament theologies there have still appeared a considerable number of important theological books which endeavour to grasp theologically the contents of the Bible as a whole, with little more than passing reference to the distinctive and self-imposed restraints of those who have chosen the narrower goal.

At other times compromises have appeared, in the form of volumes which set out to be 'Christian' theologies of the Old Testament, but where it immediately becomes clear to the critical reader that an almost impossible task is being attempted. Christian assumptions are taken to be necessary and proper to the work, but their explicit description and nature is forbidden because they cannot be made to conform to the historical limitation of dealing only with those ideas which are to be found in the Old Testament. Even here, however, it is striking to note that far too little space is devoted to noting the actual ways in which Christians have made theological use of the Old Testament, and a rather arbitrary selection is made of particular Christian connections with this literature.

Increasingly, therefore, we find that specialised treatments are being called for regarding the very nature and possibility of a subject calling itself 'Old Testament Theology'.[1] One thing at least is clear: the appropriate methodology for such a subject is much less obvious than it has frequently been assumed to be, and still calls forth a substantial debate.

We may begin our attempt to re-open the question of the proper method for an Old Testament theology by taking as our starting-point one of the simplest and most straightforward of the definitions that have been proposed for the subject. This is to be found in E. Jacob's *Theology of the Old Testament*, and is chosen for its representative character:

> The theology of the Old Testament may be defined as the systematic account of the specific religious ideas which can be found throughout the Old Testament and which form its profound unity.[2]

We may immediately seize upon those words which raise the most far-reaching questions about the subject, and the possibility of fulfilling its demands. These are: *systematic – religious ideas – unity*. In the first place we may take it for granted that a theology should be about religious ideas. But since religion is very much more than a collection of ideas, we have then got to decide what we should do with all the other information contained in the Old Testament which is only loosely related to these ideas. Are we to ignore that information, or can we in some way make use of it more effectively by drawing out from it an ideological content? This obviously affects historical narrative, but also, in a very profound way, concerns what we do in order to understand prophetic pronouncements as a form of theology.

When we go on to state that we intend to treat these religious ideas systematically the task becomes even more complicated, because it is extremely difficult to see any way in which the Old Testament as a whole treats its religious ideas in this fashion. We find ourselves, unwittingly, but of necessity, imposing a system of our own upon material which is at best more or less indifferent to an order of this kind. Moreover, the construction of such a system would suggest that it actually existed as a conscious reality at some particular time. Yet, with more than a thousand years of change and development preserved within its various writings, the Old Testament so evidently mocks at our tidy-minded desire to achieve such a system.

When we abstract the religious ideas from their context we set out on a road full of abstractions. By the time we have formed these ideas into a system we are building a great house of abstractions by the roadside. When we then go on to speak of these ideas as forming the profound unity of the Old Testament, such a house of abstractions is beginning to grow into a veritable township! The constant danger that faces us, and which we claim that all such theologies in varying degrees confirm, is that our attempts at systematising and building a unity take over the material that we are working with to such an extent that the real Old Testament becomes submerged by them. This is obviously one of the reasons why questions of introduction and methodology tend to predominate over questions of content in formulating an Old Testament theology.

We may conclude from these preliminary remarks that a theology of the Old Testament must be about the religious ideas contained in this literature. How these ideas are to be systematised, and to what extent they constitute a unifying factor in the literature, are questions that must be considered in relation to the nature of these writings, and, in turn, to the nature of the religion out of which these writings emerged. The constant temptation that faces us is to take short cuts, and in particular to assume that we can readily pick out ideas and group them together in a way which will be meaningful for us, without attention to their proper contexts. One basic danger signal which ought to warn us against doing this, is the history of biblical interpretation. Since other ages have so clearly not found it easy to isolate an Old Testament theology from the context of the literature in which it is set, should we not take warning that the task may in reality prove to be more difficult than we have supposed? Are we not in fact being guilty of showing too much confidence in our methods of interpretation, and too disdainful of older, supposedly 'pre-critical', methods of study that we fail to see obstacles that those who preceded us saw more clearly than we? It will therefore be a basic feature of our efforts to find a new approach to the problems of Old Testament theology that we pay fuller attention than is common in such volumes to the way in which Christians, and to some extent Jews also, have actually heard the Old Testament speaking to them theologically.

## I. THE ORIGINS OF OLD TESTAMENT THEOLOGY

Since the first-century beginnings of the Church, Christians have consistently retained the Old Testament as a part of their sacred literature for use in worship, and have made use of ideas that are to be found within it in their formulations of doctrine. It is certainly true that from time to time questions have been raised about the correctness of this, or about the terms in which it should be undertaken. However, with very few serious voices of dissent, it has remained the basic practice of the Christian Church. The Old Testament has formed a part of its Bible, and has been used and understood as such. Even so, whereas the Old Testament has played a part in the Church's worship and thinking for nineteen hundred years, the conviction that the best way to allow it to speak theologically is to produce an Old Testament theology is a much more recent undertaking.

The roots of such an enterprise are to be traced back to the latter half of the eighteenth century, and to the rise of a new awareness of 'historical-critical' issues which affect the study of the Bible.[3] The outstanding figures here were undoubtedly the German scholars J. S. Semler (1725–91) and J. G. Eichhorn (1752–1827), who may be regarded as the founding fathers of a new critical approach to the literature of the Old Testament. It was Eichhorn's pupil, J. P. Gabler (1753–1826), who first argued for a proper distinction between a 'biblical' theology, which would be concerned with theological ideas in the context of the biblical setting in which they emerged, and a 'dogmatic' theology, which would be free to evaluate and develop these ideas against a wider background of thought.

When we pause to think about this distinction we may note that it has both strong and weak points. It is evidently a strong point that it can take full account of the differing historical and cultural contexts which separate the biblical world from our own. Ideas are not timeless, eternal realities, which can be assumed to remain constant. They are denoted by words which are affected by what people intend them to mean, and actually conceive them to mean, at a particular time. Nowhere is this more evidently true than in the biblical field where we cannot take for granted that a biblical writer understood religious concepts in the same way that we do. Such a basic concept as that of 'holiness' was undoubtedly viewed and interpreted differently in an age where its cultic associations were more fully understood and felt than in one where these have largely disappeared. Even more dramatically, such an important concept as that of 'son of God' was capable of being understood in a number of different ways, and it is noteworthy that, even in the present, the most exacting Christian scholarship has difficulty in unravelling what it meant in the first Christian century.[4] There is clearly a necessity, therefore, that a biblical theology should be concerned to understand religious ideas in a way that is consonant with that of the biblical setting in which they are first found. In order to achieve this most of the great disciplines of biblical scholarship become necessary. Textual, grammatical, literary, and historical criticism all become important aids to establishing the proper significance of biblical ideas. So also is the comparative method an indispensable means to determining how concepts and ideas were understood at a particular time. The distinction between biblical and dogmatic theology, therefore, is to this extent justified.

Nevertheless, we should also note some significant limitations in a distinction of this kind. Most of all we must note that it tends towards the production of two different kinds of 'truth', which may, for understandable reasons, easily become confused. From a historical perspective a biblical theology is concerned with the truth of how a statement or a concept was understood at a particular time. Yet theology, as a systematic discipline of the Church, is concerned with the truth about God and his relationship to mankind. In this sense it is interested in things that may be held to be permanently true, and are not simply the expressions of one particular age.

The distinction would not be a difficult one to maintain were it not for two complicating factors. The first is that the Bible is not simply an ancient literature, but a modern one, in that it is still read and used in church and synagogue. The liturgical use of the Bible affirms that it is still capable of speaking intelligibly to the modern world, and this has to be done with the best, and most suitable, translations available. We cannot withhold the use of the Bible, nor can we easily ensure that every one who hears it takes care to hear in it only those truths that the ancient writers intended to convey.

This 'practical' obstacle to the production of a 'pure' biblical theology is strengthened by an even more important religious consideration. For all who accept the revelatory and authoritative character of the Bible, great importance attaches to the conviction that the sense that the original biblical writer intended to convey is, in some recognisable manner, still true. We can go further and argue that it is precisely the raising of this issue that lifts the statements of the Bible from the category of being 'religious ideas' and raises them to the status of 'theology' in the true sense. In other words, theology is something more than the study of religious ideas, which can be a purely historical and descriptive science, and offers some measure of evaluation of their truth. We shall have occasion to consider this aspect of the problem of a biblical theology further when we have dealt with the second step in the division of the disciplines of a biblical theology. It is sufficient here to note that the terms which Gabler laid down for the production of a biblical theology leave open a number of issues and raise the question whether what he delineated is not something less than 'theology' in the full sense.

If ideas are to be understood and interpreted in the context of the age and cultural milieu in which they are expressed, then it is not surprising that scholars should have felt that a considerable gulf separates the religious ideas of the Old Testament from those of the New. The former spans an age of almost a millennium, whereas the latter extends across little more than a century, and is for other reasons more historically compact and coherent.

It is not difficult for us to understand therefore that, shortly after the time when Gabler argued for a biblical theology, G. L. Bauer (1755–1806) went one stage further in contending that an Old Testament theology should be distinguished from one pertaining to the New Testament. The first volume presupposing this distinction[5] dates from 1796, and since that time the definition has become so commonplace as to have continued down to the present. Admittedly not every scholar has been happy with it, and some have sought to re-establish biblical theology as the basic discipline, and even to propose 'Christian' theologies of the Old Testament, as we have already noted. At one time, in the second half of the nineteenth century, the whole quest for an Old Testament theology was challenged on the ground that the goals of such a discipline can be better achieved by a history of Israelite religion. Some of the arguments in support of this are still worthy of serious reflection, even though there are few Christian Old Testament scholars today who express serious doubts about the possibility of achieving an Old Testament theology.

In spite of such a widely felt consensus that an Old Testament theology is a right and proper undertaking for a Christian scholar to pursue, we ought at this juncture at least to point out a certain strangeness in such an aim. In what sense is the Old

Testament a Christian book? By itself it has never constituted the canon of sacred literature of the Christian Church. It has always, rather, been the first part of the Christian Bible, and never considered to be the entire Bible of the Church. Even if we were to think of the very earliest Christian community, as it existed before the New Testament canon was established, we must nevertheless recognise that the Old Testament was seen and interpreted by means of the early Christian gospel and teaching. In other words something essentially comparable to the New Testament existed to provide a means by which to interpret and use the writings of the Old Testament. If we say, with full justification, that the Old Testament constituted the 'Bible' of Jesus, then this would suggest that an Old Testament theology ought, in some fashion, to concern itself with understanding how Jesus would have read and interpreted these sacred books. Yet this is certainly not what the vast majority of scholars have meant by an Old Testament theology, nor, with only minor exceptions, has the way in which the New Testament interprets the Old been accorded any significant place in such a theology. All of these issues concern historical questions about the structure and shape of the canon of the Bible, which we shall have occasion to refer to later, but they do raise far reaching questions about the possibility of an Old Testament theology.

Admittedly several scholars have noted in introducing the subject of Old Testament theology that it needs to be approached from an open avowal of Christian commitment. Yet it is this conceding of the Christian basis of an Old Testament theology that needs most careful examination. We might have concluded that some clear treatment would be offered of the way in which Christians have actually used the Old Testament in expounding Christian truth, and, most of all, in interpreting the person of Jesus of Nazareth. Yet this has hardly ever been the case, even though, in some instances, some guidelines are provided pointing the way to the New Testament interpretation of the Old. At most we are usually offered some assurance about the 'unity' of the Bible. Yet in fact is not the attempt to produce an 'Old Testament' theology in some degree a disavowal of belief in this unity? It puts asunder what we believe God has joined together.

To express the matter in this way is undoubtedly more than a little polemical, but the idea of an Old Testament theology raises questions which cannot be ignored. Certainly if we were to suppose that an Old Testament theology concerns only the 'Jewish' inheritance of the Christian Church, we should be sadly misinformed about the content of those works that present this theology. They do not recount the main ideas and teachings of Judaism as it existed in New Testament times, and it becomes important for us to learn something of these from elsewhere, if we are to come to an understanding of how there can be a unity in the Bible. We have already had occasion to mention that the pursuit of an Old Testament theology has not been a significant concern of Jewish scholarship, neither have such theologies particularly sought to show us how Judaism has used and understood its sacred literature. In fact we are pressed here back into a corner where we must face carefully what an Old Testament theology may be expected to achieve. What religion, for example, is it expected to serve – Judaism, Christianity, or ancient Israel?

To answer this might lead us, on the one hand, to answer 'all three', or on the other hand 'ancient Israel'. Since the Old Testament, as a canon, or part canon, of sacred writings, has only existed within Judaism and Christianity we ought to expect that it should reveal to us something of the reasons which have led to this canonical use. It might be expected to show us something of the way in which Jews and Christians have found theological meaning in this literature. In fact, however, the historical-critical method of approach has led to a turning away from these 'post-biblical' questions to a concern with the life and thought of ancient Israel and early Judaism in the period within which the Old Testament was in process of formation. The result is that such a theology has a barrier imposed upon it which prevents it from addressing itself to those problems which have arisen by its actual use in Judaism and Christianity.

We have already questioned the view whether we can speak at all of any systematic, or unified, theology of ancient Israel, although there undoubtedly existed something that approximated to it. The important questions would appear to be raised, however, not simply by considerations about the nature of the writings contained in the Old Testament, but by the nature of our interest in them. In the modern world, our concern with this literature and its theology arise, more or less exclusively, from the fact that we are either Jews or Christians. There seems no reason at all, therefore, why we should not be clear from the beginning that our theological interest has arisen in this way, and go on to hope that our study of Old Testament theology will illuminate and enrich our own particular religious faith. If it is the task of theology to serve religion, then these must be the two primary religions which an Old Testament theology can serve.

This carries us back to the issue of the division into Old and New Testament theologies as separate biblical disciplines. There must clearly be something distinctly 'odd' about a Christian biblical theology which deals with only one part of the Church's canon. Yet this 'oddness' may be justified for one very clear reason, and this is that the Old Testament is that part of the Bible which the Church shares in common with Judaism. In the interests of a better mutual understanding, and of a dialogue which is more than merely an entrenched polemic, there are very good reasons why Christians and Jews should study the Old Testament together, and should seek to understand how each has drawn from the older faith and writings of ancient Israel. If an Old Testament theology is to be justified as a modern theological discipline, and is to continue to have a place in the theological curriculum of colleges and universities, it must surely be on the grounds that it can provide a place of useful theological encounter between Jewish and Christian faith. In this each should have the opportunity to view its intellectual convictions in the light of the distinctive ancient religion from which they both sprang, and with a reference to the sacred literature which they both continue to use liturgically. Admittedly this is not how G. L. Bauer conceived of the discipline taking shape, which was certainly on somewhat narrower lines, but to take the narrower view appears, in the light of the many attempts to write an Old Testament theology, to do less than justice to the true nature of theology.

## 2. HISTORICAL CRITICISM AND THEOLOGICAL METHOD

To view the task of writing an Old Testament theology in this way, undoubtedly raises questions about the extent to which it is to be a descriptive science committed to the historical-critical method. It was indeed the very rise of this method in the eighteenth century which led to the search for a historical 'biblical' theology of this kind. To abandon it now would certainly be to throw away one of the most important tools of scholarship which we possess, and which it has taken almost two centuries to develop. As a consideration of the origins of the specific attempt to write an Old Testament theology shows, this goal was very directly an offshoot of the new critical approach to the Bible. There can therefore be no serious justification for abandoning this critical approach in seeking a freer and more open one in the interests of theology. The main point, however, is not whether proper regard should be paid to the historical-critical method, but whether this alone should be allowed to determine the form and structure of an Old Testament theology. As we have argued above, there are good reasons why it should be regarded as proper to theological method to go beyond this. Nevertheless there are certain basic features of the historical-critical approach to the Bible which have a very distinct bearing on the problems of an Old Testament theology.

We must note here in the first place that a fundamental aim of historical criticism is to establish what should be regarded as the correct meaning of a text. In this respect an interesting feature of the eighteenth-century background to the new criticism is to be seen in the extensive debate about messianic prophecy in the earlier part of that century. What is the meaning of such a prophecy as that of the Immanuel child in Isaiah 7.14, and to what extent can it properly be called a 'messianic' prophecy? This raises further questions in relation to the New Testament interpretation of such a prophecy in Matthew 1.23. In order to answer such questions most of the basic disciplines of historical-critical research become necessary since it becomes essential to establish the correct text and the original context of such a saying. In turn these can only be reached by a thorough examination of the literary and historical contexts in which the prophecy was originally given, which are dependent upon conclusions about the date and authorship of it. Clearly there must remain areas of doubt and uncertainty in deciding some of these issues, which is highly inconvenient for theology, but there can be no way of by-passing these questions. It is absolutely essential, therefore, that an Old Testament theology should evaluate its material and establish its conclusions upon the basis of the results of historical criticism. An Old Testament theology that ignores this would have little to commend it, or to command authority.

However, the very methods and results of historical criticism show that to speak of the 'meaning' of texts in this particular fashion is often far too simple. Our example of Isaiah 7.14, with its important declaration regarding the Immanuel child, highlights this problem very clearly. It is clear that Matthew 1.23 interprets the prophecy in a very different way, and in relation to far later events than could have been envisaged in Isaiah's time in the eighth century BC. To treat the two passages as though they were not related to each other, however, is to ignore a very important dimension of biblical faith. The appeal to ancient scripture, particularly in prophecy, becomes a widely used technique for demonstrating the divine significance and purpose that is discerned within events. If a theology is to be truly biblical then it would appear to be important to be able to show how such different interpretations of a saying, and very specifically of a name, arose. To what extent are they related to each other? Already the Old Testament shows that there is some kind of biblical 'bridge' between the Isaianic and Matthean interpretations of the prophecy since the book of Isaiah contains other interpretations of the Immanuel name (Isa. 8.8, 10; cf. Mic. 5.3). The whole question of the interpretation of prophecy becomes a complex one in which old sayings are subjected to a continuing process of interpretation and re-interpretation. The very demand of a truly historical criticism requires that we look at the biblical dimension of faith in all its aspects, and seek to proceed beyond the view that works with simple monochrome meanings for sayings. This is not to set aside the need for understanding the parts of the

Bible in their respective historical contexts, but to use it in order to link the various parts of the Bible more meaningfully to each other. One of the most deeply felt, and widely attested, canons of biblical interpretation in the Christian Church and Jewish Synagogue has been that scripture must be interpreted by scripture. An Old Testament theology should endeavour to do this, and should make use of the results of biblical criticism in order to do so more effectively and intelligently.

In some respects the kind of problem illustrated by the aid of the Immanuel prophecy represents a feature peculiar to the prophetic literature, but it is certainly not restricted to this. We find many of the same features and difficulties emerging when we come to interpret the significance of the divine promise to Abraham in Genesis 12.1–3; 15.1–6. The great importance of this in the New Testament, and its part in the Pauline formulation of a doctrine of justification by faith, need no further elaboration here. Obviously there are aspects of this which belong to the specialised area of New Testament studies, but they are not exclusive to these. In the Old Testament literature the theme of the divine promise to the patriarchs becomes a motif which re-appears in several forms and at different times. It becomes very unsatisfactory to attempt to deal with each of these in historical isolation, since there is a clear consciousness of connection in which succeeding generations of Israelites re-appropriated their own faith. A truly biblical theology ought therefore to concern itself with these connections, and to interpret leading ideas with a real awareness of the way in which they are developed in a wide biblical context. It becomes clear then that a single historical context cannot, by itself, determine the biblical meaning of a text.

This leads us to consider another way in which historical criticism has an important contribution to make to the presentation of an Old Testament theology. A basic feature of J. S. Semler's new critical initiative in biblical research was to re-examine the structure of the biblical canon.[6] No longer was its accepted form to be regarded as the sole level at which it had authoritative meaning. As critical scholarship had already begun to sense, and as its wider application was soon to demonstrate more emphatically, the canon of the Bible was the result of a long process. A great multitude of authors and editors, for the most part unknown to us, composed, revised, and shaped the Bible in the form which we now have.

This desire to probe behind the form of the biblical writings to enquire after an earlier form of them was related for Semler to a change in the conception of biblical inspiration. This was a shift from a conception of *Wortinspiration* (inspiration of the text) to one of *Realinspiration* (inspiration of the subject).[7] It led to a fresh concern with sources, and to the raising of new questions about who the original authors of a document or saying were. The result has certainly been to complicate yet further the problems associated with the interpretation of leading themes and ideas of the Bible. Instead of looking at the biblical books as relatively uniform and self-contained realities, it becomes clear that a great history lies hidden within them. The book of Isaiah, for example, is not a uniform document dictated, or penned, by one man, but a great collection of material built up around the great prophetic ministry of the eighth-century Isaiah of Jerusalem. So also the Pentateuch is formed out of a multiplicity of source material. It may be likened in many respects to an anthology of anthologies, for so much of the central core of Israelite religious tradition has been preserved there.

The result is that today, it is no longer sufficient for us to view the biblical writings as expressive of single interpretations, which may then subsequently have been added to. Already a complex history of meaning lies contained in the traditions which underlie the text of scripture. Of course not all texts are so fraught with meaning, but it becomes clear on examination, that it is precisely those major thematic conceptions such as the divine promise to Abraham, God's revelation to Israel at Sinai and his promise of rebirth out of Babylonian exile which have been the subject of such extensive elaboration and development. In some respects to speak of clear 'doctrines' associated with such themes is mocked by the great variety of insights and images which are employed to affirm them in the Bible. There is a sense, therefore, in which the theological need to provide circumscribed accounts of what the Old Testament means by such great key-words as 'covenant', 'salvation' and 'peace' is too abstract and limited an undertaking to do justice to their proper biblical setting. It is essential, therefore, that an Old Testament theology should retain a proper consciousness of the literary setting of the material it utilises, rather than to seek a body of quite abstract 'doctrines'.

All of these factors bring us back to a fundamental consideration about the aim and purpose of an Old Testament theology. It should be concerned to provide some degree of theological insight and significance in relation to the Old Testament literature which we have. This canonical form of the literature represents the 'norm', if only in the sense that it represents the way in which the Old Testament is read and interpreted in the Jewish and Christian communities. To probe behind this canonical form is important, and should provide a basis for obtaining a better understanding of it, as also is the way in which this canonical form has subsequently been understood and interpreted in Jewish and Christian tradition. The questions of tradition and canon are interrelated, since the canon of the Old Testament represents a kind of 'freezing' of the tradition that was central to Israelite-Jewish religion at a critical moment in its history.

### 3. THE OLD TESTAMENT AS CANON

All of these considerations lead us to recognise the great importance that attaches to the form, function and concept of the Old Testament as canon. It has therefore been a welcome feature of recent approaches to the problem of biblical theology to have rediscovered the notion of canon as a central feature of the Old Testament, which must be allowed to play its part in the presentation of an Old Testament theology.[8] At a very basic level we can see that it is because the Old Testament forms a canon, and is not simply a collection of ancient Near Eastern documents, that we can expect to find in it a 'theology', and not just a report of ancient religious ideas. There is a real connection between the ideas of 'canon' and 'theology', for it is the status of these writings as a canon of sacred scripture that marks them out as containing a word of God that is still believed to be authoritative. There are good reasons, therefore, why it matters a great deal that the historical and literary problems relating to the formation and acceptance of the canon should occupy a place in our discussion.

One point becomes immediately clear, and this is that the date of composition of a document, or writing, in the Old Testament does not, of itself, determine its place in the canon. Similarly where, as is supremely the case in the Pentateuch, there is evidence that a great multitude of sources have been used to create the extant whole, then we are in a real way committed to trying to understand this whole, rather than to elucidating the separate parts.

Perhaps most of all, however, the concern with canon forces us to realise that the Old Testament has a distinctive, and in many ways unexpected, shape. This becomes clearest as soon as we follow out the guideline provided by the Hebrew (Jewish) shape of the canon, which must be accorded full authority as the oldest, and most basic, form of it. The earliest Christian Church took over the Old Testament in its Greek (Alexandrine) form, whereas the separation between Judaism and Christianity led Judaism to revert exclusively to the Hebrew (Palestinian) form. In spite of many problems and historical obscurities concerning the way in which the formation of the canon developed in the first century BC and in the ensuing century, we may confidently recognise that this Palestinian form of the canon represents the oldest, and most basic, form of the Old Testament. In this it is made up of three separate parts: the Pentateuch, or *tôrâh*, the Prophets (later subdivided into the Former and Latter Prophets), and the Writings. These three parts correspond to three levels of authority, with the Pentateuch standing at the highest level, the Prophets below this and the Writings further down still. When therefore the New Testament characterises the entire Old Testament as a book of 'Law' (Greek *nomos* translating Hebrew *tôrâh*) this reflects the canonical priority accorded to the Pentateuch. In a similar fashion the characterising of the historical narratives from Joshua to 2 Kings as 'Prophets' is not without significance when it comes to understanding them as a whole.

From a literary perspective, enlightened by historical criticism, one feature becomes very marked in regard to the structure of the canon. This is that each part contains material from very different ages, spread rather broadly over the period from 1000 BC to approximately 200 BC, or a little later. Age is not of itself therefore a determinative factor in explaining why particular books are in the part of the canon where they are now found.

In addition to this we also discover as a result of source criticism that there are interesting areas of overlap between some of the circles to which we must ascribe authorship of parts of the Pentateuch and Prophets. This is most evident in regard to the book of Deuteronomy in the Pentateuch and the 'Deuteronomic' character of prominent editorial tendencies in the Former and Latter Prophets. Other literary affinities are also to be seen, as for example between some psalms and certain parts of the prophetic corpus.

Yet further literary puzzles reveal themselves, for historical-literary criticism shows us that the Pentateuch has in some respects acquired its canonical status in a curious reverse order. There is widespread agreement that the book of Deuteronomy, the last book of the Pentateuch, was the first to acquire canonical status, albeit in a somewhat different form from that which it now has. Furthermore it is now widely accepted that it once was joined on to form the first 'chapter' of a work which stretched from Deuteronomy to 2 Kings, and thus combined 'the Law and the Prophets'. The point need not be explored further here, although its consequences will be referred to again later. For our immediate concern it is sufficient to note that the canonical shape of the Old Testament cannot be assigned to the result of accident, nor to a simple process of aggregation of documentary material until it formed a massive whole. There is evidently some design and system about the shape that has been accorded to the material.

Our concern at this juncture is to draw attention to the way in which the structure of the canon affects its interpretation. As the canon is primarily made up of the Law and the Prophets, so its contents are broadly to be interpreted as either 'Law' or 'Prophecy'. In fact we quickly discover that 'Law' is a somewhat inadequate term by which to reproduce the Hebrew *tôrâh*, but a legal connotation is not altogether to be discounted.

So far as interpretation is concerned, we find that the categories of 'Law' and 'Prophecy' are not rigidly restricted to their separate parts of the canon, but each tends to spill over to affect other parts. Hence we find, for example, in Matthew 11.13 that 'the Law and the Prophets' are both said to 'prophesy', so that parts of the Pentateuch can be treated as prophecy. Similarly we find in Mark 2.23–8, for example, that a narrative from the Former Prophets is made into an affirmation of a 'law', or *tôrâh*. Even more importantly from the point of view of understanding the New Testament use of the Old we find that numerous passages from the Psalms can be treated as prophecy (cf. Acts 2.25–8, etc.). The details of these categories of interpretation need not detain us at this point, since it is sufficient for our purpose to note the way in which the shape which is given to the canon has served to establish an elementary, but significant, basis for interpretation. The literary context inevitably serves to create a basis of ideological context, for the Old Testament was not meant to be read as a collection of independent 'proof texts', but as a series of three great literary wholes. This is in line with the contention we have already mentioned that scripture should be interpreted by scripture.

Another point also falls to be considered in relation to the canon. If Old Testament theology is intended to be an examination of the theological significance of the Old Testament as it now exists as a canon, then this supports our view that it should not be a purely historical discipline concerned only with the world of ancient Israel and Judaism in which this canon was in process of formation. Rather it must address itself to those religious communities who accept and use this canon as a central feature of their religious life. This points us to both Judaism and Christianity as the religious communities who can be expected to concern themselves with the Old Testament as theology.

In this light we cannot remain altogether indifferent to the liturgical use made of the Old Testament within these communities. This, too, provides part of the context in which the Old Testament is understood. It is inevitable that the situation in worship in which the Old Testament is read, as well as the particular choice and ordering of it, play a part in its being heard as the word of God. The 'I and Thou' of scripture become readily identifiable with the 'I and Thou' of worship in which God addresses man and vice versa, and it is of the utmost importance that the theological justification for this identification should be considered. We cannot tolerate a divorce between theology and liturgy, and we cannot therefore be indifferent to the way in which the Old Testament is used liturgically. A very clear example of this need for a theological reflection upon liturgical use is provided by the Psalter and its extensive employment in Christian worship.

However, the issue does not end there, but affects the whole use of the Old Testament, as is most strikingly exemplified by the use of 'messianic' prophecies in Christian Advent services. A wide range of theological questions are raised, which relate to the canonical form and use of the Old Testament. We cannot in consequence leave the question of the canon out of reckoning in an Old Testament theology. On the contrary, it is precisely the concept of canon that raises questions about the authority of the Old Testament, and its ability to present us with a theology which can still be meaningful in the twentieth century. If we restrict ourselves solely to reading the Old Testament as an ancient text, and endeavour to hear in it nothing that the ancient author could not have intended, then we should be denying something of the tradition which asserts that God has continued to speak to his people through it. In reality we do not need to insist on such a rigidly historicising approach, if we believe that the Old Testament does present us with a revelation of the eternal God.

### 4. THE OLD TESTAMENT AND THE BIBLE

We have already pointed out that the Old Testament is not, by itself, the Bible of Christians, although it forms a very substantial part of it. On the other hand it does represent the Bible of Jews for whom it is the whole scripture. Accordingly, we have suggested that one reason for undertaking the writing of an Old Testament theology should be in order to explore that part of the biblical heritage which Jews and Christians share in common. Although this concern has played some part in the quest for an Old Testament theology, it has, however, not usually been a very large one. Rather, the overriding factor which has stimulated such a quest has been the historical awareness that a chronological gap separates the Old from the New Testament. That this gap also marks the period at which Christianity broke free from Judaism has been treated as relatively incidental to this. A number of considerations, however, lead us to suggest that it is now time to re-examine this orientation of the subject of Old Testament theology and to approach it with somewhat different aims.

The first of these is that it is in the very nature of theology to concern itself with living faith, rather than with the history of ideas, which belongs more appropriately to the field of religious phenomenology. The latter is certainly important for theology, especially in its historical aspects, but it lacks the evaluative role of theology. We are, therefore, in seeking an Old Testament theology, concerned with the theological significance which this literature possesses in the modern world, which points us to an openness to its role in Judaism and Christianity. In many respects such a theology should serve as a critique of such a role, where it is able to employ the insights of historical criticism to correct misunderstandings and errors. So also it will note differences and mark contrasts, seeking out the ways in which patterns of interpretation and continuity have diverged. This is not to abandon the historical-critical role which the founders of biblical theology so eagerly sought, but rather to relate it to those areas of religious debate in which alone it can be theologically meaningful.

Certainly we must concede that there is a place, and even a necessity, for the study of Israelite-Jewish religion in the period from its beginnings to the close of the Old Testament canon. Yet this must be the province of a 'history of religion', rather than of theology as such, if only because the form and structure of that religion now belong to the past and can never be re-covered. Most obviously this relates to the cultic nature of the ancient Jewish religion, with its centre and natural focus on the temple of Jerusalem and all the apparatus of worship that was conducted there. Questions of the significance of temple, priesthood, sacrifice, and a host of other rituals all devolve upon this. The shift from the time of the Old Testament to that of the New and beyond is a shift from the religion of a cult to the religion of a book. It is this change which raises all the essential issues of an Old Testament theology, since it gives rise to the question whether any genuine continuity of faith and tradition is possible as a result of it. Very basic questions of theology are concerned with religious continuity, and hence with the claims to continuity voiced in Judaism and Christianity.

It is not without significance in this connection that we find that the great areas of controversy which the Bible discloses to us – Israelite and Canaanite, Jew and Samaritan, Jew and Christian – are controversies of this kind. They involve questions of where the lines of continuity are to be drawn. The claim that it is through its theology that the Old Testament retains its authority and significance for us is no doubt true, but it raises the question as to what this theology is, and how it can exist and be authoritative as theology, outside of the cult which formed its cradle.

It is an outworking of this concern with continuity of tradition that reveals itself in the Christian concern with belief in the unity which binds together the Old and New Testaments. Concern with this unity, at the level of theological ideas and not simply historical conjunction, must be a basic area of interest for a Christian biblical theology. Yet it immediately faces us with one of the most far-reaching and disconcerting of problems. It was of the utmost importance to the writers of the literature of the New Testament to argue that what had been revealed to them, through Jesus of Nazareth as the Christ, was of a piece with the revelation that God had made in the Old Testament. More than this, it represented the 'fulfilment' of that earlier history of revelation. The means by which the New Testament writers endeavour to demonstrate this, by presenting Jesus as the 'new Moses', the bringer of the 'kingdom of God', and the 'Messiah' foretold by the prophets, among other such themes, involves a type of biblical interpretation which conflicts with that acceptable to a strict historical-critical science.[9] The result has been that, whereas to understand this method of interpretation has become of key importance to New Testament

scholars, it has largely been discounted in the search for an Old
Testament theology. Instead, other, often quite different, parts
of the Old Testament have been appealed to in order to show
the continuity between the two Testaments. Even more broadly
an appeal has frequently been made by Christians to a kind of
natural historical progression from the age of the Old Testament to that of the New.

The problems here are real, and are not easily to be evaded,
since it is a matter of importance to Christianity to assert this
unity of the Bible. Yet this is clearly an area in which a concern
with the structure and shaping of the Old Testament canon,
and the hermeneutical consequences of this, have a considerable
amount to offer towards a theological study of the Old Testament. So also does it lead us to a deep concern with the 'intertestamental' period of Jewish life and thought, even though such
an adjective must fall strangely on Jewish ears. It is an unfortunate consequence of the neglect by biblical theologians of
the emergence and growth of early Jewish interpretation of the
Old Testament that has contributed to this disregard of the
way in which the New Testament interprets the Old. It does
in fact bring us to recognise the real connections that exist
between early Jewish and early Christian exegesis, so that each
comes to command a new respect from the point of view of the
biblical theologian. Certainly we cannot, as Christians, be
altogether happy with a situation in which we cling resolutely
to the Old Testament as a part of our religious heritage, but
almost totally disregard the reasons and arguments which led
the earliest Christians to claim the Old Testament as their book.
The Christian therefore does not, and should not, pretend that
the Old Testament is his entire Bible, since this has never been
the case. It is, in contrast, by way of the New Testament that
he comes to claim the Old. We shall have opportunity to
explore more fully some of the consequences of this for an Old
Testament theology later.

For Jewish faith, however, there also exists a foundational
guide and groundwork for the interpretation of the Old
Testament in the Mishnah and Talmud. These lay down the
guidelines by which the continuity of Judaism with the Old
Testament is asserted. It is not necessary, nor possible, to

explore the consequences of this here. What is important to note is that some such hermeneutical 'bridge' becomes essential if we are to find a theology in the Old Testament which can be meaningful in the modern world apart from the cultic and institutional life in which it originated. The transition from the religion of a cult to the religion of a book, which we find taking place in the later Old Testament period, is an immense theological achievement. Far from regarding it as an incidental development, in which Judaism discarded a cultic dress for which it no longer had any use, we find that it lies at the very heart of what theology is. The belief that God is real, present and knowable, aside from all the rites and symbols by which the cult disclosed his activity, marks the very foundation of theology as such. No longer are religious ideas appealed to in support of symbolic actions and realities, but they themselves become a more direct avenue of approach to God. This is the development which the Old Testament made possible, and which has enabled both Judaism and Christianity to become universal religions, which are truly theological in their nature.

We noted at the beginning of this chapter that the quest for an Old Testament theology has consistently been compelled to concern itself with the grasping of unity in the Old Testament and the use of this in presenting a systematic approach to the religious ideas which are to be found there. In many respects this becomes the major question affecting the overall form of the material which is then to be presented. Yet the Old Testament has little formal unity of ideas, and does not arrange them, or relate them to each other, in any obviously systematic fashion. It is in fact the theologian, by his approach, who must do this. Ultimately we believe that it is the nature and being of God himself which establishes a unity in the Old Testament, even though this is to place the resolution of the issue beyond the actual written pages of the Old Testament. The implications of this are quite far-reaching in their consequences, for it appears that the drawing of the lines of a theology and the search for unity and a system of religious ideas are so closely interrelated as scarcely to be separable. The belief that God exists, and that he is active in the world of men, leads us to accept that we shall see the signs and effects of his activity. We

shall expect all such signs and effects to be coherent and consistent, and yet this coherence and consistency will be dependent
upon what we take such signs and effects to be. The two
questions become interconnected, and it is the importance of
not allowing one part, or text, of the Bible to override all
others that has led interpreters of past ages to insist that we
must interpret scripture by scripture. The Christian who accepts
belief in the unity of the whole Christian Bible, must inevitably
allow that this will affect his understanding of unity in the Old
Testament, yet it ought not to blind him to recognising other
ways of tracing this unity. In this regard, far from regarding as
irrelevant attention to the ways in which Jews and Christians of
post-biblical times have approached the Old Testament, such
approaches serve as an important check on more modern, and
historically critical, avenues of study.

We ought, in consequence of this, to be wary of allowing a
concern with unity and a systematic account of the religious
ideas of the Old Testament to become a determinative framework into which everything is fitted. Regrettably all such
structures seem doomed to be circular. Where we begin will
determine where we will end up. Rather we must, in the
interests of a truly historical and critical approach, submit to
becoming less systematic than this, and more open to trace the
broken lines of unity where the Old Testament draws them. In
doing this we can then see how far they connect up with the
more firmly drawn lines which later ages have found there. In
particular, this must concern the great themes of 'Law' and
'Promise' which have exercised so profound an influence upon
the understanding and interpretation of the Old Testament.

We may also note the importance of the theological study of
the Old Testament to the questions of biblical authority and its
use in liturgy. Here too the issues are interrelated, since it is out
of a sense of the authority of the Old Testament that its liturgical use can continue to be justified. Already we have sufficiently stressed that it is through its theological content that the
Old Testament can be claimed as authoritative for us. However
important we may regard its historical and aesthetic literary
qualities to be, and consequently deserving of scholarly attention, these are not the reasons which have led to its being

claimed as an authoritative part of the Christian revelation, nor as the central religious focus of Judaism. Yet the questions of how God has spoken in this literature, and how his voice may still be heard through it, are questions of theology. They are also questions which are bound up with the way in which parts of the Old Testament are used in liturgy. Especially is this a very relevant issue for Christianity on account of the great freedom with which the Old Testament either does, or does not, play a part in the multiplicity of liturgical forms in use in Christian Churches. Such liturgical use provides a very significant groundwork and context of interpretation, which may either help, or hinder, a positive understanding of the text. It is important, therefore, that some degree of theological, as well as aesthetic, insight should be accorded to the Old Testament when it is used liturgically in the Christian Church. Once again it is a question of how we are still to hear in this literature the authentic voice of one who is not simply 'the God of Israel', but more fully and universally 'God'.

# CHAPTER TWO

# DIMENSIONS OF FAITH IN
# THE OLD TESTAMENT

It is at once apparent to the student of Old Testament theology that the Old Testament does not present its faith in the form of a creed, or a set of theological treatises. Rather it is an ancient literature, stemming from a remarkably early age in the scale of world literary history, and it covers a great variety of types of writing and composition. The purposes for which these compositions were first made, the situation of their authors, and the identity and circumstances of those for whom they were written are largely matters which have to be inferred from the contents of each of them.

Careful scrutiny shows that the reality is even more complex than this, however, for it is seldom that we are faced with a complete, and separately identifiable, book in anything like the modern sense. The forty-nine books into which this literature is now split up is in large measure an artificial creation of later ages, in which very long collections of material, such as the Pentateuch, have been divided up into shorter, more manageable, 'books', or chapters. Similarly, books such as Psalms or Proverbs are collections of much smaller units in which only a relatively minor amount of editorial shaping can be discerned. In the case of the Psalms, in particular, little convincing explanation is available to show why particular psalms appear in the order in which they now do. The Old Testament, in fact, is a vast collection of material, which can loosely be called 'tradition', but which has been assembled into quite consciously arranged 'collections'.[1] Only in a few cases does any separate part of these collections resemble a book in anything like the modern sense, with a carefully thought-out theme, or plot.

If we are to make use of these great collections it is necessary to learn something about their literary, cultural and religious setting in order to fathom within them that particular quality of faith which they present to us. Nor is this quest for a rediscovery of the faith of the Old Testament necessarily made easier because there exists an immense edifice of interpretative tradition which has been built upon it. This also is so vast as to require careful sifting and categorising, and it must in any case remain one of the aims of an Old Testament theology to appeal back directly to the faith of the Old Testament in testing, and if necessary correcting, the doctrines and ideas which have been drawn from it.

It is important therefore that we should first consider the nature of the Old Testament and note some salient features about its background before attempting to elicit from it a particular theology.

## I. THE LITERARY DIMENSION OF FAITH

The Old Testament is a collection of writings, produced over a period of almost a millennium, which functions as a religious work when it is read, either publicly or privately in a religious context, and when its meaning is grasped and responded to. Yet for us to do this in the modern world requires a considerable amount of background knowledge about the circumstances and purpose of the constituent parts of the whole collection, which has largely to be discovered by a process of scholarly comparison and inference. Certainly once the principle of a canon had been accepted, and began to influence the shaping of the material, we are entitled to conclude that its use in liturgical reading and serious devotional study affected its literary form. At earlier stages, however, this was by no means the case, and we are able to see that in many cases writings that were originally written for one specific purpose or situation have been adapted to another.

Yet even at the later canonical stage of editorial shaping of the material the amount of information that has been passed down to us about the circumstances of the various writings is sparse in the extreme. Sometimes the information itself remains either unintelligible, or is indicative only of later Jewish hermeneutical interests, as in the case of the Psalm titles. Often, however, we appear to be faced with situations in which information about the sources of compositions was lost, or neglected, and where a bewildering indifference prevailed in regard to questions of date, authorship, and the many other details which are now so important in relation to the study of an ancient text.

We have already seen that questions of date and chronological sequence were never felt to be matters of overriding importance. The result now is that, in the Pentateuch for example, there is no clear pattern of order between material of a late and an early date. Nor is this true in the great 'books' of prophecy, such as that of Isaiah and Jeremiah, where again we have great assemblages of material put together in no obvious chronological sequence. Even more disconcerting for the student of prophecy is the fact that only in a relatively small number of cases have we been given any information about when, and in what circumstances, a particular prophecy was given.

These considerations pose certain difficult conclusions from the outset of our study, and make the pursuit of a literary introduction to the writings of the Old Testament a necessary, even if hazardous, undertaking. We may assume that the way in which the writings of the Old Testament have been put together is not the product of random chance, with almost no attempt made to offer any logical, or temporal, sequence of material. Yet it is equally clearly not an achievement in which any one or two clear intentions have been allowed to dominate. Sometimes there is a narrative sequence; sometimes later material has been placed directly after related earlier material; sometimes a catchword principle has been followed; sometimes sayings, or stories of a particular type, or *genre*, have been placed together. Sometimes it seems that chance has played a part, and at times too it seems that suitability for liturgical use has been considered. The point to which we must pay heed is that there is no uniform, or near uniform, pattern which reveals itself to us as explanatory of the editorial intentions of those who have given to us the Old Testament in its extant form.

This certainly ought to lead us to recognise that where such editorial information is given, as in the headings of collections of prophecy, the superscriptions of particular anthologies or collections, and in a number of general editorial comments, then they are of very real importance to us on account of their rarity. At times the information that is given is difficult to understand, especially where it conerns questions of authorship. Ascriptions to Moses, or David, or to other of the great figures of Israel's religious history cannot be equated with information about authorship in the same technical sense that belongs to modern books. Rather they must be regarded as concerned with authority and with belief in the origin of a tradition. Nor can we regard prophets as authors in the modern sense, and in no case can we regard a prophetic book as having been penned by its prophet-author. Rather we find that in most cases the prophetic books include much material showing how prophecies were believed to have been fulfilled by events; how they were re-interpreted and developed in later ages, and how they became the basis for the production of further prophecies.

All of this adds up to a situation in which we cannot regard any of the books of the Old Testament as expressive of the distinctive religious thoughts of one man. The 'faith' of Moses, or of David, as such, is simply not available to us to examine and reflect upon. Hence we cannot treat the great religious personalities of the Old Testament as theologians in the modern sense. Even though in some isolated cases attempts have been made to identify the work of particular individual authors in the Old Testament, the evidence for this, and for the expression of a single person's religious faith in a theologically rounded form, is seldom above serious dispute. We cannot therefore seek to produce a theology of the Old Testament by reconstructing the theology of specific 'authors' of books, either in the form of the books as they now stand, or in the form of sources, or documents, which have been incorporated into the extant books.[2]

Still less can we reconstruct a theology of the great prophets, in the manner once attempted by B. Duhm,[3] by seeking to elicit the distinctive contribution that each of the great prophets made in the field of religious ideas. The material of the Old Testament neither lends itself to such treatment, nor does it make the results of such reconstructions more than risky hypotheses. Even more seriously it points us in a direction away from that of the literature which we find preserved here. Consistently this is away from a concentration on the thoughts of individuals and towards the faith of the whole community, which is a message given to all, and open for all to share. It is a message about God and his people, Israel. This social dimension of the writings of the Old Testament has certainly contributed to the extensive development of them at the hands of schools of scribes and editors. A theology of the Old Testament, therefore, ought certainly to concern itself with this particular literary dimension of the faith of the Old Testament.

Alongside of this great variety of authors and editors who have contributed to the fashioning of the Old Testament literature, we also find a considerable variety of literary types within it. The great thematic titles of the parts of the canon: Law, Prophets, and Writings, are readily broken down to reveal a much wider multiplicity of types of literature. Even so broad a category as 'prophecy' easily breaks down into historical narrative and prophecy, but this latter must be divided up into the more explicitly predictive, or pronouncement, material and the admonitory and hortatory forms which serve to substantiate it. So also the Law, or *tôrâh*, includes laws of many kinds. Some correspond closely to modern civil laws, others are in the nature of religious injunctions and regulations, and yet others are more in the nature of admonitions or general ethical injunctions. They cannot all have originated in the same area of religious, or social, life, and it is their broad literary assembly under the general heading of *tôrâh* which now gives to them a degree of common connectedness. The literary formation of the Old Testament therefore has plainly exercised a co-ordinating function in bringing together different types of law, as well as a great variety of other, non-legal, material to constitute *tôrâh*.

From a modern perspective it has been convenient to classify the Pentateuch and Former Prophets, as well as some of the Writings, as 'historical books', thereby introducing a specific category which is not that of the Old Testament itself. This in itself is not necessarily misleading, although it has pitfalls which require careful scrutiny. It is important for the Old Testament, for example, that the Former Prophets are now separated from

the book of Deuteronomy to which they once belonged, and
this distinction should not be overlooked. Similarly we can
discern in the growth of the Pentateuch a series of developments
in which the historical narrative material was more and more
expanded by the incorporation of rules and regulations until
the whole balance was seriously changed. The book of Leviticus,
as it now exists, cannot be regarded as a work of historical
narrative, even though it has almost certainly been developed
out of one.

In some respects, therefore, the more neutral term *tôrâh*
serves to warn us against an over-concentration upon the more
obviously historical features of the Pentateuch. The temptation
to do this, from the point of view of a theology, has become all
the greater on account of the particular academic interest in
the history of Israel and the special philosophical concern with
history as a dimension of human experience and understanding.
Such a concern is not necessarily wrong, but all too readily
lends itself towards the support of treatments of the Old
Testament which neglect precisely those areas which have
proved to be most difficult for the modern Christian interpreter.
Particularly is this noticeable in regard to the treatment of the
cultus, and in consequence, of those large tracts of the Old
Testament which are directed towards the institutions, ordering
and life of the cult. It is salutary to recognise that the Christian
hermeneutical tradition, with all its uncritical vagaries of
typology and symbolism, has sometimes been more open in
recognising these exegetical problems, than has a more modern
'critical' interpretation.

One particular aspect of this literary dimension of Old
Testament faith is the way in which features relating to the
setting of a literary unit may have a bearing upon its meaning.
This is quite evidently the case in regard to prophecy, where a
relatedness to events is paramount, and only in its later, proto-
apocalyptic, forms does this connection with events fall more
into the background. However, it is also the case with an interpretation of many of the psalms, that very significant features
concerning this are affected by the situations in which they
were originally intended to be used. The kind of help from God
that is sought, in the form of deliverance, is seldom made

incontrovertibly clear, and the importance of examining the various possibilities of healing from sickness, acquittal from malicious accusations, or of protection from physical attacks by enemies, all play a part in obtaining a satisfactory understanding of them. Here too, therefore, the literary dimension of Old Testament faith cannot be ignored.

It is perhaps not entirely inappropriate to point out at this stage that there is an inescapable tension in the very goal of writing an Old Testament theology. The Old Testament is a literature, whereas a theology is concerned with the world of ideas and their systematic formulation. The ways in which a literature may reflect ideas are numerous, and they increase still further when many different types of literature are involved. Further, the part played in religion by ideas varies a great deal, and the rational and reflective aspects of Israelite-Jewish faith were only beginning to come to the surface in the period during which the Old Testament was formed. It is possible for us to extract the ideas, so far as is attainable, and to pay little attention to their literary setting. Conversely, we may concentrate our attention upon the literature and its complex history, giving only scant attention to the systematic ordering of the religious ideas which we find in it.

Hence we find two very different approaches current among scholars: on the one hand, it has been asserted that the most effective way of presenting an Old Testament theology is to offer a theological commentary on the text of its various writings. At the opposite extreme we find attempts to formulate a system of religious ideas which are found in the Old Testament with almost no regard for the character of the individual writings in which they appear.[4] The contention in the approach advocated here is that neither extreme is entirely satisfactory, and that something of the inevitable tension that exists in trying to satisfy both demands must be accepted. We must be as systematic as we can be, but we must allow that the form of the Old Testament literature cannot be ignored, and poses its own restraints upon our desire for a completely systematised presentation of the faith contained within it.

## 2. THE HISTORICAL DIMENSION OF FAITH

Large sections of the Old Testament are made up of historical narrative recounting the events concerning the origin and fortunes of Israel, and especially is this so in regard to the Pentateuch. There exists a firm narrative framework to this, and still the most acceptable literary explanation of this framework is that it was established by the earliest of the main literary sources from which the whole work has been built up. This is usually called J, or the Yahwist, and is thought to have originated in the early days of the Israelite monarchy, probably in the reign of Solomon. The attempt to press behind the structure of this narrative source, to find a brief summary, or credal recitation, of the foundation events of Israel's history, can no longer be regarded as proven. Instead it becomes increasingly clear that the particular texts that have been appealed to in support of this contention (chiefly Deut. 6.21–3; 26.5b–9; Josh. 24.2–13) are late summaries, dating from no earlier than the seventh century BC.[5] However, even without the support of the contention that the main fabric of Israel's history-writing originated in the setting of a confession of faith during an act of public worship, there is a clear religious dimension to such history.

On examination we discover that a considerable dimension of depth pertains to all the major narrative parts of the Pentateuch. Even in the case of J, the earliest of its larger sources, the author has acted as a collector of yet older stories and traditions, shaping them somewhat loosely into a longer connected whole. In consequence we find that even when we attempt to break down the Pentateuch into its major constituent sources, it does not present us with a single uniform picture of how God has been active in Israel's history. Instead we find a broad anthology of traditions, developed into epic proportions, but made up individually of separate episodes which are more or less self-explanatory. At this level we find a great many stories concerned with questions of the authority and significance of the cultus, the legitimacy of certain sacred sites, e.g. Bethel (Gen. 28.11–19), the appropriateness of particular offerings and the inappropriateness of others (e.g. Gen. 14.17–24; 22.1–14).

Other narratives bring out more explicit theological themes such as the divine wrath and judgment upon certain sins (cf. Gen. 19.1–29), and the blessedness of the way of obedience to God (cf. Gen. 22.15–19).

It is in the way in which these separate episodes have been woven together that there begins to emerge a religious message of a larger and more enduring kind. This is to be found in the promise to the patriarch Abraham that the land of Canaan is given to him and his descendants, who will become a great nation and a blessing in the earth (Gen. 12.1–3). Here we enter the sphere of the larger structural theme of the Pentateuch, which is concerned with the divine election of Israel, its status as a chosen nation, and the gifts that God intends to bestow upon it as a result of this. Pre-eminently the theme focuses upon the land of Canaan, as a necessary feature of Israel's national existence and the basis of its prosperity, but as the story unfolds other gifts are set alongside it. Most of all here we are directed to the institutions and organisation of worship, which are revealed to Israel through Moses on Mount Sinai (Exod. 19–40).

It is not difficult to see that the use of historical narrative of this kind is readily made to serve a theological purpose, so that a portrait of God himself is delineated. His existence and being become known through the actions that are ascribed to him, and the disclosures from time to time of his purpose and intentions. From being a hidden background figure, he appears so consistently active as to become the leading protagonist in the story, even though his 'hiddenness' is never altogether set aside.

This leads us to note that the ways in which God is presented as imposing his will upon human affairs is never reduced to any one single pattern or formula. Sometimes he is said to speak directly to men (cf. Gen. 3.9, etc.), or to exert his will directly (cf. Gen. 6.5 ff.). At other times he speaks through dreams or prophets (cf. Gen. 28.12, etc.), or acts through the mediation of messengers, or 'angels' (cf. Gen. 18.2 ff.; 19.1). At one point the necessity of his hiddenness is given a theological explanation (cf. Exod. 33.20), and is made into a basis for authorising certain features of cultic life (cf. Exod. 34.29–35). The techniques of providence, therefore, if this is how we should describe them, are variously understood and presented in the Old Testament. In themselves they stand at a nearer or farther distance from conceptions acceptable to a modern scientific world view. While they fully recognise the fact of divine immanence in the world, they do not offer any uniform doctrine of this.

Here too we encounter a complexity of language, which may be noted later in another connection. God is presented in an anthropomorphic fashion as thinking, speaking and acting like a man. Even his appearance can be taken for that of a man (cf. Gen. 32.24, 28), although that he is a being of an altogether different order is fully accepted (cf. Gen. 6.3). To what extent the language should be called analogical or metaphorical, or even whether it deserves the description of 'mythological', can seldom be determined with the kind of precision and clarity that we should desire. In the Old Testament narratives such expressions are seldom the result of a considered theological explication, but are themselves the product of traditions, which were only gradually being subjected to scrutiny and theological analysis. Most scholars therefore have felt able to discern a gradual toning down, and developing reticence, about the way in which the Old Testament portrays the actions of God in the world, the later strands of narrative being less assertively anthropomorphic and more cautious than the earlier. All of this leads us to see that the picture of the ways in which God's activity is asserted is less important than the aims and purposes for which this activity is employed. There are apparently levels of divine intervention, which have to be taken into account in uncovering the theological meaning of ancient biblical narrative.

This points us further to consider that the Old Testament does not necessarily retain a uniform interpretation of a particular event, but comes to view it in more than one light. A most obvious example of this is to be found in the account of Jehu's revolt (2 Kgs. 9.1–37), which involved a fearful massacre of the royal house of Israel. The narrative report regards this action as instigated by the divine will through the mouths of prophets, whereas the prophet Hosea (cf. Hos. 1.4–5) refers to it in a strikingly condemnatory manner.

It is seldom that a reversal of attitude of this kind appears so prominently, but it enables us to recognise an important aspect of the different literary layers within the narratives of the Old Testament. Events which at one stage appeared in a favourable light, may, at a later stage, appear very differently. The reader who seeks to learn the Israelite attitude to monarchy from the narratives of its institution in 1 Samuel 8–12, is quickly made aware of this. Expressions of both favourable and hostile attitudes appear, and in spite of the editor's attempt to weave them together into a sequence, it is difficult for the modern reader to feel that a consistent view has been maintained.

From the literary point of view we can discern in this that reports and accounts from different ages and circles of tradition have been employed in putting together the present narrative, which also attempts to offer a viewpoint of its own. Once we begin to put the different stories into some chronological order, and to note their ideological affinities, the differing viewpoints take on a valuable significance. Had only one, late, viewpoint been expressed, we should clearly have lost something of importance in understanding the history of monarchy as an institution in Israel.

The literary tangle, therefore, is not without its virtues. Even so it requires that we involve ourselves in a process of literary analysis and historical ordering, if we are to glean from the accounts any overall theological evaluation of the way in which Israel regarded the monarchy as a divine institution. That different ages may view the same event in differing perspective as its consequences and implications become more transparently obvious, is a commonplace of historical research. It is important for us therefore not to be misled through allowing a concern with the recovery of a 'factual' history, so far as this may in any way be accepted as an attainable goal, into regarding those sources which stand closest to events as always the most theologically revealing. The revised viewpoint of a later age has its own measure of theological insight to give. Nor is this always to be restricted to the view that it can tell us only about the later narrator's own age, and has little to add to the knowledge of the past it describes.

This dimension of depth within historical narrative, in which viewpoints and sources from different ages have been woven together, is a prominent aspect of the Old Testament. It marks the strongest theological feature which has arisen as a result of the source criticism of this literature. The more central the event, such as the promise to the patriarchs or God's revelation at Sinai, the more likely it is that we shall find a number of layers of narrative interpretation incorporated into the material. Clearly, from the perspective of setting out a history of Israel as well as a history of the tradition, a considerable importance attaches to our being able to sift out the earlier from the later accounts. By doing so we can obviously hope to see something of the changes and developments which affected Israel's self-understanding. Even the ways in which central figures such as Abraham or Moses are presented in the different strata of tradition have their own value in revealing to us many of the changing religious insights which affected the varying ages of Israelite history-writing.

What is less clear is the extent to which we should interpret these compoundings of tradition as a desire to put forward a comprehensive picture of the past and its heroes, and how far there is a clear development in it. Are later presentations, for example, intended in some measure to displace earlier ones? Here we come up against a repeatedly disconcerting feature of the history-writing of the Old Testament. On the one hand we have insisted that it is in the final canonical form in which it is preserved that the Old Testament speaks to us. Yet, since this final form can be split up into strata of earlier forms, it is not always easy to see what this integrated final form is saying of itself.

This presents us with a range of leading questions which relate to the theological implications of the historical dimension of faith in the Old Testament. How far are we entitled to see here progress and a consistent direction given to its changing patterns of thought? It has so often been taken for granted that a theological approach to the Old Testament can detect an upward trend of thought. In this the conception of God is progressively spiritualised and moralised so that higher and higher forms of religious understanding come before us. Such views have in the past frequently been accounted for in terms of theories of 'progressive revelation'. Certainly there are important changes of religious outlook, in which more mature and theologically reflective ideas of God and his activity in the world can be traced. Notions of the universality and transcendence of God become more prominent in the later writings and traditions, while anthropomorphic language becomes more restrained and less evident.

Yet there are other changes which cannot so readily be accounted for as the result of more mature theological insight and reflection. Conceptions of Israel's place in the world change from that of a tribal community to that of a nation, and then to a less clearly defined religious community, or 'congregation' as its altering political fortunes are reflected in its self-understanding. That these add up to any obvious pattern of development away from a religious tribalism to a nationalism and then on to a clear religious individualism is far from being clear, even though such has frequently been claimed.

We cannot attempt to sort out these problems in brief compass here, but some points regarding this dimension of historical change in thought-patterns are relevant. To recognise these patterns of change and to be able to relate them wherever possible to particular periods and situations in the development of the religion would clearly be an inestimable advantage in understanding them. At the same time to speak of 'progress' or 'development' implies some kind of coherence and direction in the way in which these changes occur. A theological approach to the Old Testament is almost bound to be committed to tracing some such directional patterns of thought. This is certainly the case if we are to be guided by the ways in which the New Testament can interpret Old Testament history in accordance with such patterns, e.g. that of a 'remnant' (cf. Rom. 11.5) or of rebellion against divine grace (cf. Acts 7.51–3). Yet we must be wary of appealing to such patterns as though some logical, or necessary, movement of thought was controlling them.

This particularly applies to the gradual decline and atrophying of the cult and its influence in favour of a more intellectual and 'spiritual' type of faith in which the formal cult played little part. The legacy of this change is to be found in both Judaism and Christianity, which each developed its own kind of apologetic to account for its dispensing with the demands and obligations of the Old Testament cultus. To appeal to a 'progress of thought' in defence of this abandonment, which was in any case necessitated by historical realities, becomes a somewhat circular argument. That which survives is always defended as that which is most fitted to survive, with little being offered by way of further explanation. In all, therefore, there are a number of aspects of the dimensions of change and movement in regard to the history of ideas in the Old Testament which prompt us to caution.

Perhaps the most salient point here is that to undertake to set out a clear history of religious ideas in the Old Testament is a particularly difficult undertaking. Those who have done so in the pursuit of a theology of the Old Testament have certainly been guilty of acting with greater confidence and assurance than the evidence really warrants. To write a history of the religious institutions of the ancient Israelite religion is a formidable enough task because of the many lamentable gaps in our knowledge of critical periods of its development. Seldom have the occasions of great changes in the cultus and its ministry been reported for us with information as to when these occurred. To attempt to go beyond this and to write an intellectual history of the growth and development of religious ideas is an even more daunting undertaking. This is not because such a growth and development did not occur, but rather because the kind of information which the Old Testament preserves for us seldom indicates how and when new religious ideas became current.

There are serious problems, therefore, which face us in appealing to trends and patterns of thought in the Old Testament as justification for the relative degree of importance which we attach to particular ideas. As we must constantly remind ourselves, a theological approach to the Old Testament involves us in a task of evaluation which goes beyond mere historical description. To explain this evaluation as simply the necessary consequence of historical development would be essentially to mask its proper theological nature. It is the presence of so many 'hidden' judgments of this kind which has enabled so much that passes for Old Testament theology to appear as more historically grounded than it really is. All in all, therefore, we must remain constantly aware of the historical dimension of faith in the Old Testament, but beware of using the breadth of ideas to which this has given rise as a means of obscuring the true nature of a theological approach.

### 3. THE CULTIC DIMENSION OF FAITH

In noting that the religion of ancient Israel was a cultic religion in the full sense, we remarked that the transition from the religion of the Old Testament to those of Judaism and Christianity was a transition from a religion of cult to book religions. We now have opportunity for noting the extent to which the religious language, ideas, and practices to be found in the Old Testament have been moulded by this cult.

Perhaps most of all is this obvious in relation to the understanding of God, for what is of paramount importance in the Old Testament is the presence of God, rather than any doctrine of his existence.[6] To seek God was to go up to see his face at a sanctuary, rather than to engage in an intellectual debate. In consequence the information that the loyal worshipper needed to know concerned where, when, and how God could be found. So much of the information contained in the Old Testament is of this kind. The God of Israel was believed to be present in his temple on Mount Zion in Jerusalem (cf. Pss. 9.11; 11.4; 14.7; 18.6, etc.) so that to worship before him there was to stand in his presence. Information concerning when to come, on the occasions of the great religious festivals (cf. Exod. 23.14; 34.23), what to bring by way of offerings (cf. Exod. 23.15, 19), and how these were to be made (cf. the Manual of Sacrifice in Lev. 1–7) formed the basic outline of a knowledge of God.

A great deal of ancillary information can be readily seen to have a dependent relationship upon this groundwork of knowledge. So traditions about the legitimacy of certain shrines, and the illegitimacy of others, the authority of the priestly families and their privileges and duties, and not least the significance attached to the symbols and rites of worship, all formed a part of this religious tradition.

When we extend this further to see how it also embraced a range of admonitions concerning the benefits and blessings that would accrue from right worship and the dangers that were attendant upon errors of religious behaviour or even its outright abuse, we find that a surprisingly large part of the tradition-material contained in the Old Testament is covered. Most of the account of God's revelation at Sinai (Exod. 19–40) falls within this category as does much of the book of Leviticus.

Because of its cultic character these traditions have frequently been given only very secondary attention in theological treatments of the Old Testament. At an early stage of its interpretative tradition in respect of the Old Testament the Christian Church came to isolate the more directly ethical admonitions, such as we find in the Decalogue of Exodus 20.2–17, and to place them on a much higher plane of authority than these cultic demands and regulations which had so obviously become obsolete in a Christian context.

The reasons and justification for acting in this way will be mentioned again later, but it is important in the present context to note the great extent of cultic material of this kind. Critical historical study of the religion of ancient Israel shows it to have been through and through a cultic religion of this nature.[7] The cult was in no sense merely an adjunct – a concession to the attitude of the times – which might later be dropped without any serious impairment of the basic religious tradition. On the contrary in origin the cult of Israel was the heart of the religion, and the more verbal and rational elements of faith emanated from this. It quickly becomes apparent in surveying the main events in the history of Israel's religion: the reform of Josiah in 622, the destruction of the temple in 587, the restoration of the temple in 520–516, the controversy with the Samaritans, and not least the separation of the early Christian community from Judaism, that these were primarily controversies about the cult and its obligations. In many respects it was in the course of these great upheavals in the cultic life of Israel and Judaism that it became necessary to bring to the surface underlying theological convictions. This is most obviously evident in the question put to Jesus by the woman of Samaria in John 4.20, 'Our fathers worshipped in this mountain; and you say that in

Jerusalem is the place where men ought to worship', (rsv). The answer that is presented by Jesus affirms in the most categorical way the necessity of a theology: 'God is spirit, and those who worship him must worship in spirit and truth' (John 4.24).

There are an abundant number of historical questions pertaining to the cult and its history in Israel which require fuller explanation and investigation. However, this is far beyond the scope of our brief notice of the subject here. What is important for us to do is to note the way in which the cult has affected the ideas and language of the Old Testament to such an extent that it is this cult which has formed the cradle of biblical theology. The basic vocabulary of religion in the Old Testament is basically a vocabulary of the cult, although we can begin to trace in the study of many of its basic concepts a trend away from this cultic association. Such words as 'holiness/profanity', 'cleanness/uncleanness' and 'acceptable gift/abomination' are all terms which belonged directly to the cult.[8] What they connoted was at first unintelligible apart from the sanctuaries of Israel and the rites that were performed there. Over a period of time, by their use as metaphors, by a natural extension of meaning, and by underlying changes in the understanding of the cult, they acquired a greater range of signification, so that we can see why, by the time the Old Testament came to be translated into Greek, they had taken on a profoundly ethical significance. Such a process of 'spiritualising' cultic concepts had already progressed a very long way by New Testament times. All of this has had the most far-reaching theological effect, since it forms a basic step in the process of moralising, universalising and theologising the religion of ancient Israel. Without it the emergence of a religion of a book – the Old Testament – would not have been possible. Yet when it comes to tracing what has made this development possible we must note more than one contributory factor.

Foremost here we must certainly place the actual course of Israel's religious development, with its narrowing down of cultic life to that of the sanctuary of Jerusalem in the seventh century, followed so shortly after by the tragic destruction of the Jerusalem temple. After this the experience of Jews in exile, which passed gradually into an experience of more permanent

Diaspora, gave rise to a situation in which a large number of loyal Jews found themselves to be effectively people without a cult. Historical reality, therefore, more and more compelled a widened interpretation of Israelite religious obligation. Yet this in itself cannot be the whole explanation, since it was in considerable measure the presence in the religion of certain theologising and spiritualising tendencies that enabled Israel's cult to survive these shocks. Other religions underwent similar threats to their cultic institutions and show no signs of having developed a theology which could take account of them.

Of paramount importance in the Old Testament we must place the understanding of God himself at the centre of this move towards the emergence of a theology. The fact that the God of Israel had no image which could be set in a sanctuary and viewed as the representation of his person was clearly one factor of significance here. So also we are entitled to conclude that the part played in the cult by verbal elements and human speech, voiced through prophets and priests as well as the worshippers themselves, all helped towards the creation of a more reflective attitude to the rites of the cult. As so many psalms reveal to us, it was possible in ancient Israelite worship to conduct a kind of dialogue with God through the agency of the cultic personnel. Yet most of all it lies in the way in which God himself was understood, and was believed to reveal himself to worshippers and to make himself accessible to them, that this reflective spiritual attitude to worship came to prevail. It is evident that when Israelites and Jews found themselves separated from the cult to which they had grown accustomed, they did not at the same time interpret this to mean that they were thereby separated from God and his power to help them. It was important therefore that a knowledge of God, which was larger and richer than a knowledge of the cult which served him, should have taken hold in Israel.

It is also noteworthy that we find in the Old Testament, alongside the direct assertions about the presence of God in his sanctuary, the development of more carefully formulated theological concepts to account for this. Hence we have in the Deuteronomic literature the development of the idea that the sanctuary was the place where God had chosen to set his 'name' (cf. Deut. 12.5), and in the Priestly strand of the Pentateuch the concept of the divine 'glory' (Exod. 40.34–8) as the means whereby God's presence on earth was effected. All of this is fully in line with the deep awareness that the traditional language about God's presence at his chosen sanctuary was an inadequate formulation of the reality since God was too great and exalted for his being to be locally restricted in this way (cf. 1 Kgs. 8.27).

We must accept therefore that a continuing process of inter-action has taken place in the Old Testament between the understanding of God and the understanding of the cult. To suppose that ideas about the cult always followed the history of its institutions would be too doctrinaire a view to carry con-viction. This may have been the case on some occasions, but at other times it seems much more probable that it was the con-ception of God which forced deep changes upon the inter-pretation of the cult. By the end of the Old Testament period it is clear that there had emerged a conception of God which was much fuller and richer than the old concepts of the cult would have allowed. As these had become obsolescent, so there had been an adequate depth of theological understanding available for later generations to recognise that 'God is spirit'.

This concern with the cultic dimension of faith in the Old Testament also raises for us the complex questions concerning the 'meaning' of cultic actions. It is obvious that such rites as the offering of sacrifice and the burning of incense were believed to effect certain necessary, or desirable, ends when properly performed in worship. In order for this to be so they had to be interpreted in a way that gave them meaning, and that was in accordance with, if not always an explanation of, the particular end that was sought. It is a fundamental fact of the history of cultus that very different interpretations, or explanations, may be offered of a particular rite. In course of time these interpretations may change in order to accommodate new ideas or new circumstances. Similarly, different com-munities may interpret the same rite differently, each in accordance with its own particular interests and concerns. Such was certainly true of Israel, where the interpretation of basic rites such as sacrifice were subjected to very substantial changes.

That there was an even older pre-Israelite history to many of the rites of sacrifice which the Old Testament records, must be regarded as certain.

It was precisely this flexibility in the area of meaning which the interpreters of the Israelite tradition within the Old Testament have so eagerly seized upon. In this area at least it is not difficult to speak of a very marked trend of thought and understanding. As a result we find that the Hebrew word for 'sacrifice' (*zebah*), which basically designates an act of slaughter, could ultimately be translated into Latin as *sacrificium*, which more broadly denotes a religious act, or oath. Throughout the development which has taken place here we can detect that the emphasis has apparently shifted from a concern with the physical and external action to a concern with the inner spiritual intention. By New Testament times a variety of actions which involved costly self-deprivation could be designated as 'sacrifice'.

The cult therefore has provided a cradle for many of the most fundamental theological concepts of the Old Testament, but it has not determined their meaning in any circumscribed way. Rather the flexibility of interpretation which the cult allowed has enabled these old concepts to acquire new meanings, in some cases far beyond the interests and expectations of the original cult. This process of theologising cultic concepts has undoubtedly taken place extensively within the Old Testament period, even though this period did not altogether witness the cessation of the cultus.

It is when we come to look at the ways in which Jewish and Christian interpreters have approached the Old Testament that we see a marked acceleration of this tendency towards theologising the cult. Within a relatively brief period after the destruction of the Jewish cultus in Jerusalem in AD 70, we find that an almost complete process of moralising and ethicising of cultic language and concepts had taken place. Ideas of holiness and purity had been transferred into a new frame of reference. The cultic dimension of faith in the Old Testament therefore is a very important aspect of its nature. The process of reinterpreting the ancient Israelite cultus, with all its rites, symbols and concepts, has gone hand in hand with the process

of establishing a religion in which its 'theology' – its understanding of the being and activity of God – forms a central part.

## 4. THE INTELLECTUAL DIMENSION OF FAITH

This regard for the deep changes in the attitude towards cultus
which are to be found in the Old Testament raises for us some
of the most profound questions about the nature of religion and
the role of rational, theological and philosophical thought
within it. Very markedly the religions which have been strongly
influenced by the Old Testament (Judaism, Christianity and
Islam) have been profoundly reflective 'theological' religions.
In many other religions this rational and reflective aspect plays
only a very minor part.

It is not surprising therefore that the study of the faith of the
Old Testament has often been set within a wider context of the
history of ideas, and especially of the history of religious ideas.
The move away from an explicitly cultic world of thought
towards a more subjectively rational and ethical one has
frequently been claimed to mark a natural 'evolution' of
religious ideas, and to relate to a natural 'progress' in human
thinking. It may indeed be claimed that this is so, although it
would carry us beyond the proper area of an Old Testament
theology to assert, or defend, such claims. What we should note
at this stage is their inevitably doctrinaire character, and the
dangers that are attendant upon establishing too early an
interpretative scheme of this kind.

In particular we must beware of the tendency that is inherent
in such schemes to establish a pattern of evaluation which
forces the historical evidence which the Old Testament provides
into a fixed pattern. All too easily such schemes become self-
justifying, and exercise a more far-reaching control over the
ideas of the Old Testament than a stricter historical criticism
can properly support. There seems little ground for disputing
the claim that it has been the presence of such convictions about
the natural history of ideas, often unconsciously held, which
has in the past led to a great under-estimation of the role and
significance of the cult in ancient Israel.

Not only here, however, but the adherence to related theories about the natural history of religion, with belief in its propensity to move through certain necessary stages of development, have also tended to affect the study of Old Testament theology. Especially here we are concerned with the popularity of such ideas that religion moves through necessary stages from animism, through polytheism to monotheism. Comparable schemes are to be found asserting that religion moves through recognisable stages from a tribal to a national, and then on to a universal, frame of reference.

All of these are interesting suggestions which have at varying times affected the study of the history of religion and which have found their way into the study of Old Testament theology. It is not necessary here to do more than note the fact that they have at times gained currency and support in regard to the Old Testament. In noting them, however, we must also take some warning against allowing them to intrude their own interpretative patterns upon the study of the religious ideas of the Old Testament. The result all too often of failing to heed this warning has been that the study of Old Testament theology has developed into a form of apologetic for various semi-philosophical theories, which are relatively modern in their appearance. By doing so, the historical and critical function of such a theological task in relation to the use of the Old Testament in church and synagogue is set aside.

We cannot engage in the study of an ancient literature like that of the Old Testament without being made conscious that it has arisen in a culture and world of ideas which is strikingly different from our own in many respects. The very necessity of translating the Old Testament from its ancient Hebrew and Aramaic original into modern English raises questions which are more than simply textual and grammatical, and which reflect upon wider areas concerning the relationships between language, culture and ideas. We may pause therefore to consider three very prominent features in which significant aspects of the relationship between language and ideas has been thought, in varying degrees, to be reflected in the Old Testament.

The first of these relates to what has been termed 'primitive thinking', to use the terminology made current by the French anthropologist Lucien Lévy-Bruhl.[9] This concerns the view that primitive societies, both in the ancient and modern world, do not think in the same rational categories as more sophisticated communities but in a more intuitive and symbolic manner. Hence there is a tendency towards collective thinking, in which the individual does not readily isolate his own thought-processes from those of the community to which he belongs. The validity, or otherwise, of Lévy-Bruhl's theory from an anthropological point of view is not our concern, but we must note the way in which his ideas have influenced Old Testament studies especially in relation to the belief that we find there signs of the 'corporate' thinking of ancient Israel. The role of the tribe and clan, the solidarity of the family, and even the complex interchange between 'I' and 'we' in the language of psalmody and prophecy have all been adduced as evidence of such corporate thinking in the Old Testament. The case is far from being proved, and the general distrust of such theories from an anthropological point of view, warn us against any firm reliance upon them in order to understand some of the particularly complex features of the Old Testament's world of thought. In general, the belief that there can be delineated any such rounded and clearly definable category of 'primitive thinking' remains unproven. In any case the evidence of the Old Testament must be examined and interpreted in its own context, and not be made subject to explanation by dubious theories which have arisen elsewhere.

A somewhat similar word of caution regarding the possibility of our tracing in the Old Testament a number of firmly recognisable categories of primitive thinking must be made in regard to the analyses of basic categories of thought presented by J. Pedersen in his volumes on Israel.[10] Here we find repeatedly an emphasis upon a distinctively 'dynamistic' pattern of thought in ancient Israel in which words, symbolic gestures and rites were thought to be capable of a measure of self-realisation. Certainly there is strong evidence in the Old Testament that an importance was attached to the spoken word and to the demonstrative gesture far beyond that which is normal in more modern societies. However, the evidence that is adduced by Pedersen in respect of categories of curse, blessing and prophetic pronouncement all appeal to a certain 'primitiveness' in relation to processes of thought and speech as to raise questions about their validity. For all the greatness of Pedersen's achievement in bringing to light many of the strange and unexpected processes of thought which have given rise to particular cultic and social patterns of behaviour, the picture he offers goes too far in the direction of irrationality and primitiveness. Furthermore, it is often difficult to detect how deeply submerged some of these thought processes are held to be, and to what extent they had long since been forgotten by the time they make their appearance in the Old Testament.

For all the insights that are to be obtained therefore from this analysis of a primitive culture, the very concern to uncover its irrational, symbolic and dynamistic elements has led to a rather exaggerated neglect of its more reflective and rational features. On the one hand, such an approach has been of benefit in challenging the assumption that we find in the Old Testament an almost idealistic world of theological reflection. Yet on the other hand, it has set against this a picture of primitive and irrational thought patterns which allow too little for the remarkable discernment, maturity and often sophistication of thought which comes to us through the pages of the Old Testament. That there is a genuinely theological dimension to the faith of the Old Testament seems assured, else the quest that so many have set themselves in recounting this would be in vain. Even so, such a theology has to be viewed in a context of religious life and behaviour in which much was taken for granted which the more critical outlook of the modern world finds hard to understand.

The second feature of the thought world of the Old Testament which has been seen to bear illuminatingly upon the relationship between language and ideas is that of mythology. That certain stories and episodes concerning a rather vaguely defined past can be classed as 'myth', and that such myths formed an important part of the intellectual life of antiquity, is clear.[11] It may be frankly accepted that there are stories in the Old Testament which should be properly classed as 'myth', and few would deny this. In this category we should certainly include such episodes as the marriage between the sons of God and human women (Gen. 6.1–4), and the story of the confusion of languages at the Tower of Babel (Gen. 11.1–9). Most scholars would go far beyond this and find a consistent mythological element in Genesis 1–11, and note wider mythological allusions also in other parts of the Old Testament. Yet others would go so far as to see the entire world-view of the Old Testament as predominantly mythological. Against this we also find claimants to the view that myth plays a relatively small part in the Old Testament, and that the predominant trend is away from mythology towards a more positively historical type of thinking. The subject itself is sufficiently complex for more than one viewpoint to maintain a reasonable credibility, and for different approaches to its complexities to appear plausible. So far as an understanding of the intellectual world of the Old Testament is concerned we may take note of two important points.

The category of myth is itself so difficult of definition that it is improbable that any one single attempt at this is likely to obtain widespread assent. The nature of myth is many-sided, and how it is to be differentiated from saga, and even from a highly metaphorical type of language, is not easy to determine. The portrayal of God as 'the Rider of the Clouds' (cf. Ps. 18.10–11) may appear to be self-evidently mythological, or it may be interpreted as no more than a particular example of metaphor, with a complex tradition-history underlying it. Similarly, in comparison with the very extensive myths from a Mesopotamian sphere which have come to light (as in the Enuma Elish and the Epic of Gilgamesh), it is evident on even a relatively superficial examination, that the narratives of the Old Testament are of a very different order. To insist that the Old Testament belongs to a markedly mythological world of thought, therefore, would appear to be a highly exaggerated claim. At the same time to deny the presence of myth altogether, or to insist that the clear trend of the Old Testament is to discard myth in preference to a more historical type of thinking is likely to be in excess of the truth.

In this field in particular the value of a proper literary criticism comes to light, since it is important to make some distinction between 'myth' as a category of literature, and 'mythological thinking', as though it were an easily identifiable stage in the history of ideas and thought. The modern world is perfectly capable of creating 'myths' from a literary point of view, even though it cannot restore to them the kind of authority which ancient society accorded to them. That mythical thinking is itself a natural precursor of rational thought, or that rational thought naturally dispenses with or overcomes myth, are themselves theories of a complex literary and philosophical kind as to remain outside the scope of a study such as this.[12] Certainly it appears hazardous to make the dispensing with myth a leading feature of an Old Testament theology, even though the very nature of theology makes it critical of the role of myth in religion. Furthermore, it is scarcely satisfactory to endeavour to understand the Old Testament from the assumption that it is through and through coloured by mythological processes of thought. All too easily the manner of defining the questions tends to determine the kind of answers that the Old Testament is then made to yield.

In a somewhat similar vein we may note the third area of contrast in which the ideas and language of the Old Testament have been thought to be especially revealing in relation to the history of religious ideas. This concerns the role of magic, and the problems of differentiating between the world of magic and the world of religion, where often very similar aims and assumptions can characterise the two spheres. The belief that man may, by his words or actions, influence the outcome of events by supernatural means, and without directly participating in them, inevitably means that there is a degree of similarity between religion and magic. The distinctions between a curse and a spell, a word of good omen and a prophecy, or between a ritual and an incantation are far from easy to draw. Certainly in comparison with the kind of picture that emerges of the ancient Babylonian religion, it is clear that whatever magical element there was present in Israelite religion was of a very much more restrained kind.

Hard as they are to draw, distinctions are nevertheless important, and it seems that certain features of Israelite faith have tended to combat and reject the more overtly magical features of much ancient religion. In this area two features stand out, and render the contrast a very meaningful one. First of all, the Old Testament's strong insistence on the personal nature of God, especially as this has been brought yet more into the forefront by the recognition of his oneness, has led to a restraining, and ultimately a discounting, of the more impersonal and coercive features that belong to magic. Secondly, the awareness of the moral nature of God, and that his blessing and power are morally governed, has overthrown the beliefs, associated with magic, that divine power can be in any sense available to man for his manipulation through magical techniques. Morality, not magic, has gradually influenced, and eventually completely dominated, the belief in the presence in the world of divine power and energy. In this regard the influence of the Old Testament against any magical interpretations of religion has been very pronounced, both in the formative stages of the literature, and in the way in which it has been understood.

It is probably going too far, however, to suppose that there is an identifiable magical stage through which religion passes before its more moral and spiritual features come to the fore. Rather it seems that the temptation to relapse into magic, and magical assumptions, is constantly present in religion, and that it is one of the tasks of theology to challenge this. To this extent therefore the Old Testament, when interpreted theologically, has a valuable function to fulfill.

In all of these three areas of the history of religious ideas – primitive thinking, mythical thinking, and the realm of magic – the Old Testament has had a significant perspective to offer. As subjects of investigation they all touch upon areas of learning which range far beyond the pages of the Old Testament. Yet they are of relevance to the Old Testament, or have at least been held to possess such relevance, and it is useful to note here that they impinge directly upon the task of presenting an Old Testament theology. It would be wrong, however, to allow them, either separately or together, to exercise a dominant role in determining the way in which the theology of the Old Testament is presented.

# CHAPTER THREE

# THE GOD OF ISRAEL

The literature of the Old Testament is fundamentally religious in its character, assuming the reality and activity of God even where it does not explicitly mention him. This is so most notably in the otherwise exceptional book of Esther, which is the only one of the Old Testament writings which does not overtly mention God. More often he is mentioned very frequently in these writings, referred to either by the generic title 'God' (Hebrew *'elōhîm*) or by his distinctive name 'Yahweh' (Hebrew *yhwh*). A number of other names and titles also appear, and these all have value in enabling us to see something of the complex religious history through which this Old Testament concept of God has passed. In many cases they undoubtedly reflect distinctive local, and sometimes international, traditions about gods which were current in the ancient Near East. However, in its preserved canonical form the Old Testament certainly intends to present God as one unique supernatural being who had revealed himself to Abraham, Moses and other of the great figures of Israel's life, and who is the Lord and sole Creator of the universe.

More than a millennium of religious history, therefore, anchored firmly in an even older stream of religious tradition deriving from the ancient Near East, is guided and interpreted for us by the Old Testament. This literature contains a revelation of God who is one unique uncreated Creator of all that is. At a literary level the canon itself serves to bind together various local traditions, to link together experiences from different ages, and to lay down a unifying pattern of insights to show that it is the same God that is being described and referred to here. To some extent the use of the same names and titles serves to establish this uniformity of identity, although this could at times be misleading, especially where the use of the title *'elōhîm* alone is concerned. Sometimes *'elōhîm*, a noun plural in form, is used to refer to alien 'gods', who are held to be apart from, and even hostile to, Yahweh, the God of Israel. They have no part to play therefore, except a negative one, in the building up of the tradition about the revelation of God in the Old Testament.

Thus there is a very distinctive identity given to God in the Old Testament, which is on the one hand remarkably broadly based, because of its undoubted universalist elements, but which on the other hand is sufficiently circumscribed to assert again and again that particular rites, cultic traditions, and even sanctuaries, do not belong to him and have no place in a true knowledge of his being and will. A very careful line is drawn between a broad syncretism which could claim almost any and every religious tradition as in some sense attributable to 'God', and a narrow exclusivism, which owned allegiance to only one local, or community, tradition.

How this line came to be drawn, on what principles it was established, and by what means and insights its competing interests and tensions were resolved, cannot be reduced to any simple formula. In a very real sense the emergence of *tôrâh* – instruction – was a way of establishing this line of demarcation which became all the more important to grasp once a large number, and ultimately the majority, of Jews came to be living among gentiles in the Diaspora. Yet the nascent Old Testament was not the only means of drawing this line, since we find earlier that an important element of cultic uniformity was established by restricting the legitimate cultus of Yahweh to the sanctuary in Jerusalem. Paradoxically, however, this restriction came at a time when other pressures were forcing the faith of Israel to become more and more conscious of the universal and supra-national power and sovereignty of its God. The very tensions inherent in this meeting of the unversalist and exclusivist tendencies in the religious tradition of Israel may be seen to have borne a distinctive fruit in the Jewish and Christian religions.

The Old Testament possesses no one single definition of God, nor any one formula by which he is to be identified, although probably 'Yahweh, the God of Israel' would come closest to this. In consequence the opening self-introductory formula of the Decalogue may be taken as the broadest and most basic affirmation of the distinctive identity of God in the pages of the Old Testament: 'I am the LORD (Yahweh) your God, who brought you out of the land of Egypt, out of the house of bondage' (Exod. 20.2).

This formula draws our attention to three elements which recur with such frequency in the Old Testament as to make them a groundwork of the Old Testament faith in God. The words 'your God' identify him as the God of Israel, for there can be no doubt that the situation in worship in which this formula grew up ensured that these words were spoken by a duly authorised priest to the worshipping community of Israel. The question of who constituted this Israel, and on what conditions, will concern us in another chapter. It is sufficient here to note that this relationship to Israel is regarded as fundamental to a knowledge and understanding of God.

The second element, however, also has a bearing on this, for the words 'who brought you out of the land of Egypt' tie this knowledge of God to an event in the national past of Israel, which we find elsewhere was understood to be the foundation-event by which Israel was given birth as a nation. In this way the rise of the nation was attributed to Yahweh its God, so that the entire dimension of national existence and life was held to derive from him. Certainly this ties the knowledge of God to a historical event, but it is misleading to make this historical interest the dominating theological concern. It is not simply that in this event, as event, the hand of Yahweh was revealed, but that all that has ensued from this event, in Israel's very existence, is regarded as dependent on his action. It makes a sense of gratitude, and of obligation deriving from gratitude, fundamental to man's response to God.

To enter into the more narrowly historical question about what actually happened in Egypt to make the departure of Israel's ancestors from there the single most important feature in the tradition of the nation's origin need not be examined here.[1] There must certainly have been some such event, even though the tradition has obviously magnified its significance in all kinds of ways. It was a religious event, rather than a political one in which great numbers of people were necessarily involved.

That there is no independent corroboration for it outside the Old Testament, therefore, should hardly surprise us.

The third element in this formula of God's identity is also interesting for the way in which it modifies the second. The words 'out of the house of bondage' identify Egypt with the conditions of slavery which Israel's ancestors had experienced there, and give to the fact of escape from thence a moral, as distinct from a more narrowly political character. Certainly the whole political side of Israel's existence, with its territorial and governmental claims, was regarded as dependent on the gracious will and actions of God. Nevertheless the overt mention of freedom from slavery, with all its implications in the free development of personal life in accordance with God's will, lend to this formula a peculiarly ethical dimension. Yahweh, the God of Israel, is the God of freedom, the champion of the oppressed, the guardian of the poor and the avenger of those who have been unjustly treated. It is not surprising therefore that later generations of Israelites could be reminded of this ancestral experience as a basic motive for their own obligations to show a like defence of the poor and oppressed (cf. Exod. 22.21; Deut. 15.15). The effect is certainly to give the Old Testament conception of God a very distinctive quality of moral insight and concern. Particularly is this so when we find that the national and political aspects of Old Testament faith come into tension with its more explicitly ethical and personal features. With a reasonable consistency the tensions tend to be resolved in favour of the ethical aspects, so that God's commitment to Israel is not allowed to run out into an unqualified nationalism.

That Yahweh is the God of Israel is at once both the strength and weakness of the Old Testament. It is a point of strength because it gives its doctrine of God direction, detail, and a concrete relatedness to events, personalities and human affairs which belong to a known and identifiable historical past. There is here no vague, other-worldly, spirituality which can dissipate itself in misty sentiments and subjective longings. It possesses an extraordinary robustness, and at times an almost too immediate relationship with the realities of this world in war, politics, intrigue and commerce. Yet on balance this immediacy of contact with life and history is a major part of the attractiveness of the Old Testament presentation of God. It gives to it an extraordinary vitality which makes the expression 'the living God' no empty title.

At the same time an element of weakness is apparent because the concept of 'the God of Israel' links him very directly to one particular nation and religious community. Furthermore, from the theological point of view, this conception relates the Old Testament understanding of God to a past that is no longer with us, and to certain national and territorial aspirations which must inevitably call forth careful scrutiny. The modern Jew, if he is to see in the God of the Old Testament one whom he can still call 'my God', must come to some understanding of how he himself stands within the community of Israel. For the Christian the link with the God of Israel may appear even less direct, since it involves some understanding of the Christian community as 'the Israel of God' (cf. Gal. 6.15) and raises important issues about the relationship of Jesus to the Old Testament. Some essays in Old Testament theology have sought to overcome this apparent limitation in the Old Testament conception of a 'God of Israel', by arguing that there is a discernible trend in the literature towards a more universal faith, in which a pure religious individualism displaces the older national dimension of faith.[2] That there is some movement in this direction is discernible, but to make this a conclusive pattern of development is certainly to exceed the evidence. In this regard the way in which the New Testament interprets the Old must inevitably exercise a profound effect upon the way in which the latter is interpreted by Christians. The problem, however, is not an exclusively Christian one, since any belief in monotheism must raise these questions, as Jewish interpretation has readily recognised.

If we are to find in the Old Testament a theology – a word about God which still holds good for us today – then we are in some measure committed to asking how the picture of God that the Old Testament gives to us can be properly regarded as true of the One whom we still call 'God'. In other words we must expect to find in the Old Testament truths about God which are more than historical truths, tied to the beliefs and events of a world that has long since passed. To do this we should not expect to find arguments and theories about his existence, of which we may still approve, but rather a general picture, often in the form of analogies and images, which provide us with a worthy and recognisable portrayal of the God whom we worship.

## I. THE BEING OF GOD

The Old Testament uses a number of impersonal images to convey a sense of the majesty and restless activity of God, with which we readily become familiar in seeking language to describe the Ineffable. So God is like 'light' (cf. Ps. 104.2; Ezek. 1.27, 28), and 'fire' (cf. Exod. 19.18; Deut. 4.32, 36), and 'wind', or 'spirit' (Hebrew *rûaḥ*; cf. Hag. 2.5; Zech. 4.6). All of these convey something of the power and transcendence of God, while holding close to the conviction that an inevitable hiddenness remains in his dealings with men and their world.[3] Significant as such images are, however, the overriding impression given by the Old Testament references to Yahweh is that which concerns his personality. No other facet of his being stands out as strongly as this. He plans, wills, speaks, acts and feels like a human being. No other description of his being can so adequately describe him as that which calls him a 'person'. In a number of ways his senses are referred to as being entirely analogous to those of other persons (cf. God's eyes, Deut. 11.12; God's ears, 1 Sam. 8.21; God's nose, Exod. 15.8). While in a number of telling phrases, therefore, an importance is attached to the assertion that he is a different kind of person from human beings, who may be vacillating and deceitful (cf. Num. 23.19), the striking fact about Yahweh the God of Israel is that he possesses personality.

Two features of this vigorous personal life of the deity, as it is presented by the Old Testament, have given cause for reservations, and even theological objections. In many instances the anthropomorphic way in which God's being and actions are described seems to border on the creaturely and the naïve. Thus when he is said to 'walk' (cf. Gen. 3.8), to 'laugh' (cf. Ps. 2.4), and even to 'pant' and 'groan' (cf. Isa. 42.14), the analogical function of such language seems clearly to be stretched. It is evident in the later parts of the Old Testament literature that a serious effort has been made to tone down some of this language and to describe God's actions in a more restrained manner. This process becomes even more marked in the Greek translation of the Old Testament, and was evidently an aspect of Israelite faith which underwent some modification through Jewish encounter with Hellenism. Yet it is never seriously given up, nor indeed could it be if the ascription of personality to God, which is so essential a part of the Old Testament understanding of him, was to be retained.

A second feature concerning the personal nature of God which has occasioned difficulty is the suggestion of male sexuality in the description of him as like a man. A very careful avoidance appears to have taken place of any suggestion that God was feminine, or even that he combined a kind of male–female nature. Yet this objection, relevant as it may seem in a cursory glance at the gender of nouns and pronouns that are used to describe him, is really only superficial. The avoidance of any suggestion that Yahweh possessed female sexuality must certainly owe a great deal to the need for shunning any association with the sexual elements of the cults of Canaan in which the female element, through the goddesses Anat and Astarte, was very prominent. The sexual practices of the cultus associated with these conceptions were strongly abhorrent to the Israelites, as a prominent stream of Old Testament polemic shows (cf. 2 Kgs. 17.16 f; Ezek. 16.15 ff).

In reality, in spite of the gender of nouns and pronouns that are used to describe God in the Old Testament, it is scarcely true to say that any prominence at all is accorded to his masculinity. On the contrary, the very sharpest attack is made by the prophet Ezekiel upon those of his fellow countrymen who had so misinterpreted their faith as to worship their God with the aid of male images (Ezek. 16.17). Such explicit sexuality, in this case most probably associated with images devoted to Yahweh, was regarded as a doubly false representation of God. The sexual element as a whole, whether male or female, does not obtrude in any significant way in the Old Testament portrait of Yahweh. That the underlying religion may once have accorded more place to it is possible, but, if so, the Old Testament tradition has effectively expunged it.

Comparable to the avoidance of any explicit sexuality in God, is a marked antagonism in the Old Testament to any suggestion that he may appear in animal form. This is particularly relevant because of the frequency with which the form of a bull is associated closely with both El and Baal in Canaanite religion. Although at times the Old Testament uses the image of a lion (cf. Hos. 11.10; Amos 1.2) or an eagle (cf. Exod. 19.4) to describe the actions of God, it is clear that these are straightforward comparisons. It is expressly forbidden to use images of any animal form in an effort to represent God (Deut. 4.16–18), so that the Israelite tradition contrasts markedly with that of Egypt where such animal images, especially in mixed forms, abounded in the representation of deities.

The most prominent consequence of this insistence upon the personal nature of God, with severe restraint as to the more physical aspects that might be associated with such personality, is that it enables the emotional and intellectual aspects of his nature to be vigorously presented. Hence the most telling and moving pictures of the relationship between God and his people are those which draw upon the realm of human relationships. Most noticeable here are the splendid analogies drawn from the father–son relationship (Hos. 11.1–9; Jer. 31.20) and those of the husband and his bride (Hos. 2.2; Jer. 2.1–3). More than anything else it is images such as these which have tended to characterise the Old Testament conception of God, and have enabled a warm sensitivity to soften its compelling moral earnestness.

The personal nature of God leads naturally forward into an awareness of the morality which colours all the understanding of him. He is a God of justice (Hebrew *mišpāṭ* Pss. 33.5; 36.6, etc.), righteousness (Hebrew *ṣedeq* Pss. 7.19, 11.7, etc.) and truth (Hebrew *'emet* Pss. 25.5, 10, etc.) so that no deviousness, or corruptness mars his dealings with men. He is the completely impartial judge (Pss. 7.11; 9.4, etc.) whose knowledge of the secret reasonings and plans of the human heart (cf. Ps. 44.21) ensures that no craftily laid scheme can escape the just penalty he will impose (Ps. 64.1–9). Such an unrelenting maintenance of justice might appear cold, and almost aloof from human emotions, were it not for the fact that it is entirely out of his desire to uphold 'love' (Hebrew *ḥeseḏ* = RSV's 'steadfast love') and 'loyalty' (Hebrew *'emûnâh*) that he acts in this way. In a remarkable formula, which originated in the sphere of Israel's worship, it is the gracious, patient and loving aspect of his nature, including his desire and willingness to forgive (Exod. 34.6–7), which is brought most into prominence. Justice itself is no cold and impartial reality, where Yahweh is concerned, but a basis for peace and loving relationships.

The particular concern of Yahweh with the weak and oppressed sections of society has already been noted, which has certainly had the effect of making the assisting and delivering of the weak a strong facet of the religious life, as seen from the Old Testament point of view. In the Old Testament itself this sensitivity to the plight of the weak, especially widows, orphans and aliens finds a significant place (cf. the book of Ruth). It readily moves in the direction of overstepping the more markedly nationalistic features of Israelite faith (cf. Amos 2.1). Certainly as significant, however, is the way in which the strong moral emphasis in the understanding of God has influenced, and ultimately, remoulded the conception of the cult. This is most forcibly to be seen in the way in which the concept of 'holiness' is progressively moralised, even though it does not altogether lose its cultic associations in the Old Testament.[4] Not only in its effect upon cultic vocabulary, however, but in its whole approach to the interpretation of the use of the cult, does this moral emphasis make itself felt:

> For thou art not a God who delights in wickedness;
>> evil may not sojourn with thee.
> The boastful may not stand before thy eyes;
>> thou hatest all evildoers. (Ps. 5.4–5)

In consequence we find an interesting development in the way in which the right of access to the cult and the enjoyment of its benefits came to be made subject to moral demands (cf. Pss. 15; 24.4–6). The effects are to be seen in two ways. First, the gifts which the cult was believed to bestow in prosperity, divine protection and good health, which were all aspects of divine 'blessing', came themselves to be seen as morally conditioned. There could be no enjoyment of life with God, experienced in the bounty of his presence among men, which was not a profoundly moral life. Secondly, in the later Old Testament period, when the cult of Jerusalem became more and more remote from many Jews, we can see that the fulfilment of the moral demands with which God's presence in the cult had been associated, still occupied a dominant place in the thought of man's duty to God. It gave to belief in God's presence a deep moral relevance, and an element of universal appeal, which profoundly affected Judaism and contributed to a continuing sense of the importance of *tôrâh*, even for such Jews who had no expectation of sharing more directly and personally in the Jerusalem cult.

Whatever the many factors are which have contributed to this development, there is no doubt that the Old Testament period witnessed a profound moralising of religion. The conception of a righteous and moral God has influenced at the deepest level the interpretation of the rites, forms and institutions through which he could be worshipped. Ultimately it has so transformed the understanding of religion that this was able to survive, and to find new forms for itself, when the cultus in which it was originally nurtured was swept away by events. At the same time it has enabled a religion of *tôrâh*, contained in a collection of sacred writings, to become an effective and meaningful way in which God's approach to man can be declared.

## 2. THE NAMES OF GOD

Besides the generic title 'God' (Hebrew *'elôhîm*), which occurs frequently in the Old Testament, we find over six thousand occurrences of the distinctive name Yahweh (Hebrew *yhwh*), which is consistently translated as 'LORD' in RSV, following an old Jewish tradition which substituted the title 'Lord' (Hebrew *'adōnay*) in public mention of the name.[5] The Old Testament contains a very distinctive interpretation of this name in Exodus 3.14, when God declares to Moses what his name is and its significance: 'God said to Moses, "I AM WHO I AM".' This connects the Hebrew letters with the verb 'to be', so that

God is described as the self-existent One. Moreover, the particular construction used (*idem per idem*) appears to signify that God is a category of being that cannot be defined by reference to any other category. He is unique.

It is improbable, however, that the interpretation of the name given here reflects the actual origin of its form, although this may, in fact, have had some connection with the verb 'to be' (Hebrew *hāyāh*). In spite of a great deal of research, how the name originally arose can only be a matter of conjecture.[6] In any case it is unlikely to have been a specifically Israelite achievement, since it is likely that the name was already current when the Israelites adopted it for their God, and effectively filled it with a new content by the distinctiveness of the tradition concerning the exodus from Egypt.

While its original meaning and pre-Israelite currency would be of great value for us to know more clearly from the perspective of the history of religion, it is improbable that much of the Old Testament's theological understanding of God would be greatly affected by it. The exodus tradition, together with the new Mosaic content of the religion, have become such constitutive features of the understanding of who Yahweh is that they have given to the name a new content. Although the Old Testament retained a clear awareness that the Kenites too had worshipped Yahweh (cf. Gen. 4.26), throughout the Old Testament generally it is accepted that Yahweh is the special name of the God of Israel.

In view of the strength and frequency of this tradition regarding the distinctive name of God in the Old Testament, it is at first surprising that other names should also appear to the extent that they do. The most notable here is the title *'elōhîm* (= God), and its much less common singular form *'elôah*. The latter is certainly a relatively late construction deriving from the fact that *'elōhîm* is unusual in being plural in form. In spite of various attempts to explain this as either a 'plural of extension' or a 'plural of majesty', neither explanation is likely to be correct. The plural form is more convincingly to be explained as a consequence of the Hebrew establishing of the cult of Yahweh, as sole God, at sanctuaries where previously a pantheon of several deities (*'elōhîm*) had been venerated. In order to ensure compliance with the demand that no other deities should be worshipped 'beside Yahweh' (cf. Exod. 20.3) the plural title was subsumed under the one new deity.

Etymologically the title '*elōhîm* is connected with the name 'El', who appears as one of the two most prominent deities in Canaanite religion, and whose name, through the form *ilu*, relates even more widely to a popular high-god of ancient Mesopotamian religions. The name 'El' is identified with the Israelite Yahweh, especially through the identification of the latter with the gods worshipped by Israel's ancestors in the land. These bear such names as El-Elyon (cf. Gen. 14.18 ff.), El-Roi (cf. Gen. 22.14), and El-Shaddai (cf. Gen. 17.1), which must be regarded as local forms of the god El, venerated in the land of Canaan in pre-Israelite times. The Old Testament makes a point of very strong emphasis concerning the identity of these gods worshipped by the nation's ancestors with the God Yahweh (cf. Exod. 3.13, 16). Since the Old Testament also witnesses firmly to the original Mesopotamian homeland of the nation's ancestors, a good deal of historical uncertainty remains concerning the precise nature of the El deities worshipped by them.[7]

To what extent an older religion concerned with 'gods of the fathers' had survived alongside, or subsumed under, the local Canaanite El deities of the land is difficult to determine. Conversely, it could be argued that these Canaanite religious traditions had been much modified by the patriarchal inheritance. In any case, that there was asserted a basic element of continuity of tradition between the worship of Yahweh and the El deities of the Israelite patriarchs is a prominent feature of the Old Testament tradition. It marks an important aspect of the broadening and even 'universalising' of the Old Testament religious tradition.

This contrasts rather markedly with the very much more negative attitude of the Old Testament to the cults of Baal, which formed a parallel, and in some respects more vigorous, part of the Canaanite religious tradition. Although there are some relatively minor traces of attempts to identify Yahweh with Baal (cf. 2 Sam. 5.20 and the names Ishbaal/Ishbosheth, Meribaal/Mephibosheth; 2 Sam. 2.10; 9.6 ff.), these are largely eliminated by the developing Old Testament tradition. Evidently aspects of the cult of Baal were felt to be so inimical to the Yahweh faith that the very name of Baal, and with that any suggestion that Yahweh could be identified with him, has been rejected. In this we see the very real consciousness in the Old Testament that Yahweh, the God of Israel, is unique, and that not all religious traditions are identifiable with him. At the same time, the exclusivism which we should expect to see deriving from this is not applied with the rigour which we might have anticipated. The use of the title *ᵉlōhîm* is itself a witness to this, as also are other features of the history of Israel's religion.

When we come to ask, therefore, how and why these distinctions have been drawn, we are not provided with any very explicit explanations. So far as the 'how' of the making of distinctions, it appears that this has very largely been achieved by the careful protection and the use of the divine name Yahweh. This name alone defined the extent and legitimate authority of the worship of the God of Israel. In respect of 'why' other traditions, or aspects of them, were felt to be hostile and unacceptable to the worship of Yahweh, we can only learn this by examining the polemic which the Old Testament directs against the cults of these other gods.

We shall have opportunity of considering the significance of this polemic later, in connection with the uniqueness of Yahweh, but two features come to the fore. First, we must note the marked hostility felt by Israel to the immorality associated with certain cultic traditions. Most obvious here is the sexual immorality associated with the cult of Baal (cf. Hos. 4.13–14; Num. 25.1–17). Here then the ethical element in the Old Testament religious tradition has exercised its effect. The second feature in the formation of the distinctiveness of the tradition about Yahweh is the sharp opposition to the use of images in worship, which has made their widespread use in other traditions a focus of the sharpest antagonism. So much is this so that the very word 'idolatry' has virtually come to sum up all that is false and unacceptable about the non-Yahwistic forms of religion. In the outcome all that is unacceptable to God can be described as 'idolatry' (cf. Col. 3.5).

One other feature has played a part in moulding the way in which the name of the God Yahweh has been used in the Old Testament. This is the directly political factor, which naturally infers from the assertion that Yahweh is the god of Israel that the gods of other nations are not to be identified with him. Hence the gods of Egypt, of Assyria and of Babylon are, in various ways, evidently assumed to be the rivals of Yahweh. In this factor in the tradition we can see that the political conflicts between Israel and these nations have undoubtedly been reflected in the ways in which their respective deities have been understood. The rivalry of the nations has led to the portrayal of a rivalry between their gods. Important as this feature is, it is not as prominent as we might have expected, and is certainly not the decisive factor in creating the unique Old Testament portrayal of Yahweh. Yahweh's superiority to the gods of Egypt becomes an integral part of the exodus tradition (cf. Exod. 7.11, 22; 8.7, etc.), and even more strikingly, the exilic prophet of Isaiah 40–55 makes a vigorous and effective attack upon the gods of Babylon, especially the supreme Babylonian god Marduk (Isa. 40.12–14, 18–20; 41.21–4, etc.).

All in all, however, it would be mistaken to regard the political conflicts between Israel and various of its neighbours and other great powers of the ancient Near East as the leading factor in creating the unique conception of Yahweh in the Old Testament. Where necessary the Old Testament writers have not been afraid to draw upon elements of the wider Near Eastern religious traditions in filling out the portrait of the God of Israel. At the same time they have not made themselves dependent upon any single one of these traditions to the extent that would enable us to regard it as a major 'source' for the Israelite conception of God. Perhaps it is most in the conception of creation that this wider tradition has had its part to play.

### 3. THE PRESENCE OF GOD

It is an oft-noted feature of the Old Testament that it contains almost nothing by way of argument to assert the existence of God. Even those who deny his existence are subjected to rebuke, rather than to any counter-arguments in defence of his reality.

This has sometimes been taken to imply that the existence of God is 'taken for granted', and H. H. Rowley comments that, in the Old Testament, Yahweh is 'the God of experience and not of speculation'.[8] This is in fact only partially true since there is a very clear reason why the existence of God is not made the subject of enquiry or discussion in the manner that we might expect of a theology. The reality of God, and the possibility of man's knowing him and dealing with him, are taken care of by the cult.

First and foremost in the Old Testament God is a presence to be sought and experienced at a sanctuary in an act of worship, rather than the postulate of any particular argumentation. Time and again we find that the sanctuary is the place where God's presence (Hebrew *pānîm*, literally 'face') is to be found. Hence the layout of the sanctuary, the rites and symbols used in worship, and the whole tradition concerning why the place was sacred, served to support the claim that the sanctuary was a place where men could meet with God.

We have already pointed out that a considerable proportion of the information contained in the Old Testament, especially about the origin of sanctuaries in the book of Genesis and the origin of Israel's cult in the book of Exodus, is of this kind. Certainly God was not the object of speculative thought in the Old Testament, but his existence and accessibility by men was in no way taken for granted. What we find throughout the pages of these writings is evidence that the cult itself was progressively 'theologised', and the traditions that served to authorise the cult have eventually become more important than the cult itself. So such a story as that of Jacob's founding of the cult at Bethel (Gen. 28.11–19), which originally belonged to the use of the sanctuary at Bethel, has become transformed into a tradition about the blessedness of Jacob and a confirmation of the truth that God was with him (Gen. 28.20–2).

In the earliest forms of the religion of Israel not only did the traditions preserved at the sanctuaries of Israel serve to interpret their religious authority, but the presence of certain major symbols also served to affirm the fact of Yahweh's presence among his people. Three such symbolic institutions stand out most prominently. First of all we find mention of the sacred ark (Hebrew *'ārôn*), the name of which indicates that it was a box of some kind, and which was used in leading Yahweh's people into battle. The ancient rubric that is associated with this institution shows that the ark could be addressed very directly as though it were Yahweh himself:

Arise, O Yahweh, and let thy enemies be scattered; and let them that hate thee flee before thee. (Num. 10.35)

Later, in the Deuteronomic literature, this older view of the ark is subjected to a theological development, which almost entirely discards the implication that Yahweh's presence is directly associated with it (cf. Deut. 10.1–3).

The earliest tradition about the ancient tent-shrine of Israel shows the same kind of immediacy regarding the way in which God's presence was believed to be related to it (Exod. 33.7–11). In the later tradition this too was subjected to a theological development which came to invest it with all the apparatus and significance of a much more elaborate shrine (Exod. 26.1–37). The Tabernacle is in fact a rather idealised portrait of a sanctuary, in many respects reminiscent of the great temple building of Jerusalem. This latter building (cf. 1 Kgs. 6.1–36) also shared in the elaborate traditions of religious symbolism and iconography that had grown up in the ancient Near East. Solomon's employment of Phoenician architects and craftsmen almost certainly was reflected in the style, layout and symbolism of the building. In particular the cherubim, which formed the most prominent of these symbols (cf. 1 Kgs. 6.23–8), must be regarded as guardians of the way to the divine throne (cf. Gen. 3.24). They, like the sanctuary as a whole, expressed the specific assumption and purpose of the cult, which was that, through his chosen shrine, God was present with his people. The language of the Psalter abundantly testifies to the way in which the hymns and prayers of worship reflected and interpreted this belief. Only later, in the seventh century, do we begin to find a determined effort to recast in more refined theological concepts how this divine presence could be known and experienced through the cult. This appears in the Deuteronomic theology which asserted that it was God's name which was present at his sanctuary (Deut. 12.5 ff.), and which could re-interpret the temple as essentially a house of prayer to the God who dwelt in heaven (1 Kgs. 8.22–53).

A further development in the same direction towards the 'theologising' of the cult and its symbols is to be seen in the post-exilic Priestly theology which regarded the cloud of the divine 'Glory' as the means by which God's presence could be found on earth (cf. Exod. 24.15–18; 40.34). In many ways the particular vocabulary and imagery used to describe how the cult could serve to mediate the divine presence is of less importance than the fact that such a process of 'theologising' was felt to be necessary at all. Underlying this development we can discern a greatly enhanced awareness of the transcendent nature of God, and a growing loss of faith in the power of the visual and spatial symbolism of the cult to mediate his presence.

It is difficult to avoid the conviction that this progressive rejection of symbolism, and its replacement by the development of theological concepts was related to the entire rejection by Israel of the use of any image of Yahweh. We shall need to consider the reasons for this in examining the unique features of the worship of Yahweh, but for the present it is worthy of note that the rejection of the use of any image of Yahweh came to be associated with the specifically spiritual and transcendent nature of God. 'Idolatry' summed up that which was felt to be flagrantly pagan and hostile to the true nature of Yahweh. It seems improbable that any one single feature of a historical or theological nature has alone been responsible for this development. Rather a feature which belonged to the very earliest stages of the Yahweh religion has acted as a catalyst, and has drawn to itself a number of insights and convictions about the true nature of God which have ultimately proved to be among the foremost theological assets of the biblical tradition.

Not only has the process of theologising the cult affected the way in which this was itself interpreted and understood, but it has also served to strengthen several other concepts and images concerning the activity of God upon earth. Increasingly this activity came to be expressed through concepts and language of a decidedly a-cultic character. Foremost here we must undoubtedly place the concept of God as 'spirit', or 'wind' (Hebrew *rûaḥ*), which gave a remarkable realism to the sense of his vitality and omnipresence. Nowhere is this more effectively expressed than in the words of Psalm 139.7:

> Whither shall I go from thy Spirit?
> Or whither shall I flee from thy presence?

What is so remarkable about this assertion is not simply that it makes 'spirit' a leading concept for the portrayal of the divine presence on earth, but that it does so with an apparent complete independence of the concepts and symbols of the cult. Later, in the post-exilic age, the concept of spirit became an important part of the vocabulary concerning the nature of God, and enabled the language and ideas concerning his presence with Israel to develop outside the narrower confines of the cult (cf. Hag. 2.4–5; Zech. 4.6). The role this played in sustaining and fostering a strong religious life among Jewish exiles and those in the Diaspora can only be guessed at, but must have been quite profound.

Alongside the concept of 'spirit' we find other concepts of divine mediation coming into vogue, notably those of Word and Wisdom. Later still, by the first century of the Christian era, the concept of the Shekinah, the tabernacling presence of God among men, became a richly used means for explaining the language and ideas of the Old Testament which referred to God's presence on earth.[9] In its own way it both witnesses to the way in which this language had given rise to the need for fuller theological explanation, and also sought to supply that explanation by the formation of a concept in which the immanent and transcendent aspects of the divine nature were linked together.

In another way also the ideas associated with the concept of the divine presence have undergone a considerable development in the Old Testament. The belief that the institutions of the cult could themselves mediate this presence carried with it certain very important consequences concerning the relationship of the deity to space and time. The sacred area of the sanctuary was 'holy' because of the divine presence there, and the physical consequences of this were a prominent aspect of all that was understood by the term 'holiness'. To be near the sanctuary was to be close to God. In the Priestly stream of cultic legislation in the Old Testament the exact location of this presence could be given with remarkable precision (cf. Exod. 29.42; 30.6; Lev. 16.2). This stands in a measure of tension with belief in the divine omnipresence to which Psalm 139.7 witnesses. Increasingly the emphasis upon the ubiquity and omnipresence of God seems to have prevailed, so that the spatial language concerning the 'nearness' of man to God has taken on a new dimension of interpretation in relation to a spiritual, and almost mystical, sense of man's communion with him.

A comparable effect on the cult has taken place in regard to God's relationship to time. The Psalms attest very strikingly the sense of immediacy and directness with which God 'appeared' to his people when they came into the sanctuary to worship him at the set festivals (cf. Ps. 96.13). So marked is the language that attempts have been made to explain it in terms of a tradition about a cultic theophany.[10] The sanctuary was not only the place where God 'dwelt', but to which he 'came', and no inherent contradiction seems to have been felt between these two metaphors for the manner of God's acting through the sanctuary.

Nevertheless we observe two developments occurring in relation to this language. In the first place the language of a direct 'coming' of God to his people during the great festivals has been set aside. In its place we find that the whole understanding of the cult was gradually transformed to make its rites and praises into acts of 'remembering' the work of God in the past (cf. esp. Deut. 16.3, etc.). By such a subjective act of 'remembering' the past the worshipper appropriated its benefits and meaning for himself anew. The related development was to project the language concerning God's 'coming' to his people into the future to make it an expression of the hope of the blessing which would belong to Israel when God fulfilled his declared purposes for it. The language of God's 'coming', therefore, has been transformed into the language of an eschatological hope which originated in all its main essentials with the prophets. Concepts of sacred time and sacred space have thereby both been profoundly affected by the way in which the understanding of the presence of God in the cult underwent a process of change. In many cases the most marked effects of these changes do not become manifest until a very late Old Testament period, or even beyond this. In other cases, however, we can see, as most noticeably in the way in which the book of Deuteronomy interprets the cult, that the initial stages of such a development began to make their appearance quite early. As we have had occasion to mention earlier, it is no easy task to establish any kind of clear chronology to the course of Israel's intellectual and theological development. Changes which were of the greatest importance to the Jews of the Diaspora seldom appear to have originated with them. Rather it was because certain far-reaching theologising tendencies were already present in the religion that so much of the tradition of Israel's religious past, which had been nurtured in the cult, retained its meaning for Jews in the much changed circumstances of the post-exilic age.

### 4. THE UNIQUENESS OF GOD

The Decalogue of Exodus 20.2–17, which sums up so much that is central in the Old Testament religious tradition, makes the foremost of its demands upon Israel: 'You shall have no other gods beside (RSV, before) me' (Exod. 20.3). This command not only prohibits the giving of precedence to any other God, but it firmly precludes the acceptance by an Israelite of any allegiance to another god alongside Yahweh. In a situation in which the Canaanite religious tradition usually regarded the god of its major sanctuaries as the head, or 'king', of a pantheon of gods, this prohibition was particularly meaningful. It effectively meant that the loyal Israelite was to be a person who had dealings with only one God. That this obligation had existed from the very beginnings of the religion is scarcely provable, but is hardly to be doubted. So marked a change as its introduction would have entailed could scarcely have taken place without leaving its mark in the tradition. Because of this demand the sense of uniqueness attaching to Yahweh, and an awareness that other cultic traditions could not simply be combined in his worship, belong to the very essence of the religion of Israel. Yahweh is a unique God, who is held to be unlike other gods.[11]

Eventually this sense of uniqueness finds its fullest and firmest expression in the Old Testament in the monotheism of Isaiah 40–55 (cf. esp. Isa. 40.18, 25; 41.21–4; 43.11; 44.6–8). Here with this exilic prophet the ultimate consequence is clearly drawn that Yahweh alone is God, and that other gods that men seek to worship do not in reality exist. However, the path from the earliest Mosaic sense of the uniqueness of Yahweh to the polemical monotheistic assertions of the exilic prophet is a very difficult one to trace. Some have argued that the sense of uniqueness concerning Yahweh amounts to a monotheistic faith all through, while others have regarded the unknown exilic prophet as the first of the truly monotheistic thinkers of the Old Testament.[12] Others have sought to coin a suitable expression by which to define the particular Israelite understanding of God, such as 'incipient monotheism'. There are indeed recognisable stages at which various of the writers of the Old Testament accord to the belief in other non-Israelite deities some measure of reality (cf. Deut. 32.8–9; Judg. 11.24). Perhaps little is to be gained by either attempting a suitable definition of the Mosaic conception of God, or of a precise outlining of the 'stages' by which this developed into a full monotheism. Two points, however, deserve some special attention.

The first of these concerns the helpfulness, or otherwise, of such a relatively speculative concept as monotheism. Many have pointed out that it is in many respects a rather abstract concept, and one which, for this reason, is not very suited to the more pragmatically oriented faith of the Old Testament. More than this, however, it is a concept which is capable of several interpretations. One possible conclusion that could be deduced from it is that all the names, titles, forms and traditions by which men have venerated their separate deities, must in reality have been offered to the one true God, who alone exists. In this way the sense of multiplicity and variety which everywhere faces us in looking at religion, and nowhere more than in its ancient Near Eastern forms, is treated as an illusion. The 'One' that exists behind the 'many', is regarded as the reality which has become overlaid by an appearance of variety. Israelite monotheism was certainly not of this kind, else its antagonism to other religious traditions, especially those which it found in Canaan, becomes quite inexplicable.

At the other extreme, the idea that the apparently rather insignificant deity of a nation that was historically a very small one among those that emerged, and briefly flourished, in the ancient Near East, is alone the true God, can appear quite ludicrous. There is some necessary sense in which a realistic monotheism compels a concern with the other forms of god that men worship. There is no doubt that the Israelite tradition was fully aware of this, and was willing to identify its faith with aspects of other religious traditions where this was appropriate. We have already drawn attention to this in regard to the identification of Yahweh with El, and there is ample evidence to support the view that this carried with it some very significant elements of the religious tradition of ancient Mesopotamia. The Israelite conception of the uniqueness of Yahweh managed to create a surprisingly homogeneous tradition out of a great variety of separate parts, and to bring together a coherent picture of one unique deity. This retained both universal and particularist elements in a measure of tension which we can believe has ultimately proved profoundly fruitful and convincing. The more abstract concept of monotheism would not, by itself, have necessarily been particularly helpful in enabling this picture to emerge.

A second feature concerning monotheism is also important. We find a number of tendencies present in the polytheistic religions of Canaan and Mesopotamia which can best be termed 'monotheistic'. This is in no way to claim that we find here a clear-cut and comparable monotheism in the background of ancient Israel from which its own conception of God might be held to have been adopted. This is not the case. Nevertheless we do find both in Babylon as well as in Canaan tendencies to exalt one deity to a position so far above all others that he comes to exercise a kind of supreme authority. The most notable example of this is in connection with the Babylonian god Marduk, who was the supreme deity of Babylon, but the exaltation of El in Canaanite religion shows some comparable tendencies. Furthermore the cultic celebrating of the role of one god as 'king', follows in the same direction. We find therefore in religious traditions that have been generally regarded as polytheistic that a strong trend is often apparent in the direction of elevating one god to a position of greatest eminence, and even supremacy.

So far as the Old Testament tradition of Yahweh's uniqueness is concerned, a marked emphasis was placed by the tradition upon his superiority to other gods. Hence the narratives regarding the plagues in Egypt greatly exalt Yahweh over the gods of Egypt. Furthermore we find in the prophets and their interpretations of events that they regard Yahweh as controlling the actions of non-Israelite rulers, even when they do not acknowledge him (cf. esp. Isa. 10.5 ff.; 41.2–4; 45.1–5).

The feature in the Israelite tradition about the uniqueness of Yahweh that has achieved most prominence is undoubtedly that which concerns the prohibition of the making or worshipping of any image of him. The origin of this prohibition goes very far back, but, surprisingly, the earliest layers of the Old Testament tradition offer no clear explanation for it. Various suggestions have been put forward, most plausibly, that the setting up of an image could be thought to convey to the worshipper some measure of direct access to, and even control over, his god. The freedom and transcendent nature of Yahweh could then have been felt to have been prejudiced in this way. By the time that clear explanations are offered in the Old Testament, we find that a more historical reason is given (cf. Deut. 4.15–18). It is, however, in the exilic age that the sharpest polemic against the use of images emerges, in which the whole understanding of the reason for the prohibition is set on a profoundly theological plane (cf. Isa. 40.18–20; 44.9–20). The creation of an image is taken to suggest that the workman who makes it must in some sense be thought to be making a god. Against this the whole idea of God who is himself the Creator and source of all things stands in opposition. Ultimately it is this line of polemical argument which comes to predominate in the discussion about the making and use of images. They are taken to be images made 'with human hands', and therefore as created things, cannot serve to represent the Creator (cf. Philo, *De Decalogo*, 58–61).

Certainly the prohibition of the use of any image for the

deity grew to be regarded as the most characteristic feature of the cult of Yahweh. It naturally came to enjoy prominence as an expression of the uniqueness of the theological conception of Yahweh held by Israel. Conversely 'idolatry' was to express all that was hostile to him, and all that was palpably 'false' in the religious traditions of the non-Israelite nations. That there is underlying this theological development a very much more complex history of religious controversy concerning the use and legitimacy of symbolism in worship is evident. Since the immense wealth of symbolism and iconography in the religions of the ancient Near East can only be brought with difficulty into clear categories of meaning and significance, the precise course of these controversies are far from easy to trace. So far as the Old Testament is concerned, the period when the most forceful attack on idolatry was made, in so far as it had been accepted at all in early Israel, regards it as already so expressive of an alien tradition that it is condemned in the sharpest possible terms (cf. Jer. 2.27; Ezek. 20.7, 18, etc.).

The uniqueness of Israel's conception of Yahweh its God might easily have led to a narrow and exclusive attitude in regard to him, so much so that such a faith would in no way have broadened out to become a universal religion. Yet this it has done in Christianity and Islam, and, with some limitations, in Judaism also. Several factors have contributed to this wider understanding of God, which was not content to think of him as 'the God of Israel' in a restrictive and purely nationalistic fashion. First of all we must certainly place the belief in Yahweh's role as Creator of the material universe. That there are two separate creation narratives in Genesis (1.1–2.4a is ascribed to the source P, and 2.4b–3.24 to J) has gained almost universal acceptance among scholars. One of the consequences of this is that it points us to a relatively early date for the emergence of the earliest of these (the J narrative), to a time when the buoyant nationalism of Israel was very strong. That Israel's faith should have incorporated this concern with Yahweh's role as Creator has undoubtedly been an important factor in widening the theological horizons of the tradition to a universal dimension. When we survey the arguments adduced to affirm that Yahweh alone is God, we find that the claim that he alone has created the world unaided is foremost among them (cf. Isa. 40.28; 42.5; 45.18, 22). That the theme of creation in the Old Testament should have drawn upon even older elements of Near Eastern tradition, involving a connection with creation mythology, is in no way surprising. What is particularly striking about the Israelite reminting of this is the genuinely universal character that is accorded to the material. Neither in the early (J) nor late (P) accounts is there any suggestion that the order of creation has been fashioned to give some special precedence to Israel, or its geographical setting. In spite of some minor echoes of the tradition that Jerusalem lay at the centre, or 'navel', of the universe, the Old Testament fully recognises the openness of the entire created order to Yahweh's control. Israel is not accorded any exclusive 'right' or 'privilege' in respect of the created order, even though its history then unfolds in a unique way. That other nations also have their own role to fulfil within creation is fully accepted in the narratives of Genesis 1–11.

A further element in the direction of widening Israel's understanding of God has certainly been contributed by the prophetic insistence upon Yahweh's control of all nations and their histories. This is particularly brought out in the inclusion of large collections of 'foreign nation' oracles within prophecy (esp. Amos 1–2; Isa. 13–23; Jer. 46–52; Ezek. 25–32). God's interest in the changing political fortunes of the world do not cease at the borders of Israel. Nor was it necessary for Israel to be directly involved with the fortunes of other nations for such a concern on Yahweh's part to become manifest. Sometimes this is the case, but by no means is it true in every instance. The genuine universality of Yahweh's concern with the affairs of men is accepted as a presupposition of the prophets and their preaching.

A third element in the move towards a universal faith must be accorded to the unique moral emphasis in the Israelite understanding of Yahweh. Morality itself is a supra-national reality, and the needs, sufferings and ambitions of all men, as men, were thought to come before Yahweh. We have already had occasion to touch upon this aspect of Old Testament faith, and it is apparent that it has found its way into the prophetic

preaching. There is an unbounded note of universality in the
address of the prophet to mankind in Micah 6.6–8:

> He has showed you, O man, what is good;
> and what does the LORD require of you
> but to do justice, and to love kindness,
> and to walk humbly (or 'circumspectly') with your God?

# CHAPTER FOUR

# THE PEOPLE OF GOD

If the primary point of reference in the understanding of who God is in the Old Testament is that he is 'the God of Israel', then the natural correlate of this is that Israel is to be understood as 'the people of Yahweh'. This clearly involves some understanding of the identity, scope and purpose of the people called 'Israel'. From the point of view of the Old Testament the answer to this question of identity is resolved very simply by the portrait of Israel as the patriarchal ancestor of the nation, whose twelve sons produce offspring which become twelve tribes, who themselves ultimately grow and prosper until they become a nation (Gen. 35.22–6). Such is the simplicity of the tradition, although the theological implications of understanding it are not resolved by its form. For one thing Israel comprised a single nation for only a remarkably small part of the period covered by the Old Testament. After less than a century the united nation split into two, the larger part of which survived for two centuries, and the smaller for little over a century more. After this the time when all Israel, or all who claimed descent from Israel, could be defined as a nation ceased, and has never been recovered. Although for a brief period a new national entity of Judah emerged in the late Old Testament period, this never embraced all those who felt themselves to be Jews, nor even a majority of them. In the modern world the revival of the state of Israel since 1947 has not incorporated all Jews into its citizenry. The national dimension therefore has remained something of an 'ideal' point of reference for an understanding of the people of God.

The claim that the people of Yahweh have all been descended from one man asserts, by its nature, a 'racial' theory of identity and membership within this community. Yet we find that, precisely because it is understood as a religious community, the racial criterion alone has seldom sufficed to resolve all questions about the nature and role of 'Israel' in relation to Yahweh. Other factors of a moral, spiritual and political kind have all played their part. Indeed the importance of the concept of Israel's nationhood in the Old Testament witnesses to a measure of overstepping of the straightforward 'racial' theory of accounting participation in this community. There is therefore, even at a surface level of understanding the situation, no easy resolution of the difficulties which emerge once the question is raised 'who is a Jew?' (cf. Rom. 9.6–8).

In fact, however, the situation becomes more complex once the Old Testament evidence is examined in critical detail. First of all we find that the picture of the origins of Israel from the twelve sons of one ancestral figure is a kind of 'image' or 'structure' imposed upon a tradition which was historically very much less clear. The Old Testament itself does not know more than a few features concerning the historical origins of many of its member tribes. Furthermore, how and why the 'image' of the descendants of the twelve sons as twelve tribes arose in the way it did has been a matter of considerable debate.[1] Even the time of origin of such a portrayal has been strongly contested. Whether it does accord with some kind of prenational social and institutional structure, or represents a later 'idealised' picture of a past are views which have each gained adherents.

The world of the Old Testament was one in which the political and social mechanisms of government were much less developed and sophisticated than they are today. As a result the Old Testament does not possess a technical vocabulary to define what constituted a 'state', and who qualified as a 'citizen', with anything like the precision that we should desire, or find necessary in the modern world.[2] Such vocabulary as existed in ancient Israel was of a broader, and more loosely defined kind concerning such entities as a 'people' (Hebrew *'am*) a 'nation' (Hebrew *gôy*), a 'tribe' (Hebrew *šēbeṭ*) and a 'father's house' (Hebrew *bet 'āb*). It is only when we come to look at aspects of a more pragmatic nature concerning the structure of a nation that we obtain a clearer picture. This particularly concerns the aspects of territory and government, so that for Israel questions of its land and kingship become of outstanding importance. Alongside the interest in, and emphasis upon, racial descent these two features each played a vital part in establishing the nature and identity of Israel as the people of God.

Nevertheless all three aspects – race, territory and government – are not in themselves, or in combination, necessarily religious in their nature, so that a more directly religious quality of 'faith', or 'allegiance to *tôrâh*', also came to play its part. How this occurred, and how differing emphases came to be placed upon each of them, is a feature of the unfolding of the tradition in the Old Testament. The ability to interpret the history of this tradition by reference to the actual course of Israel's political and social history, enables us to see it in a fuller light. It does not of itself, however, enable us to resolve the tensions that are apparent between the different factors. Even more important from the theological point of view, it does not enable us to single out any one feature of the Israelite tradition so as to make it possible for us to establish this as the 'norm' or the 'ideal' of what constitutes Israel.

It is in this regard that considerations that were raised in an earlier chapter regarding the ability to trace 'development', or some natural line of progress, in the Old Testament must be borne in mind. The fact that the earliest form in which Israel appears is that of a tribal community does not mean that this must be considered the norm for all time; nor does the fact that by the end of the Old Testament period the 'national' stage of Israel's life had been severely reduced mean that the hope of restoring it in full measure had been abandoned.

From the Christian perspective the understanding of Israel came to be interpreted in a more exclusively 'religious' light, with the emphasis falling upon the people as religious 'community', or *ekklēsia*. All we can hope to do in examining the theological aspects of Israel's belief in its calling to be the people of Yahweh is to try to understand better the varying factors that played their part. This requires not only some attention to the political fortunes of Israel in the Old Testament period, but also some awareness of the social factors that were involved as well. Above all, however, it requires that we should endeavour to single out those institutions in the people's life, and those concepts by which they interpreted them, which have a particular bearing upon the way in which Israel came to understand itself as the people of God.

From this basis we can then begin to see that the formulae that have tended in the past to dominate the discussion of these issues are seldom in themselves entirely adequate. It is not true that universalism eventually predominates over nationalism, or that 'religious community' naturally displaces the 'territorial state'. Nor is it clear that the Old Testament maintains any single interpretation of what constitutes the ultimate 'goal' of Israel's election. The images that are used to describe the future eschatological Israel are not of a kind that can be easily recast into explicit theological categories.

### I. PEOPLE AND NATION

Within the Old Testament tradition a very clear presentation is made of the occasion when Israel became a nation. It is the moment when Yahweh made a covenant with the people whom he had delivered out of the bondage of Egypt:

> Now therefore, if you will obey my voice and keep my covenant, you shall be my own possession among all peoples; for all the earth is mine, and you shall be to me a kingdom of priests and a holy nation (Exod. 19.5–6).

This report of the institution of the covenant with Israel on Mount Sinai is certainly not contemporary with the event it describes, but represents a reflection upon it from a much later age. The question of the date when this particular presentation emerged will call for discussion later in considering the history of the use of the concept of covenant in this connection. What is important here is to notice that Israel is understood to be a 'holy nation' (Hebrew *gôy qāḏôš*) and a 'kingdom of priests' (or a 'kingdom in respect of priesthood'; Hebrew *mamleḵeṯ kōhᵃnîm*) from the time that God made his covenant with the people on Sinai. The making of this covenant is more or less synonymous with the constitution of the nation.

What exactly 'kingdom of priests' means, whether it concerns the special role that priests were to play within the nation's need to maintain its holiness, or whether it denotes a 'priestly kingship', or whether, as is more usually understood, it points to a unique priestly role that Israel is to play in respect of other nations, cannot be determined with certainty. What is striking about this particular tradition is that it makes the covenant between Israel and Yahweh a basic and conditioning element in the existence of Israel as a nation. The origin of the nation, therefore, is pushed back to the relatively distant moment in the past of its constituent tribes, before it had acquired its territory or government. The tradition makes the institution of the covenant the decisive moment in the nation's life. In this way the religious element has very dramatically been set in the foreground. The view that Israel's life as Yahweh's people can be understood from this far back in the history of its origins is further supported by the tradition of Deuteronomy 26.5: 'A wandering Aramean was my father; and he went down into Egypt and sojourned there, few in number; and there he became a nation, great mighty, and populous.'

This summary, which probably comes from the seventh century BC, looks back on the nation's past and sees the natural growth in Jacob's descendants while they were in Egypt as the point at which they became a nation. Such a view is also that suggested by the account of the oppression in Egypt, which looks upon the sheer growth in numbers of Jacob's descendants as making them into a people (Exod. 1.7–8). From the point of view of the Old Testament tradition, therefore, there is a near unanimity in regarding the time spent by the nation's ancestors in Egypt as the period of growth into the proportions of a nation, with the actual moment of constitution coming at the time when Yahweh made his covenant with them on Mount Sinai.

All of this contrasts somewhat with a critical historical view of the time and circumstances in which the nation of Israel appeared on the stage of history. If we take 'nation', which is the closest counterpart to the Hebrew *gôy*, to mean 'territorial state', then we do not really encounter this as an established reality until the time of David. Until this period the land upon which the tribes of Israel were settled was shared by them with other ethnic groups, as the Old Testament itself is fully aware. In particular also we know that the Philistines had come to exercise a powerful political hold upon much of the land, exercising their control even where they were not in direct occupation. Furthermore, from the perspective of imperial politics, it appears that the Egyptian empire had by no means conceded that the land of 'Canaan' was no longer a vassal province under their suzerainty. Competing interests and conflicting claims existed until the time of David, when for the first time Israel gained sufficient internal political strength to establish a stable government, to lay claim to reasonably firm borders, and to introduce some basis of unity among the mixed ethnic groups occupying the land. If our criteria were to be those of modern statehood, then we should first find that a state of Israel became a reality under David. As such, however, it flourished for only a short time, since after Solomon's death the youthful nation split apart into the two separate kingdoms of Israel and Judah.

It is characteristic of the Old Testament that it should take a rather different viewpoint in its own approach to understanding the origins of Israel, for its concern is to look more deeply into the religious meaning of such events. As a consequence it offers only a piecemeal and incomplete record of how the land as a whole was brought under Israelite control, the rival claims of other factions countered, and even how the Egyptian claim to control was overthrown. Instead, the Old Testament tells us about the divine purpose which had brought about the rise of Israel. This it does by recounting the providentially governed lives of the patriarchs, the divine miracle of the exodus from Egypt, and the chastening and educative value of a period spent in the wilderness before entering the promised land. The focus is less upon the political realities than upon the hidden theological purposes which are seen to have been at work. So the account of the conquest itself, which brings the nation into full possession of its land, is more theological than political in its orientation. It is more concerned to demonstrate the great power of God that was at work in making this act of conquest a reality, than in narrating how all the different regions of the land of Israel were occupied.

On one point, however, the tradition is very clear and positive. This is that Israel existed as a people, and spent some time in occupation of the land, before it set up a firm central government in the form of a kingship. The aspect of government, therefore, which would appear to be indispensable to any modern concept of what constitutes a nation, is set in a relatively secondary position. Israel had been a people before it introduced a monarchy, so that this latter was not to be regarded as essential to the life of the nation. In fact, as we shall see when we examine this institution, it was a part of the national life which came to be looked at very critically.

Just what feelings of unity existed between the tribes before there was a monarchy, and what means of common action in war and social affairs enabled them to express this unity in concrete policies, are far from clear. According to a widely accepted and attractive hypothesis, this period, which the Old Testament views as one in which Israel was ruled by 'Judges', was that of an amphictyony.[3] Others see it as a tribal federation, and the two social patterns are not entirely identical. Certainly it was one in which the nascent Israel was moving towards a greater feeling of solidarity, and a growing awareness of the need for unified government for military and defence needs. In a number of ways we can see that politically it was ultimately the need for effective military action against the threat of the Philistines that forced Israel to introduce a monarchy and from this to move towards the establishment of a full territorial state.

The fact that the Israelite tradition came to view its life as a 'people' as older than its acquisition of its land or the founding of its monarchy was of inestimable importance when the time came that both realities were lost. When, in 587 BC, the last remnant of the state of Judah fell to the Babylonians, we find a new phase of the life of the people of God coming into being. Jews who had been deported to Babylon came to form a community in exile, and this cherished the hope of returning to its old homeland to re-establish the nation and rebuild its cities. Its goal was clearly the complete restoration of the people of Israel, which it believed still remained the intention of God, now re-affirmed through the mouths of prophets.

In spite of an initial attempt at restoration in the late sixth century, this hope was never fully realised in the Old Testament period. The exile instead grew into the Diaspora, with an ever-

increasing number of Jews scattered throughout the Mediter-
ranean and Asiatic lands. In time they outnumbered the Jews
who lived in Judah under Persian and subsequently Hellenistic
rule. So far as the Diaspora was concerned two conflicting
interests become apparent. On the one side it was of the utmost
importance to show that the tradition of the people of God, as
it had come to be accepted, did not disinherit these Diaspora
Jews from their part in God's election, nor release them from
their obligation to live in obedience to him, nor deprive them
of their hope of sharing in the final blessedness of Israel. Yet on
the other side the national dimension of Israel's life could not be
forsaken, nor the hope abandoned which had grown up among
the early exiles that the nation of Israel would be fully restored.
The result was that the tensions arising from these conflicting
interests could only be resolved by projecting the hope of the
restoration of the nation more and more into the future. For
some the concept seems to have lost much of its appeal, while
for others it awakened the deepest and most searching of
desires for the final 'salvation' of Israel. Much of the sectarian
conflict in later Judaism can be seen as a reflection of these
competing desires. When we find that the Old Testament is a
book concerning the promise of salvation, therefore (cf. Luke
1.30–2), it is essentially this understanding of the ultimate
salvation of Israel that is referred to.

From the point of view of historical development we can see
that the period when Israel existed as a single nation was a
relatively small part of the time-span covered by the Old
Testament. Yet it established an important point of reference
and brought into being many of the central concepts and ideas
by which the belief in 'the people of God' was understood. At
no point in the later Old Testament literature is the hope of
restoring the nation altogether given up, even though a new
emphasis came to be placed upon the organisation and life of
Jews as a religious community. Similarly the period before the
nation became a full political reality under David is viewed by
the Old Testament tradition so completely from the point of
view of this emerging nationhood that the separate nature of the
events that led up to it is entirely overlaid. Everything is seen
from the perspective of 'all Israel'.

This fluidity in the structure of Israel during the Old Testament period is one contributory factor in the difficulty of
writing a 'history' of the people. The entity that is itself to be
studied does not remain constant, but has a surprising varia-
bility of form. Even more strikingly the major historical sources
in the Old Testament view this reality of Israel from very distinctive perspectives. So the period of the two kingdoms –
Israel and Judah – is recounted in the books of 1 and 2 Kings
as though the people still remained one ideal entity, and had
only temporarily been split into 'two houses'. The view that
there ever were two separate 'nations' (Hebrew *góyim*) is
conceded only in retrospect (Ezek. 37.22). In the history of
1 and 2 Chronicles, which was written later still, but which also
covers this period of division, the belief in the unity of Israel is
brought out as forcibly, although in a rather different way.[4]

There is a very real measure of conviction throughout the
Old Testament, therefore, that the belief in Israel's special role
as 'the people of Yahweh' was to be seen as something that
reached to a deeper level than a simple nationalism. It did not
regard nationhood alone as the criterion by which the role of
Israel was to be understood. The implications of this for
Judaism and for Christianity have been immense, enabling
each to retain a vital sense of continuity with the community of
the Old Testament. At the same time the important consequences this has had upon the understanding of God are hard
to over-estimate, since it has ensured that Yahweh is thought
of as much more than simply a national God. Just as the 'people'
of Israel are constantly pressed into becoming something more
than a nation, so the God of Israel was never a God whose
popularity might rise and fall with the fortunes of the nation of
Israel. Had this been the case then all effective regard for him
would have ceased long ago, engulfed by the catastrophes that
overtook the Israelite-Jewish people.

## 2. THE THEOLOGY OF ELECTION

When we come to ask the question why Israel is the people of
Yahweh in this unique fashion, the Old Testament presents us
with the answer in the form of a theology of election.[5] The most

striking affirmation of this is to be found in Deuteronomy
7.6–8:

> For you are a people holy to the LORD your God; the LORD
> your God has chosen you to be a people for his own possession,
> out of all the peoples that are on the face of the earth. It was
> not because you were more in number than any other people
> that the LORD set his love upon you and chose you, for you
> were the fewest of all peoples; but it is because the LORD
> loves you, and is keeping the oath which he swore to your
> fathers, that the LORD has brought you out with a mighty
> hand, and redeemed you from the house of bondage, from
> the hand of Pharaoh king of Egypt.

The theology of election that is given here, with the assertion
that Yahweh has 'chosen' (Hebrew *bāḥar*) Israel, marks a very
prominent feature of the teaching of the book of Deuteronomy.
As such it cannot be clearly shown to have arisen in this form
before the seventh century BC, when this particular vocabulary
of 'election' becomes current. Yet the main ideas of such a
theology are certainly very much older, and the belief that
Israel is Yahweh's people carries with it many of the essential
elements of such an election faith. The whole tradition concerning Abraham and the other patriarchs of the nation (Gen.
12–50) is viewed from the perspective of belief in such an
election. The promise made to Abraham that his descendants
would become a nation, possess the land of Canaan, and be a
blessing to other nations (Gen. 12.1–3, etc.) conveys most of the
ideas implicit in such a theology of election, even though the
special vocabulary of 'choosing' is not actually employed.
There is a very real sense, therefore, in which the whole of the
tradition about Israel's ancestors that has been preserved in the
book of Genesis must be seen as a theology of election, since it
is strongly coloured by this particular forward-looking interest
in the rise of Israel as a nation, and a promise of its greatness.
From the point of view of the actual written form of the history,
there is a virtual unanimity among scholars that this national
existence had become a reality when the main outlines of the
account were established.

What the vocabulary of election adds in the book of Deuteronomy is a more conscious relating of this special bond between Yahweh and Israel to the existence of other nations: Yahweh 'has chosen you ... out of all the peoples ...'. What in fact this is to mean for these other nations is not made the subject of any special reflection in Deuteronomy, although later it was to become an important point of concern in understanding the divine choice of Israel. It raised a number of questions about what Israel's role was to be in regard to these nations. The theology of election, in the strict sense, is therefore a very particular facet of the teaching of the book of Deuteronomy. This work, which is the product of a school of thought which emerged in the seventh century, shows throughout a sense of crisis and threat. It is very conscious that Israel might, at this stage in its history, come to grief altogether, and lose everything that Yahweh had given to it: land, freedom, holiness and its special destiny among the nations. A pervasive assumption throughout the book is that Israel is a nation, and it can scarcely be said to countenance the possibility that Israel might continue to live as Yahweh's people in some form other than that of a nation. For its authors, to be thrown out of the land and scattered among the nations would be death (cf. Deut. 4.25–8).

If the book of Deuteronomy brings into the forefront of Israel's understanding the concept of a 'chosen nation', it also witnesses in a rather different way to the importance of three institutions which served in their separate ways to give content and visible reality to this belief in divine election. These were the kingship, the central sanctuary, and the land.

The introduction of a monarchy into Israel is described in a hesitant and critical manner, firmly recognising that it was not of itself essential to the salvation of Israel (1 Sam. 8–12; cf. esp. 1 Sam. 12.15, 25). Yet this rather negative approach to the ideology of kingship in the Old Testament is countered by the very strong and positive emphasis which is placed upon David and his dynasty as the divinely chosen royal family of Israel (cf. 2 Sam. 7.18–29). All the good and beneficient aspects of monarchy which belong to a favourable view of the institution are centred upon David and his descendants. Here in fact we find a surprisingly rich vocabulary, which could view the king as 'the son of God' (Ps. 2.7), a priest of a unique order (Ps. 110.4), and even the very breath that gave life to his people (Lam. 4.20). The king could, if he remained obedient to the divine will (cf. 1 Sam. 12.14; Ps. 132.12), be a source of life, salvation and blessing for Yahweh's people.

Yet the Old Testament is careful to insist that it is not the institution of monarchy as such, but the special 'chosenness' of the Davidic family (cf. 1 Kgs. 11.32; 2 Kgs. 19.34) which can accomplish this. The governmental aspect of the life of the people of God, therefore, is, from the point of view of the Old Testament, very firmly put into the hands of David and his descendants. Once this distinctive outlook concerning the role of the Davidic dynasty is understood, we can see that within this limitation the Old Testament retained a quite positive attitude towards the kingship. When the disaster of 587 BC overtook the nation, the hope of the restoration of the Davidic monarchy became the focal point of the hope of restoring Israel's political independence (cf. Jer. 33.14–26; Ezek. 37.24–5). In very many respects, therefore, we can see that the Davidic kingship became a visible symbol of Israel's election, and served as a witness to the special bond between Yahweh and the nation. The relationship between God and the king, which could at times be described as a 'covenant' (cf. 2 Sam. 23.5; Isa. 55.3; Jer. 33.19–22), was a central point of contact and mediation between God and his people.

It is quite in keeping with this that once the political possibilities began to fade, after the exilic age, of restoring one of David's descendants to the throne of Judah, the figure of the coming messiah ( = Anointed One) of David's line was thought of in increasingly transcendental terms. The frustrated political hopes forced attention back to the theological groundwork upon which all such hope was built. This lay with the belief in Yahweh's purpose for his chosen people Israel.

Certainly we can see very important points of criticism directed against the monarchy, sometimes on account of its moral and social failures (cf. 1 Sam. 8.11–18); sometimes on account of its religious and cultic shortcomings (cf. 1 Kgs. 11.7–13; 12.26–33); and sometimes because the people put greater trust in the institution than it properly warranted (cf.

1 Sam. 8.7; 12.15, 17, 25). Yet these criticisms do not lead to a complete rejection of the institution from the perspective of the Old Testament writers. It was believed to have its special part to play as an embodiment and representation of the unique relationship between Yahweh and Israel.

The second of the great institutions which served as a visible sign of Israel's elect status was the chosen sanctuary set on Mount Zion. Primarily this was in the form of the temple, built by Solomon (1 Kgs. 6.1–38; 7.15–51), destroyed by Nebuchadnezzar (2 Kgs. 25.9, 13–17), and rebuilt by Zerubbabel (Ezra 3.8–13; 6.13–22). Yet the particular vocabulary of the Old Testament speaks more broadly than in terms of the magnificence of the temple as a sanctuary, and develops a distinctive theological view of the chosen status of Mount Zion (Pss. 84.5–7; 87.1–3; 132.13–14).

The roots of this theological development are to be sought in the widespread importance attached to sacred mountains and to temple-mountains in the ancient Near East. From the Israelite historical situation a special strengthening and vindication of the belief that Mount Zion had been chosen in this way to be Yahweh's abode was supplied by the installation of the Ark there (2 Sam. 6.1–15; 1 Kgs. 6.19). Most probably, however, we should also recognise some prophetic oracular utterance as a part of the origin of the belief.

There is no sure support for claiming that it was a simple Israelite adaptation of an older Canaanite tradition, since this fails to account for many of the distinctively Israelite features that belonged to it.[6] As with the kingship, so also with the Zion theology, the development of the tradition came to see in the temple of Jerusalem, the sacredness of the temple hill, and ultimately the special holy nature of all Jerusalem (cf. Jer. 3.17; Isa. 62.1–12), a visible sign of the elect status of Israel. The nation's election, and the visible testimony to this in the sanctuary on Mount Zion, were related aspects of the belief in the unique bond that related people and God to each other.

What we have said earlier about the significance of the cult in ancient Israel and the particular way in which the blessing and holiness of the cult were conceived of in a quasi-physical fashion has a special importance in its application to Jerusalem.

It encouraged the view that Jerusalem was itself the source of life, light and prosperity for God's people (cf. Ps. 92.12–15; Ezek. 47.1–12). From it justice would be dispensed to the nations (cf. Isa. 2.3–4); light and truth spread abroad among them (Isa. 60.1–14), and in the peace and prosperity of Jerusalem the well-being of the people of Israel, and ultimately all mankind would be advanced (cf. Zech. 14.16–21).

Here is a distinctive area in which the traditions and symbols of the cult took on a unique form in Israel, and from this became the basis for a quite remarkable kind of theological understanding. The chosenness of Mount Zion came to be seen as a special aspect, and in its own way a special guarantee, of the chosenness of the people of God. As the cult had been regarded as providing a point through which divine blessing and life could flow into the nation, so now in a broader, and less cultically oriented fashion, the political and social well-being of Jerusalem came also to be thought of as contributing to this. The very name 'Zion' became a part of the special vocabulary concerning the elect status of God's people (cf. Isa. 40.9; 51.3, etc.).

In a further extension of this meaning and symbolic significance attaching to the concepts of Zion and Jerusalem we find them later being used as images of heaven, and in particular to express the final state of blessed fulfilment which would attend the destiny of the people of God (cf. Rev. 21.2). Alongside this we find too that Jerusalem came to be linked in a very special way to the eschatological expectations of Judaism so that the names acquired both concrete and symbolic meanings, which at times are not all that easy to distinguish from each other.

The third of the institutions of Israel's life which acquired a very special significance as a visible expression of Israel's elect status was that of the land.[7] Already at a very fundamental stage in the growth of the Israelite tradition we find that the promise of the land was a constituent part of the promise to Abraham that his descendants would become a great nation (Gen. 12.1–3). This land then became the subject of the basic theme of divine promise which binds together the patriarchal traditions. Its extent is set out in idealistic terms to cover the maximum area of control which the Davidic empire attained

(Gen. 15.18–21; cf. 2 Sam. 8.1–15; 24.2). The extent of Israel's actual boundaries at any given time and the effect that the nation's diminishing political fortunes had upon these territorial claims can be pursued historically only with the greatest difficulty. The sparseness of information precludes our drawing more than very tentative boundary maps for much of the historical period covered by the Old Testament. Certainly, by the time of the Assyrian conquests in the latter half of the eighth century, little was left of the immense territorial area that the Davidic-Solomonic empire had claimed.

However, from the perspective of Old Testament theology it is not the extent of the land, but the particular theological significance that was attached to holding it, that concerns us. Here it is once again the book of Deuteronomy that provides the fullest theological treatment of the conditions and consequences of Israel's holding of its land. This land is interpreted as the nation's 'patrimony', or 'inheritance' (Hebrew *naḥªlâh*), which stood in the forefront of God's gifts to his people:

> And you shall eat and be full, and you shall bless the LORD your God for the good land he has given you (Deut. 8.10).

> Know therefore, that the LORD your God is not giving you this good land to possess because of your righteousness; for you are a stubborn people (Deut. 9.6).

As the gift of the land is so important to Israel, so its loss would be synonymous with the destruction of the nation. To be driven out of the land was the direst of the consequences that could follow from Israel's disobedience to God's commands:

> If you act corruptly ... you will soon utterly perish from the land which you are going over the Jordan to possess; you will not live long upon it, but will be utterly destroyed (Deut. 4.25–6).

Although, therefore, there is a less articulate tradition underlying its special significance, such as we find in the cases of the kingship ideology and in connection with the Mount Zion temple theology, yet the land also served for Israel as a visible symbol of its special relationship to God. The people were never to forget the God who gave them this land (cf. Deut.

8.11 ff.), and were to take steps in their worship to ensure that they displayed a proper gratitude to him (cf. Deut. 26.5–11, esp. v. 10). To live long on the land that God had given was the reward of an obedient and responsive life (cf. Deut. 5.16). As in the case of the kingship, so with the land, the particular aspect of national life that it represented was regarded as so important that without it Israel would no longer be a nation (cf. Deut. 11.26–32; 28.15–68). To be driven out of the land was consequently seen as the forfeiting of all that God's election of Israel had brought to the people. The land was not only a gift of God's election, but to some extent it was also an expression and confirmation of it.

It is in this respect that we discover a gradual change developing in the interpretation of the significance of the land during the time of the exile. Once the people had been driven out from their inheritance they did not completely perish, but retained, with the encouragement of prophets, a very real expectation that they would one day return to it. Surprisingly also the exiles in Babylon came to regard themselves, rather than those who had actually survived on the land, as more fitted to retake possession of it (cf. Jer. 24.1–10; Ezek. 33.23–9). The land became for these people a sign of hope, and an object of promise. That they would one day be able to go back to this land, purge it of all its unclean elements, and rebuild within it a new community which would truly be the chosen Israel of God was their deepest spiritual longing (cf. Jer. 29.10–14; Ezek. 40–8). From being the gift of God, the loss of which would spell disaster, it became the central object of hope and eschatological expectation. It became impossible to think of a restored Israel, and a cleansed and purified community, except in relation to this land. Even more than the hope of a messiah it appeared as an indispensable part of the life that was anticipated as the fulfilment of Yahweh's choosing of Israel.

Even within the later period of the Old Testament literature we find the formative stages of that faith emerging which regards this land as necessary to the fullness of Israel's salvation (Isa. 65.17–25).

We have already mentioned that it is an unexpected feature of the teaching of Deuteronomy in regard to Israel's election

that, although it consciously considers Israel's position in relation to the nations, it does not develop from this any role or
service that Israel is to play in regard to them. Yet in the earlier
tradition of God's promise to Abraham there is an assertion
that Abraham's descendants are to be a 'blessing' to the
nations (Gen. 12.2). This may be taken simply in a reflexive
sense to mean that the nations will swear by the 'blessing' of
Israel as an example of what such a rich destiny may mean.
More probably, however, we should see in this a wider affirmation that in Israel's blessing other nations too will be blessed. If
so, then it would appear to be through Israel's rise to nationhood
and imperial greatness, with a Davidic king at its head, that
this promise was believed to find fulfilment (cf. Ps. 72.8–11, 17).

The earliest model that we find for the interpretation of what
Israel's election means for other nations is that of an imperial
power bringing peace, prosperity and righteous government to
those over which it ruled. For a brief period such a 'political'
interpretation of the goal of Israel's election prevailed. Yet the
realities of the actual historical situation after the division into
two kingdoms made such a hope hollow and pretentious. We
find, in consequence, that it re-appeared in a modified, and
much more directly religious, form.

The most striking expression of this religious re-interpretation
of Israel's imperial expectations is to be found in Isaiah 2.2–4
(= Mic. 4.1–5), with its picture of a great pilgrimage of the
nations coming to Mount Zion to hear God's law (tôrâh). In
the preaching of the later exilic prophet of Isaiah 40–55 we find
this understanding of the special religious purpose which Israel
is to fulfil among the nations brought yet further to the fore
(Isa. 45.14–17, 20–3; 49.6, 7; cf. 60.1–9; 61.5–7). It is clear
that in part the strong emphasis upon the subservient role that
was to be given to the nations, which made them into Israel's
servants and slaves, tends to detract from the higher level of
the prophetic vision as it first appeared. Yet it still retains
something of an expectation that Israel's election is an election
for service to bring other nations to a knowledge of Yahweh.

Most fully is this brought out in the interpretation of Israel's
role as 'servant' which is to be found in the 'Servant Songs'
of Isaiah 42.1–4; 49.1–6; 50.4–9; 52.13–53.12. Broken and

incomplete as the images are of the servant's work that are set forth here, they look for Israel's blessing to be carried beyond the boundaries of the survivors of the old nation (esp. Isa. 49.6). The light that God had given to Israel would become a light by which other nations also might live. Strikingly too the servant-master image is reversed, and it is Israel's task to be the servant in order that God's truth and righteousness might be made known to the nations. The picture is not that of a 'mission' in the strict sense of a going out to the nations, but rather that, when Israel returns to its homeland, it will bring the faithful of other nations in its train.[8]

### 3. THE THEOLOGY OF COVENANT

If the concept of election represents the basic Old Testament viewpoint on why Israel is Yahweh's people, then that of covenant stands as the most widely used of the concepts, or analogies, to express the nature of the relationship between them.[9] It is not, however, the only analogy that is used, and we find that the image of Israel as Yahweh's 'son' has a deeply embedded place (Exod. 4.22–3; cf. Hos. 11.1–9; Jer. 31.20). So also the marriage imagery of Israel as the 'bride' or 'wife' of Yahweh finds employment (cf. Jer. 2.2–3).

Prominent as the sonship imagery is in parts of the literature, it remains very much a metaphor, and undergoes little in the way of theological explication and reflection. It hints at the 'naturalness' of the bond between Yahweh and Israel, without defining this in any explicit fashion, or adducing any mythology to support it. Evidently too the use of marriage symbolism was restrained on account of the antipathy to the strong sexual overtones that were current in the cult tradition of Baal.

All of this points to 'covenant' as the most flexible and convenient of the analogies by which the relationship between God and people could be expressed. Such at least is suggested by the prominence which the term receives in certain parts of the Deuteronomic tradition. It comes to provide as full and as considered a theological account of the God–nation relationship as the Old Testament anywhere presents. Of added significance is the fact that this particular covenant theology has exercised a profound effect upon the growth and shaping of the literary tradition of the Old Testament.

Before examining this theology and its antecedents it is necessary to consider the main features of the Deuteronomic movement and its literature. It has long been recognised by scholars that the book of Deuteronomy represents a seventh-century revision of the Mosaic tradition of Israel, with a special focus on a revised edition of the Book of the Covenant (Exod. 20.22–23.19).[10] This Deuteronomic law-book was certainly, in some form or other, the law-book discovered in the Jerusalem temple which became the basis of the great reform under king Josiah (2 Kgs. 22–3). Yet the book of Deuteronomy is not the work of a single author, but of a circle of writers and reformers which was active over an extended period, leaving marks of progressive expansion in the book. This same circle has clearly had a considerable hand also in shaping the writing of the history of Joshua to 2 Kings, which has frequently been termed the 'Deuteronomistic (or Deuteronomic) History' in consequence. It was composed in the first half of the sixth century BC, although many scholars detect in it signs of a revision, apparently made after the destruction of the Jerusalem temple in 587 BC.

A third literary product of the Deuteronomic movement is to be seen in the book of Jeremiah, where both an extensive narrative tradition about the work and preaching of Jeremiah, as well as a number of 'sermons' based on themes from the prophet's ministry show signs of Deuteronomic editing. Evidently the Deuteronomic movement had found in Jeremiah's preaching an important source of authority for its own work. All three literary works, therefore, the book of Deuteronomy itself, the history of Joshua to 2 Kings, and the edition of the book of Jeremiah reflect the hands of the Deuteronomic 'school'. These writings can also be seen to reflect some progressive development of certain themes, which is most noticeable in the case of the theology of 'covenant'. It is apparent that the tradition of the covenant of Horeb (Deut. 5.1–21) has become the centre of an elaborate covenant theology in these different literary works which have passed through the hands of the Deuteronomists.[11]

We noted earlier that the birth of Israel's life as a nation is ascribed by Exodus 19.5–6 to the moment when Yahweh instituted his covenant with the nation on Mount Sinai (= Horeb). The language of covenant in this passage has certainly been incorporated into it by the Deuteronomic movement, as also is the central theme that makes Israel's obedience to the covenant a condition of the continuance of its life as a nation (so especially Exod. 19.5). Here we encounter a marked feature of the covenant theology of the Old Testament, and one which has occasioned considerable discussion.

A covenant, as normally understood, points to a compact, or agreement, between two or more parties to which all are bound. As Exodus 19.5–6 affirms, and as other aspects of the covenant tradition corroborate (cf. 2 Kgs. 23.3; Jer. 11.1–8), the idea of a covenant that was binding upon both parties is clearly presented by the Deuteronomic teaching. Yet there is in the Old Testament a stream of tradition regarding the making of covenants which speaks of them as virtually synonymous with the making of a solemn promise. This is most noticeable in connection with the covenant made by God with Abraham (Gen. 15.18), but it is also reflected in the tradition which interpreted the divine promise to David and his descendants as a covenant (cf. 2 Sam. 23.5).[12] How are we to reconcile these apparent differences between the conception of a covenant which was that of an unconditioned promise and that which saw in it a conditioned agreement in which the mutual obligations were prominently declared? No entirely satisfactory answer has been forthcoming, although a number of important suggestions have contributed to a better understanding of the different patterns of covenant. We may note the following three main lines of investigation:

(1) It was suggested by J. Begrich as long ago as 1944[13] that the original Hebrew meaning of 'to make a covenant' was 'to make a solemn promise', and that no conditions would be attached to this. Later, under the influence of Canaanite commercial practices, this was changed to make the institution that of a 'conditioned' agreement, thereby seriously weakening its theological clarity. However, this view reconstructs a history of the concept which is largely a matter of supposition, and it

fails to take account of the fact that by far its greatest theological development in the Old Testament is based upon the understanding that it denotes a conditioned agreement.

(2) A somewhat different approach has been argued for in an extensive series of studies by E. Kutsch.[14] He defends the view that 'to make a covenant' was originally a unilateral action, tantamount to meaning 'to impose an obligation'. This could either be upon oneself, in the form of giving a promise, or upon another in which a 'binding' of the other person would be undertaken. Eventually the situation in which each of two, or more, parties gave and accepted obligations to each other gave rise to a situation in which a mutually conditioned covenant agreement arose. It is in this form that the belief in a divine covenant between Yahweh and Israel has ultimately been developed. This, like the view of J. Begrich mentioned above, depends upon the reconstruction of a rather uncertain semantic history of the vocabulary of covenant-making in ancient Israel. It also fails to allow enough room for the appearance of both types of covenant alongside each other. A quite different approach to the problem has been advocated on the basis of a study of the forms of covenant-making.

(3) A large number of scholars, led by G. E. Mendenhall,[15] have detected in the forms of covenant-making in the Old Testament a dependence upon an ancient Near Eastern form of vassal-treaty. In this political form of treaty a suzerain power granted a covenant to a subordinate (vassal) power, but stipulated certain conditions in doing so. Hence the superior position of the suzerain was fully acknowledged, whose initiative was stressed, but an element of bilateral obligation was present. Mendenhall distinguished such vassal-treaty covenants from promissory covenants, such as that with Abraham, where no explicit obligation on the part of the recipient was acknowledged. This hypothesis has been extensively explored, both in its implications for the date of origin of covenant concepts in the Old Testament, and in the particular significance that the borrowing and adaptation of this form may be thought to reveal about Israel's religio-political ideology. Only a brief summary of criticisms may be put forward here.

Of itself the claim for an Israelite dependence upon this

special ancient Near Eastern treaty form has failed to establish a convincing basis for showing the Mosaic introduction of such a covenant ideology into Israel. It is abundantly evident that the mainstream of covenant language and ideas enters into the Old Testament tradition with the Deuteronomic movement.[16] It may be that some influence was felt here from contemporary political ideology, but, if so, it was much modified. In consequence this particular hypothesis does little to assist us in understanding the unique way in which the Deuteronomic movement has developed the concept. In fact, most of the features of this Deuteronomic ideology can be adequately explained without resort to this particular hypothesis of a borrowing of a form, coupled with a major modification in its purpose and significance.

Furthermore, the marked differences between such treaty-covenants and promissory covenants are noted, without any clear explanation being offered why the same term is used to describe them. Not least we may also mention that so many features of Israel's distinctive covenant ideology have been held to derive from this ancient oriental form that it has come close to overwhelming the features it has been adduced to explain. We must therefore regard it with considerable caution. Once the Old Testament tradition is looked at critically, then the parallels that have been adduced to support a dependence upon this treaty form are much less prominent than has been maintained by its advocates. The amount of light that can, in consequence, be brought to bear upon the Old Testament by appeal to such a borrowing becomes drastically reduced. Whether such a hypothesis can be sustained at all, therefore, remains in question, and it can offer little elucidation of the distinctive way in which the Old Testament interprets Israel's relationship to Yahweh after the analogy of a covenant. We are entitled to assume that covenant-making, both in the political and the social sphere, was sufficiently well known in ancient Israel for the use of such an analogy to be ready at hand.

When we come to look in detail at the origin and nature of the Israelite covenant theology, we find several points emerging with reasonable clarity. First among these we must put the fact that, in spite of a number of earlier instances where the term 'covenant' (Hebrew $b^e r\hat{\imath}t$) is used in a uniquely religious way (especially in Gen. 15.18 and 2 Sam. 23.5),[17] it is with the Deuteronomic movement that it becomes the major term by which to describe Israel's relationship to Yahweh. It is unlikely that this Deuteronomic vocabulary was an entirely novel introduction in the seventh century to describe the relationship, but it clearly acquired a quite new emphasis then. It is in any case in the Deuteronomic History and the development of Jeremiah's preaching that the concept of a covenant between God and people receives its fullest development.

In covenant ideology two points stand out very prominently, and have greatly influenced all subsequent development of it in the Old Testament. The first of these is that Israel's existence and continuance as a nation is made dependent upon its obedience to the covenant (cf. esp. Exod. 19.5–6; Deut. 4.13–14; 2 Kgs. 17.15). In particular, as we have already noted in connection with Israel's beliefs about the land, its occupation of the land of Canaan is singled out as the most prominent of all the features by which this nationhood is signified. The supreme punishment is seen as that of being driven out from the land to perish among the nations. The conditional nature of the covenant is therefore taken very seriously and no hesitation appears in drawing the direst consequences from the threat which this inevitably brought. Just as Israel had been given birth as a nation by the election of God, so its death could be brought about by disobedience to the covenant through which the election had been given expression.

The second major point about Deuteronomic covenant theology is that the stipulations of the covenant which are binding upon Israel are set out in the form of a written 'law'. This 'law' is called a tôrâh (Deut. 4.44), and contains obligations of a legal, social and more directly religious nature. The actual scope of this tôrâh is defined in more than one way, since supremely it is made to refer to the Ten Commandments of Deuteronomy 5.6–21 (= Exod. 20.2–17; cf. Deut. 4.13). However, the broader commands of Deuteronomy 4.44ff. are also included as tôrâh, in which the Deuteronomic law-code proper of Deut. 12–26, must be seen as having a special place.

There are signs therefore that the precise scope of *tôrâh*, and the injunctions that it contained, was itself the subject of development and elaboration. This was to have a great bearing upon the growth of the Old Testament. Of particular significance is the fact that from the beginnings of this covenant theology there was an acceptance that this *tôrâh* was written. Indeed, we find that 'covenant' (Hebrew *bᵉrît*) and 'law' become such close synonyms that 'to obey the law (*tôrâh*) and 'to obey the covenant' become virtually synonymous expressions (cf. Jer. 11.6, 8).

When we ask why a covenant theology of this kind, which certainly raises some far-reaching theological issues, was so appealing to the authors of the Deuteronomic movement, we can draw only one conclusion. The particular moment in history in which the Deuteronomists saw themselves and their people to be standing was a moment of crisis. The loss of the Northern Kingdom to the Assyrians in 722, followed by progressive and appalling deportations of so many inhabitants of that kingdom, left only a small remnant of what had been the great empire of David. All could yet be lost, and in the hour of threat the Deuteronomists stressed the danger that faced their fellow countrymen. They hoped that by learning the lessons of the past and recognising the threat of the present, Israel might yet be saved. The conditions of salvation were consequently very fully spelt out.

We find, however, that as the crisis unfolded and Judah's darkest hour came with the fall of its king and the destruction of its temple in 587 BC, a message of hope remained for the people. Central to this message was the preaching of Jeremiah, who had prophesied a future for his nation and people (Jer. 32.1–15, esp. v. 15; cf. 31.2–9, 20). As the Deuteronomic school came to develop its covenant theology in the light of events, and with a deep consciousness of the importance of Jeremiah's preaching, so they came to look beyond the uncertainties of a conditional covenant agreement with God to the greater certainties of the divine grace and love. A new message of hope developed which did not discard the old covenant theology, but which came to extend it in very distinctive directions.[18]

The most direct and memorable way in which this hopeful development is to be found is in the promise of a new covenant, or more strictly a 'renewed covenant', as we find it set out in Jeremiah 31.31–4. The famous prophecy takes up the substance of Jeremiah's assurance of a future for the nation, but sets it in the distinctive theological language of the covenant ideology. What it promises is a new kind of covenant:

> But this is the covenant which I will make with the house of Israel after those days, says the LORD: I will put my law within them, and I will write it upon their hearts; and I will be their God and they shall be my people (Jer. 31.33).

God will not only set the conditions of the covenant in his *tôrâh*, but he will himself, by his action within the human heart, give the power and strength to fulfil them (cf. Ezek. 36.26–7). In this way a covenant, which is recognised by the tradition to be a bilateral obligation, becomes effectively a unilateral one, since God himself ensures the fulfilment of the obligations that he makes. It becomes synonymous in effect, though not in name, with a covenant of promise.

This is not the only way, however, in which the covenant theology of the Old Testament was developed during and after the exile. More prominent in some respects is the appearance of a changed emphasis, in which the whole weight of the tradition of Israel's election is placed on the covenant between God and Abraham and the 'conditional' nature of the Sinai covenant given a much reduced place.[19] We shall note some of the wider consequences of this in considering the growth of the Old Testament and the particular importance of its role as *tôrâh*.

Throughout the Old Testament a special relationship between God and Israel is assumed and made the basis for its own distinctive presentation of the knowledge of God. In a very deep and inescapable fashion the belief that there is a special revelation of God in the Old Testament is related to the belief that he has chosen and used Israel in a special way to bring this knowledge to all mankind. Each of the different forms in which Israel appears – tribal community, nation, and a remnant scattered among the nations – brings to light some facet of the nature and activity of its God.

# CHAPTER FIVE

# THE OLD TESTAMENT
## AS LAW

We remarked in considering the problems of method associated with the writing of an Old Testament theology that it is of great importance to the subject that it should take fully into account the nature of the Old Testament as literature. This must necessarily include some attention to the literary form and structure of its constituent books, but also it should look at those broad categories by which the Old Testament as a whole has been understood. The importance of doing this is all the greater on account of the far-reaching consequences that develop from the way in which the unity of the canon is understood.

Two factors can assist us in finding this basis of unity. One is the structure of the canon itself with its division into three literary collections of Law, Prophets, and Writings, in a three-tier level of authority. The second factor is provided by the way in which the early Jewish and Christian interpreters of the Old Testament have set about their task, with the indications which they give of the particular assumptions and presuppositions which they bring to the literature. Here immediately we encounter the most widespread and basic category which has been employed to describe the nature of the material which the Old Testament contains. This is that of 'law', or more precisely *tôrâh* since the question of how far 'law' is a very satisfactory translation of the Hebrew *tôrâh* remains to be considered. Certainly it raises the question of what kind of law, and what legal authority and sanctions it may be thought to possess.[1]

In the New Testament a quotation from Psalm 82.6 is said to be written 'in your law' (John 10.34). Thus even the third part of the Old Testament canon, the Writings, could, by a kind of extension, be regarded as falling within 'the Law'. Evidently the priority and importance of the first part of the canon was felt to be such that it carried over to affect other parts also.

Certainly we readily discover other indications that this was so
for the Prophets. In Mark 2.25–6 we find the citation of an
incident regarding David and the eating of the Bread of the
Presence which is recorded in 1 Samuel 21.1–6. This incident
from the Former Prophets is interpreted as an example of the
fundamental principle, applied to Old Testament laws and
regulations, that the humanitarian demand for preserving life
is of greater importance than the more specifically cultic demand
of respect for holiness. The background and assumptions of
this interpretation need not detain us. It is simply a clear
illustration of the way in which the record of narrative incidents,
which were originally preserved for specific purposes of quite
another kind, could later be interpreted out of the basic presupposition that they are *tôrâh* – law. Nor is this approach a
uniquely Christian one, for we find very strikingly that it
pervades almost completely the mainstream of Jewish interpretation of the Old Testament. The Mishnah, and later the
Talmud, are full of citation and interpretative comment upon
the Old Testament which regard it as *tôrâh*.

Certainly we cannot put aside this fundamental category by
which post-Old Testament Jewish and Christian interpreters of
this literature have set about understanding it as though it were
imposed upon it entirely from outside. We have already noted
that the literary structure of the Old Testament supports such
a pattern of interpretation by its three-tier ordering of the
canon. From a literary point of view the Old Testament is
*tôrâh*, and the fact that it contains a great deal else in addition
to this, has to be understood in some kind of relationship to this
*tôrâh* structure.[2] What has evidently happened is that the concept
of a *tôrâh* literature has been used to provide some element of
co-ordination and unity to a very varied collection of writings.
It offers a unifying guideline, or motif, which has served to
impose some degree of order upon what would otherwise be a
rather strange miscellany of writings.

As we move further away in time from the editorial and
redactional activity which has shaped the Old Testament into
its present form, so we tend to find that the assumption that it
is all *tôrâh* has tended to become more and more dominating in
its effect upon the way in which the material is understood.

More diverse elements tend to become submerged under the weight of conviction that all the literature is *tôrâh*. At least this is so in respect of Jewish interpretation, since we find that in the mainstream of Christian exegesis a rather different category came to predominate. This is that of 'promise', which we must discuss later. In considering the structure of the Old Testament, therefore, we find ourselves facing a number of questions about its role as *tôrâh*. How far is this category endemic to the literature itself, and how far is it simply a structural framework, lightly built around writings of a more diverse character? Secondly, if we find that the category of *tôrâh* does have a real and fundamental place in the formation of the Old Testament, what exactly is this *tôrâh*? What kind of 'law', or 'instruction' is it?

### I. THE MEANING OF TÔRÂH

The word *tôrâh* occurs very frequently in the Old Testament to denote 'instruction' of various kinds. Its etymology is contested, and two possibilities present themselves. Either it has been formed from the verb *hôrâh* (√*yārāh*) with the meaning 'to direct, aim, point out', or it is a Hebrew counterpart of the Babylonian word *tertu*, 'oracular decision, divine instruction'. Most probably the former is correct, in which case the word means 'guidance, instruction'.[3] As such it could be the kind of instruction which any person might give in a whole variety of situations. However, we find that the word is predominantly used for religious instruction, and especially for the kind of instruction which could be given by a priest. The clearest confirmation of this is to be found in Jeremiah 18.18:

> Then they said, 'Come let us make plots against Jeremiah, for *tôrâh* shall not perish from the priest, nor counsel from the wise, nor the word from the prophet. Come, let us smite him with the tongue, and let us not heed any of his words.'

The assumption here is evidently that *tôrâh* would especially be given by a priest. Yet we find in the Old Testament that others besides priests give *tôrâh*. Hence the prophet does so (cf. Isa. 8.16); so also does the wise man (cf. Prov. 3.1; 4.2), and also apparently the king (cf. Isa. 2.3). To what extent any clear

development or extension of meaning can be traced over a
period is hard to determine with confidence. Evidently a word
of *tôrâh* was particularly the kind of instruction that the ancient
Israelite expected to learn from a priest, so that it was a
religious direction, the ultimate source of which was to be
found with God.

What kinds of rulings might be the subject of such priestly
*tôrôth* can only be inferred from the particular duties and concerns which fell to the priest to take care of in ancient Israel.
Obviously matters concerning the protection of the holiness of
a sanctuary, the obligations of worshippers at the major
festivals, and what perquisites belonged to the priests and their
families would form a part of this. The fact, however, that a
much wider range of concerns dealing with the health of the
community, the avoidance of unclean foods, and even sexual
and social manners, counsels us against drawing any very
narrow conclusions about the nature and scope of *tôrâh*. Cultic,
ethical and hygienic interests could all be made the subject of
priestly *tôrôth*. That the word could readily be extended to
cover matters where the traditions of the past, most naturally
thought to be in the custody of the priest as the guardian of the
community's lore, could all be included is not difficult to see.
What is noticeable is that it does not specifically apply to
juridical traditions in the narrower sense of 'law', nor is it a
broad word for general ethical admonition, although it could
include this.

So far as the formation of the Old Testament is concerned a
quite fundamental development is to be found in the book of
Deuteronomy, where *tôrâh* becomes applied to the law-book
itself:

> This is the *tôrâh* which Moses set before the children of
> Israel; these are the testimonies, statutes, and the ordinances,
> which Moses spoke to the Israelites when they came out of
> Egypt ... (Deut. 4.44–5).

This summarising introduction to the central part of the book
of Deuteronomy is particularly helpful to us in showing the
way in which the idea of *tôrâh* was developed and extended. It
must once have formed an opening introduction to an edition

of the book, and so clearly was intended to apply to a written text. Hence it has carried over the idea of an orally given *tôrâh*, delivered as occasion demanded, to a more permanently recorded account of what constituted the *tôrâh* of Israel.

There is clearly also a very marked effort present to achieve comprehensiveness, as is shown by the definition which follows and the wide range of rulings and injunctions which the book contains. The definition in terms of testimonies (Hebrew *ʿēḏôṯ*), statutes (*mišpāṭîm*) and ordinances (*ḥuqqîm*) is interesting for the way in which it brings together words denoting laws, decrees, and admonitions under one all-embracing category. From this time onwards *tôrâh* came to signify the most comprehensive type of instruction in which legal, cultic, and more loosely social obligations were brought together. To obey *tôrâh* was to satisfy the demands of religious, social and family life in the broadest possible compass. Even quite directly political obligations would appear to be included.

The definition that is given in Deuteronomy 4.44 f., therefore, provides a valuable summarising note about the kind of duties that are brought under the heading of *tôrâh* in the book of Deuteronomy. When we look at the contents of this book this anticipation is fully borne out. Very decidedly the book is addressed to each and every Israelite, who bears the responsibility for bringing its contents to the attention of his children (cf. Deut. 6.7; 11.19), and of reflecting upon them carefully himself (cf. Deut. 11.18). No exceptions are envisaged or allowed for. Included in the book are rulings of a markedly legal character concerning the processes of law and the way in which serious crimes are to be dealt with (cf. Deut. 19.14–21). Murder, theft, adultery, and the problems arising therefrom about the trial and punishment of offenders, are all included. But so also are matters of an exclusively religious kind such as the observance of cultic festivals (Deut. 16.1–17), which even incorporates notes on how the festivals are to be interpreted. Perhaps more surprising in a document of this kind, which is concerned to spell out precisely the nature of the individual's responsibilities and obligations, is that moral attitudes are commanded, particularly those of love and respect (cf. Deut. 15.7–11). Even more prominently is this carried over into the religious realm, so that it becomes a prime duty to love God, and to feel and express gratitude to him (cf. Deut. 6.5; 9.4–5). Beyond these broad ethical admonitions, we find that a wide area of life comes under the heading of *tôrâh*. Obligations for military service, the care of buildings, the conservation of the environment and the protection of slaves are all included (cf. Deut. 20.1–20; 21.10–17; 22.6–7; 23.12–14).

So far as the threat of punishment for disobedience to particular *tôrôth* is concerned, two points call for comment. The first is that the entire machinery of the state, with all its sanctions, is involved in dealing with all offences against the injunctions laid down. Hence religious offences, especially apostasy, are to be dealt with by the most severe sanctions (Deut. 13.5, 8–11). In some cases, as for instance in that of failing to show a right attitude, it would clearly have been impossible to adjudicate the fault. Yet this highlights the second feature concerning punishment, which is that, over and above the particular punishments and sanctions that society could impose, there stood a larger sanction. This is that Israel would have shown itself to be disobedient to the covenant with Yahweh, and would forfeit all its privileged status as his chosen people. We have already considered this earlier in relation to the Deuteronomic teaching concerning Israel and the covenant.

This brings us to note the wider theological context in which the book of Deuteronomy places the notion of *tôrâh*. This is not treated simply as 'good advice', which might, through social pressure and the good sense of the hearers, be accepted by men of good intention everywhere. It is directed specifically to Israel and is the *tôrâh* of the covenant by which Israel's relationship to God is governed. It is as a consequence of belonging to the elect people of Yahweh that the Israelite finds himself committed in advance to obedience to *tôrâh*. Hence he found that it was imperative for him to know *tôrâh*, to understand it correctly, and to be reminded of it regularly, if he were to remain as a member of his people. Furthermore, it was upon the sincerity and willingness of each individual Israelite that the well-being of the whole nation was made to depend.

When we come to ask the question 'What is *tôrâh*?', therefore, the clearest and fullest answer that we have is that which is

provided by the book of Deuteronomy. *Tôrâh* is the comprehensive list of instructions and stipulations by which Israel's
covenant with God is controlled. What we have now to do is to
enquire further how far this understanding of *tôrâh* has affected
the Old Testament as a whole.

## 2. THE PENTATEUCH AS TÔRÂH

In the book of Deuteronomy the structure of the work, and its
role as *tôrâh*, is reasonably clear. This is much less so in the case
of the Pentateuch as a whole, however, on account of the wide
range of source material that has been incorporated into it, and
the less unified structure that has ensued as a result. On two
points scholarship has become confidently clear in regard to the
Pentateuch. The first is that the origins of the Old Testament
as canon are to be traced back to the book of Deuteronomy and
to the particular authority that was accorded to it in the great
reform of king Josiah (2 Kgs. 22–3). The second is that the
Pentateuch was the first major section of the present Old
Testament to be accorded canonical status in anything like its
present form, and that its consequent pre-eminence is a continuing reflection of this.

The process of forming the Old Testament as canon, therefore, can be traced through three major stages. Its beginning is
to be seen in the book of Deuteronomy, or at least that part of
it which acquired special significance on account of its role in
Josiah's reform. The second is that this canonical work grew
until it took on the proportions of our present Pentateuch; and
the third stage is that in which two further collections had been
added to this, the Prophets and the Writings, until our present
Old Testament had been formed. The seed-bed of the belief that
the Old Testament as a whole can be called *tôrâh* is then certainly to be found in the way in which the *tôrâh* of Deuteronomy
has cast its influence upon the whole literary collection.[4] The
concept of a canon and the concept of a written *tôrâh* go hand
in hand and become part of one and the same development.
There is every reason therefore why we should see the concept
of *tôrâh* as exercising a profound unifying influence upon the
formation of the Old Testament.

That the Old Testament concept of a canon begins with the role of the Deuteronomic law-book in Josiah's reform stands out in a number of ways.[5] To say that the book was officially 'canonised' at that time would be to anticipate too many later developments, but one major step was taken. The book that moulded the reform was regarded above all other contemporary agencies of divine revelation and media of religious authority. In the written *tôrâh* of its covenant with Yahweh Israel possessed a vehicle of revelation and divine truth which exceeded that which could be given by prophet, priest or king. This in itself marks a great shift in the understanding of *tôrâh*, for this now became relatively fixed, and could be appealed to in matters of doubt and conflict involving other religious officers or institutions. The old *tôrâh* had been delivered orally, and could be adapted to take account of particular circumstances and changing needs. The new *tôrâh* was written and required to be interpreted and applied, but could not itself be changed (cf. Deut. 31.24–9). No more profound change than this had taken place in Israel's religion, for it marks the first and most momentous step in the development of a religion centred on a book. Eventually the scribe, rather than the priest, was to be the deciding arbiter of disputes and uncertainties concerning man's duty to God.

This awareness of a canonical authority is fully borne out when we look at the content of Deuteronomy, for we find here that the king is very pointedly made subject to the demands of obedience to the written *tôrâh* (Deut. 17.18–20). He is no longer the supreme law-giver of Israel, but is himself a man subject to the *tôrâh* of God. Yet this is made true also of the prophet, where previously we should have expected to find the greatest freedom of expression in allowing the prophet to be the mouthpiece of God. Now there is a strong awareness that the prophet could be a false interpreter of God's will (Deut. 13.1–5; 18.15–22). Against this the true prophet is to be one who will speak God's word 'like Moses' (Deut. 18.18). Although this still allows considerable freedom to the prophet, it firmly ensures that his prophesying is set alongside, and not above, the teaching of Moses. Furthermore, it strongly suggests that the role of the prophet is to preach *tôrâh*, in a way that could be likened to the work of Moses. The office of the prophet is thereby seen in a new light.

Admittedly the book of Deuteronomy did not suggest the abolition of the cult in favour of a religion directed towards *tôrâh*. Far from it, for with Deuteronomy and its use in Josiah's reform, the role of the cult acquired a new dimension of authority. All sacrificial worship was restricted to one sanctuary, at 'the place where Yahweh had chosen to set his name' (Deut. 12.1–14). This too, however, was to enhance the concept of a canon, for its introduction of the belief that only one sanctuary was properly authorised by God swept aside much of the great variety that had previously marked the cultic life of Israel. The forms of worship too, therefore, were made subject to a new canonical authority in this way. Such a restriction was to have a profound effect upon the development of Israel's priesthood (cf. 2 Kgs. 23.9). The canonical *tôrâh* was beginning to act like a leaven which was destined to transform eventually all of the religious institutions of Israel.

We might have expected that such a far-reaching change in Israel's life would have provoked strong opposition, and left a legacy of division which would have healed only gradually. Such was no doubt a possibility, but we should note that several factors contributed to the success of Josiah's reform. Not least we can see the strong range of support which it acquired, from the priests and political leaders of Jerusalem (2 Kgs. 22.3 ff.), the king himself (2 Kgs. 22.9), and the voice of the prophetess Huldah (2 Kgs. 22.14–20).

Yet behind it all we can only feel that the time was ripe for such a reform, with the first signs of weakness in the Assyrian sovereignty, which had dominated Judah and its affairs for a century. The kingdom was ready for political and religious change, and the appeal back to the name of Moses conferred its own element of transparent authority. Josiah's reform made a canonical *tôrâh* a central and necessary feature of Israel's life. Behind it we can discern that a new era of hope aroused expectations that it might mark a new beginning in the history of Israel's political greatness. Such did not materialise, but rather the tragic death of Josiah in 609 BC, marked the beginning of the end so far as Judah's political hopes were concerned.

Yet this tragedy, followed by the fall of Jerusalem in 587, served
to highlight the timeliness of the changes that had occurred.
That section of the Judean community which went into exile
in Babylon found in the conception of a Mosaic *tôrâh* a relevant
and flexible guide to its own religious duties. The hope of the
eventual restoration of Israel could draw from it a source of
support and a blueprint for planning. Hence the introduction
of a *tôrâh* by Josiah's reform, which possessed all the outline
essentials of a written canon, became no temporary shift of
interest, but rather a more lasting change of direction, which
provides us with a formative step in the transition from the
religion of Israel to the birth of Judaism.

In the years that followed Josiah's reform we find that the
conception of a written *tôrâh* became an increasingly central
presupposition of the religious life and organisation of Judaism.
The process of change which had begun with the reform became
an increasingly influential feature of religious life until eventually Judaism became, when the Jerusalem temple was yet
again destroyed in AD 70, the religion of a book. Accompanying
these external changes in the forms of the religious life, a great
literary undertaking was set in movement. This was to see the
book of *tôrâh* added to, revised and progressively extended,
until the present Pentateuch resulted. The book of *tôrâh* was
destined to become a great literary work, and, as we have
already argued, the conception of *tôrâh* that originally applied
to the law-book of Josiah, became applicable to the Pentateuch
as a whole.

The process by which this great literary achievement was
brought about was sufficiently complex for many of its stages
to have become entirely lost from historical knowledge. Such
information as we possess is largely what can be inferred from
a careful critical analysis of the structure of the Pentateuch.
However, all that concerns us in the present theological context
is to note the main lines of growth, and to perceive the way in
which this has contributed to the understanding of the Pentateuch as *tôrâh*. It was this step which has led on ultimately to
the understanding that the entire Old Testament may be read
as such a book of *tôrâh*.

The next steps in the literary development of Josiah's lawbook were not directly connected with the Pentateuch, but, surprisingly, with the formation of the great historical narrative work of the Former Prophets. The book of Deuteronomy became the first chapter in the history which described the fortunes of Israel from the days of Moses to the fall of Judah. The books of Joshua to 2 Kings at one time formed a continuous work, to which Deuteronomy provided a beginning. Only at a relatively late stage in the formation of the Pentateuch was the step taken which severed Deuteronomy from this position, and joined it instead to the book of Numbers to form the present Pentateuch. When this was done some significant readjustments were necessary in order to accommodate the change.

To speak of Deuteronomy being joined to the book of Numbers, however, is somewhat misleading for what at that time existed was not divided up into the four books from Genesis to Numbers which we now have. To detail the history and structure of these books, and to note their major sources, would be only partially relevant to our present concern. Especially is it difficult to undertake this at a time when quite radically new conclusions are being put forward regarding such sources and structure.[6] The most widely accepted critical view is that these books have been formed out of a major narrative work which is older than Deuteronomy (J E) and one which is later (P). This latter is essentially a post-exilic work, which its contents firmly bear out. For our present purpose it is sufficient to note that material from a wide span of time has been brought together and assembled into a coherent work. How and when this unified work took shape is a matter of contention. For the past century scholars have worked on the basic assumption that four basic source documents have been woven together in a series of editorial redactions, the last of these taking place probably in the fifth century BC. Now, however, it has become increasingly accepted that this is too tidy a view and that a rather more extended process must be assumed. This certainly means that a considerable number of additions and revisions have been made, in which a basic nucleus of material has been built up into the large work which the Pentateuch now is. However, the source-document hypothesis should not altogether be discarded, since it appears that quite extended written narrative works have formed a substantial basis for the overall composition. It is likely, therefore, that the main narrative outline of the Pentateuch was already established at an early stage, and that this has remained basic to the structure of the whole.

So far as the understanding that the Pentateuch as a whole is to be regarded as *tôrâh* is concerned, two points are of significance. The first of these is that the main source documents which may be posited as underlying the work (JE and P) were essentially works of narrative history. Although both of them contained series, or codes, of laws, these formed only a relatively minor part of the material. Furthermore, it is rather questionable whether the later of these sources, the so-called P, or Priestly, document was all that much more full of cultic and priestly regulations than the earlier. A greater interest in the origin of Israel's cultic institutions was however present.

The second point is that it is in the later stages of the formation of the Pentateuch that the great bulk of priestly rules and regulations have come in, many of these being added once the major narrative structure was already complete. In this regard the book of Leviticus must be viewed as largely the product of such an expansion to include substantial blocks of cultic rules and instructions. The shift of balance, therefore, in the general make-up of the Pentateuch would appear to have been a gradual and progressive development. From being a work of historical narrative the emergent Pentateuch has progressively become a framework into which a great wealth of traditions and regulations of an ethical and cultic nature have been woven. In the end the main features of narrative history have become less prominent as the growing mass of instructional material has taken over. Surprisingly too, we find that the inclusion of an extended code of civil laws (Exod. 20.22–23.19) almost certainly belongs to the oldest major narrative source (JE). To call the Pentateuch 'law', therefore, in anything like the sense that this word most usually bears as 'civil law', hardly does justice to the actual contents of the work. It is evidently a *tôrâh*-law of a rather different kind. However, one thing is clear: the title *tôrâh* is a reasonably appropriate one for the material that is to be found in the Pentateuch, especially once we bear in mind the heavy preponderance of rules, regulations and ethical injunctions that have been incorporated into it in its later stages.

We may now raise two important questions concerning the interrelationship between the literary formation of the Pentateuch and its theological classification as *tôrâh*. The first is the question of why and when this literary collection came to be called *tôrâh*, and the second is dependent upon the answer to this. Which has come first, the classification as *tôrâh* or the inclusion of such a wide range of instructional rules and regulations?

The answer to the first question has, in fact, already been strongly suggested above. It is that it was the carrying over to the whole Pentateuch of the title that was first applied to the book of Deuteronomy that has made the whole work a book of *tôrâh*. This most probably took place when the book of Deuteronomy was combined with the basic material of Genesis to Numbers.

The answer to the second question is certainly more difficult, but it is hard to escape one very probable conclusion. Once the main substance of the Pentateuch as a book of *tôrâh* had been established, the necessity was felt to include many of the traditions and collections of *tôrâh* that Judaism had built up. Probably a great deal was already incorporated into the work, but certainly the need for comprehensiveness was now felt more acutely than ever. The exact chronology of this literary growth of the Pentateuch cannot, however, be established with any certainty.

Nevertheless, from the theological point of view, our main concern is to establish the recognition that the labelling of it as a book of *tôrâh* is not an extraneous imposition from outside, but does have a recognisable appropriateness in describing the material that is to be found within it. Furthermore, this awareness of the need for a book of *tôrâh* has undoubtedly contributed to the way in which the Pentateuch has taken shape. It may be held, therefore, to be an important clue to the way in which those who shaped and formed the Pentateuch into its present wholeness intended it to be understood. When we speak and think of the Pentateuch as *tôrâh*, we are therefore interpreting it in accordance with the aims for which it was formed.

This digression into some of the complex literary issues that concern the origin and structure of the Pentateuch may appear a little abstruse, and to have little to do with the more central theological issues which relate to the Old Testament. All the more is this so on account of the inevitable tentativeness that surrounds these literary conclusions. Yet this apparent abstruseness is misleading, since in reality a number of points of very direct theological concern are bound up with these conclusions. The Old Testament was assumed by early Jewish and Christian interpreters to be a book of law, and we have seen that this must first be clarified to the extent that 'law' is to be understood as a rather loose translation of the Hebrew *tôrâh*. We can now see that this categorisation is substantially borne out in regard to the structure of the Pentateuch, and that it is from this foundation that the treatment of the whole Old Testament as *tôrâh* has been built up. How then is *tôrâh* to be understood in this context?

In the first place it must be frankly conceded that to make *tôrâh* loosely equivalent to 'historical narrative' would be quite misleading. Although there is undoubtedly a good deal of historical narrative in the Pentateuch, and on this account Christian tradition has labelled its five parts as 'historical books', this was not the main characteristic of *tôrâh*. This discovery in itself is very significant on account of the widespread popularity of the assumption that an Old Testament theology can be a 'kerygmatic' one, in which the central emphasis is placed upon the use of historical narrative as a form of theological expression.[7] Such at least would not appear to be the main emphasis of the way in which the Old Testament has actually been put together. It is also relevant to note that the more weight that is placed upon the main literary 'sources' of the Pentateuch (especially J E and P), the more 'history' appears to predominate. Yet the more we take seriously the final form of the Pentateuch the more evident it is that this historical dimension is only one aspect of *tôrâh*. The books of Leviticus and Deuteronomy are as basic to the Pentateuch as are the books of Genesis and Exodus. We must take full account, therefore, of the elements of instruction and regulation that appear as a fundamental part of the *tôrâh* of the Pentateuch.

A second point is also relevant to this recognition, and concerns the fact that the areas of life and religion that are covered by *tôrâh* are very extensive and are not all of one kind. What we have seen to be true in the relatively circumscribed compass of the book of Deuteronomy is even more true of the Pentateuch as a whole. Matters concerning the cultus, as well as wider religious duties, are all included. So also are broad ethical admonitions and very explicit laws concerning behaviour in society and the identification and punishment of particular crimes. To be obedient to *tôrâh* is a broad, life-encompassing demand. This is important both for the way in which it shows *tôrâh* to be a very comprehensive form of instruction, and in no way limited to those aspects of life which might be thought of as distinctively 'Israelite', or 'Jewish', such as circumcision. Many of its demands are evidently of a universal moral character, and this was to have an important bearing upon the way in which it came to be understood and interpreted by later ages of Jews and Christians.

However, when we come to ask what exactly this *tôrâh* is, and how it is to be applied, the answer given by the Pentateuch as a whole is as clear as that which is presented more narrowly by the book of Deuteronomy. The *tôrâh* of the Pentateuch presents those demands which God has set before Israel as a consequence of his election of them, and as the conditions of the covenant by which this election has been constituted. The Pentateuch therefore is a covenant literature. We are brought face to face here with an issue that has aroused no small amount of discussion in recent years, and which concerns the degree of centrality which may be ascribed to the concept of covenant. Ever since W. Eichrodt made this concept a basis for a theological unity in the Old Testament,[8] the question has been raised whether it can be considered as pervasively unifying as such an approach requires. Already we have seen that the disproportionate frequency with which the word 'covenant' is used in the Old Testament shows that it was not always regarded as a concept of paramount significance by all ages of Israelite-Jewish life.

Yet now we find an important clue to putting the issue in a fuller perspective. It is the structure of the Pentateuch as *tôrâh*, and supremely as containing the *tôrâh* which God gave to

Moses when he instituted the covenant on Mount Sinai, that has made the concept of covenant a central one to the Old Testament.[9] It is in fact the natural correlate of the literary recognition that the Old Testament is built up around the Mosaic *tôrâh*. This is provided with a meaningful context when it is seen as the range of instructions which God gave as the conditions of his covenant. To recognise this is in no way to seek to minimise the importance of the narrative record by which the election-will of God was made known to his people. Nor should it be held to place all the weight upon the aspect of Israel's response to God's saving activity, rather than upon the grace that is evident in that activity itself. Salvation and *tôrâh* are naturally related to each other by the very nature of God's saving work which calls his people to live in responsive obedience to himself. To insist on a separation where none is intended would be to falsify the perspective of the Old Testament.

It is from within this literary perspective that we can see that the concept of a covenant between God and Israel is central to the Old Testament, even though the idea of covenant may not always have been used with comparable frequency throughout all ages of Israelite-Jewish religion. When therefore we speak of an Old Testament, with the word 'testament' arising, by way of the Latin *testamentum*, as a translation of the word 'covenant' (Hebrew *bᵉrît*), this is in all essentials entirely appropriate. The Old Testament is a covenant literature because it recounts as its focal point the making of the covenant between God and Israel, and central to its structure is the presentation of the demands that fall upon Israel as a consequence of this covenant. First and foremost, therefore, the Old Testament is addressed to those who are members, or partners, in this covenant.

We may note here that it appears to have been a direct consequence of this sense of the centrality of the Sinai covenant that has given rise to one rather strange feature about the literary form of the Pentateuch. This is the unexpected repetition of the Ten Commandments, the primary summary of the covenant's demands, at two separate places in the sequence of the Pentateuch (Exod. 20.2–17 and Deut. 5.6–21). Only minor differences of wording distinguish the two presentations. The result is particularly awkward from a literary point of view since it results in the recounting of the contents of the two tablets of *tôrâh* which were lost, and which needed a subsequent replacement by Moses (Exod. 34.1–28). This repetition would appear most readily explicable as a result of the felt need to place these commandments in a position of prominence, which they would have lost once the book of Deuteronomy was united with Genesis to Numbers. From being in a position of great prominence in the original book of Deuteronomy, they would have been unintentionally relegated to come very late and out of order had they been kept only in their original position. They were therefore brought forward and repeated in Exodus 20, quite in keeping with their important role in outlining the main summary of demand which the covenant of Sinai entailed. This particular position of eminence, and the fact of their consequent repetition, has certainly contributed to the singling out of the Ten Commandments as the *tôrâh*, or law, *par excellence*, which the Old Testament contains. We shall have occasion to note this further in considering the consequences of the development of the Old Testament *tôrâh* as law.

### 3. THE TÔRÂH AND THE PROPHETS

So far we have concentrated upon the categorisation of the Old Testament as *tôrâh*, and the way in which this is reflected in the literary structure of the Pentateuch. Yet the Old Testament is more than just the 'Law', or Pentateuch, and also contains the very substantial collection of writings known as 'the Prophets'. In fact the title 'the Law and the Prophets' is by far the most common way in which the New Testament refers back to the scriptures of the Old. A very significant point of theological interest therefore hinges upon the relationship between these two collections.[10] Indeed the theological concern amounts to an issue of paramount proportions, because the category of 'prophetic promise' becomes another major theme by which the entire Old Testament can be understood. It appears in the New Testament so prominently as to become the leading Christian theme in interpreting the Old Testament. If on the one hand the Old Testament is a book of *tôrâh*, or law, on the

other hand it is certainly also to be understood as a book of
prophetic promise, the fulfilment of which the early Christians
claimed to have taken place in the life and passion of Jesus of
Nazareth.

The idea of 'prophetic promise' belongs particularly to the
second part of the canon, but it became so extensive in its
influence as to enable other parts of the canon, the Pentateuch
and especially the book of Psalms in the Writings, to be interpreted also as prophetic promise. We must therefore deal with
this theme separately in a later chapter. For the moment our
concern is in a different direction, and is to discover how far
the theme of *tôrâh* may be held to appear in 'the Prophets'. The
issue is not by any means a hypothetical one, since it matters
greatly to any attempt to establish a measure of unity in the
Old Testament that what we find in the collections of the
Prophets can be brought into some kind of conceptual relationship with the contents of 'the Law'. Even more broadly, however, as soon as we obtain some awareness of the main lines of
interpretation which have dominated Jewish and Christian
understanding of the Old Testament, we see that the relationship of the Prophets to the Law becomes an issue of far-
reaching importance.

We may begin this brief study by noting a point which has
already been touched upon in another chapter. The Prophets,
as a part of the canon, are divided between the Former and the
Latter Prophets, the Former Prophets being in reality a very
extensive work of narrative history (Joshua to 2 Kings). At one
time this was joined to the book of Deuteronomy, which formed
its opening 'chapter'. At this very early stage in the growth of
the canon, therefore, it is abundantly clear that 'the Law and
the Prophets' were believed to belong together and to form a
very appropriate and harmonious single work.[11] It was a later
age which split them asunder and joined Deuteronomy to
Genesis–Numbers, and the Former Prophets to a very extensive
collection of the sayings of the great prophets of Judah and
Israel. The division has, in effect, come after the unity. From
this basic perception about the literary growth of the Old
Testament we can see that there exists a very substantial basis
for contending that the Law and the Prophets belong together,

and that the Law (the *tôrâh* of Deuteronomy) is an essential presupposition for understanding the prophets.

This is certainly borne out when we look at the content of the narrative of Joshua to 2 Kings. At a great many significant points in the telling of the story of the rise and fall of Israel reference is made back to the *tôrâh* of Moses which God had given to his people Israel (cf. Josh. 1.7–8; 1 Kgs. 2.3; 11.11). The transition to the age of Joshua makes positive reference to this *tôrâh* as the charter by which the emergent nation is to be governed, and the institution of the monarchy provides further occasions for recalling the existence of this law. The greatest moment of triumph in the nation's history after the death of Solomon is seen as the rediscovery of the book of *tôrâh* in the temple in Josiah's time (2 Kgs. 22–3). The history is through and through interpreted against the basic conviction that Israel is to be regarded as the people to whom God had committed his *tôrâh* as a part of his covenant with them. Nor is this simply a matter of a few explicit references to the existence of the 'book of *tôrâh*'. Rather it affects the whole presentation of the history at a fundamental level, for it enables the whole course of events to be seen from the perspective of this law. Kings are judged by it, and the fortunes of the nation in general are interpreted as determined by the measure of obedience or disobedience that the people display towards the *tôrâh*.

It is when we turn to consider the collections of prophecies which make up the Latter Prophets that the position becomes more complicated, and no such simple answer to the problems is forthcoming, as in the case of the Former Prophets. Even more confusing is the fact that a major facet of the modern critical approach to the study of the literature of the Old Testament and its underlying religious history has proceeded on the assumption that the 'Prophets' must really be seen as the historical presupposition of the 'Law'. To examine all the arguments, or to attempt to survey the way in which scholarship has dealt with the various questions, is quite impossible in a brief summary. However, a number of points can be noted and the relevance to the overall perspective assessed.

Certainly we find that prophecy as a phenomenon is built up around two main types of saying, or written pronouncement.

The first is that of a foretelling, or pronouncement proper, in which some future event is foretold in terms of its good, or evil, nature. The second type of saying is that in which some motive, or reason, is given in explanation of this coming event. In its own way this 'reason' serves to corroborate the certainty of the foretelling by its ability to show the rightness of the events that are to come. They are made into an intelligible revelation of the divine will. In explaining the coming of woeful events as judgments from God, is was natural that prophets should appeal to all kinds of moral and religious offences as necessitating some punitive action on the part of God. There is therefore a wide area in which the preaching of the prophets may be held to presuppose *tôrâh*, when this is taken in the very broad sense that we have seen to apply in the book of Deuteronomy for example.

However, from a literary point of view it appears that much of this denunciatory material, or invective, in the preaching of the prophets can be seen to be older than the comprehensive collections of written *tôrôth* which we find in the Pentateuch. Even more it is clear that the main period of activity of the greatest of Israel's prophets, in the eighth to sixth centuries BC, antedated the period in which the greatest emphasis came to be placed upon *tôrâh* in Judaism. This latter was certainly the post-exilic age. From a literary-historical perspective, therefore, there is substantial justification for claiming that the preaching of the prophets antedates that of the scribes and editors who have made the Pentateuch a great work of *tôrâh*.

Scholarship, however, has come increasingly to recognise in recent years that behind both the 'Law' and the 'Prophets' there lie long traditions of laws, admonitions and regulations, which make it a rather distorted conclusion to claim that an absolute priority can be given to one or the other. Instead, particular attention has been devoted to the Ten Commandments as representative of a kind of fundamental tradition of law that existed in Israel. Attempts have been made, therefore, to claim that it was this central stream of *tôrâh* tradition, explicitly regarded as belonging to Yahweh's covenant with Israel, that stands behind the prophetic preaching.[12]

Yet increasingly the attempt to establish a certain date for the Ten Commandments, which would ensure that it could be assumed to be older than the earliest of the canonical prophets has foundered. The secure evidence needed for such a conclusion is simply not available. In any case, it must be argued against an approach from this direction that to single out the Ten Commandments as the particular collection of *tôrôth* which can be seen to underlie the prophets is not entirely convincing. The particular offences for which the prophets rebuke their contemporaries cannot be limited in any precise way to those covered by the Ten Commandments. It is true that there is a substantial measure of overlap, but this can more readily be explained by the fact that just as the prophets naturally single out very serious and clear-cut offences to justify their pronouncements of woe, so also can the Ten Commandments be seen to be a conscious singling out of such major matters of religious and moral behaviour. There is a common denominator behind both which is to be found in the nature of the Israelite tradition as it had been since the days of Moses, and the particular problems and features of Israelite society as it developed in its encounter with the Canaanite culture of the land. The literary questions, and the issues concerning the history of ethical ideas in Israel, do not of themselves allow us to resolve the issues in dispute about the priority of the Law or the Prophets.[13] Yet this is not altogether surprising in view of the dimension of historical depth which is present in the great literary collections of the Old Testament. Seldom can the rise of specific theological or ethical ideas be dated with any great confidence.

We may suggest, however, that it has not been altogether appropriate to try to resolve the tensions between the 'Law' and the 'Prophets' in the Old Testament solely from the perspective of the history of ideas. It is essentially a question about the structure of the canon itself. We may be content to establish two main conclusions. The first of these is that there is evidently a very real basis of moral and religious concern in the preaching of the prophets which overlaps with similar concerns which we find in the rulings of *tôrâh*. Once there was a full and decisive acceptance that the tradition of this *tôrâh* could be traced back

to the days of Moses, then it was entirely in order to regard the
great prophets of Israel and Judah as having presupposed this
*tôrâh* in their preaching. No other perspective could possibly
have satisfied the basic structural patterns of the tradition as it
came to be enshrined in writing. From the viewpoint of the
canon as it now exists, therefore, it is entirely correct that we
should read the prophets in the light of the *tôrâh*, rather than
the other way round. Without this *tôrâh* the full significance of
the denunciations of the prophets would be lost upon us. It is
this perspective that shows that by these offences the very
covenant relationship between God and Israel had been
jeopardised.

The perspective which sees the tradition of *tôrâh* in Israel as
antedating the preaching of the prophets and as providing some
basis of explanation for their threats of woe is, therefore, an
important part of the Old Testament understanding of the
work of the prophets. It provides a background and frame of
reference, based on a theology of Yahweh's covenant with
Israel, which gives added significance to what the prophets
said. Essentially we must admit that this perspective is provided
by the structure of the canon, rather than by any very clear
recognition of the actual course of Israel's religious development, with a specific chronology of the emergence of religious
and ethical ideas. Even so, much as we shall have to admit that
this canonical perspective is imposed upon the great literary
collections of the Old Testament, it does not appear to be in any
way false. It simply makes explicit many of the ideas and
concepts which the preaching of the prophets left as implicit.
Overall it brings out, by the way in which the canon of prophecy is structured, the convictions about the nature and role
of prophecy which we find in the history of the Former
Prophets.

This brings us to note the great importance for an understanding of the theological perspectives of the Old Testament
of the interpretation of prophecy given in 2 Kings 17.13–18:

Yet the LORD warned Israel and Judah by every prophet
and every seer, saying, 'Turn from your evil ways and keep
my commandments and my statutes, in accordance with all

the law (*tôrâh*) which I commanded your fathers, and which I sent to you by my servants the prophets.'

This very compressed summary of the significance of prophecy is remarkable for two prominent features which it contains. First, it sets this preaching very firmly against a background of the Mosaic *tôrâh*, to which it can be referred for elucidation. Secondly, it views the work of the prophets as primarily that of those who worked for the salvation of Israel by calling the people back from their transgressions, to live in accordance with the Mosaic law. In this way it sees the prophetic pronouncements of doom and woe as admonitions designed to spur the people to repentance. Perhaps too we can see here, in the manner in which the prophets can be regarded as an easily identifiable group, the foundations of a clear differentiation between true and false prophecy, and the beginning of a conception of a series of canonical prophets.

The understanding of prophecy which saw it as a means of preaching repentance and of calling Israel back to the Mosaic *tôrâh*, can certainly be seen, therefore, to have an authentic place in the Old Testament theological tradition. It has undoubtedly contributed to the way in which the canon has taken shape, and it serves to confirm the appropriateness of using it as a basic framework of theological reference by which to understand prophecy.

There is, however, a rather different, and more radical side to prophecy, which must also be noted. This is that which saw the prophets as the heralds of the new Israel, the preachers who foretold the coming of a great new age of salvation in which a remarkable fulfilment would be achieved of all that God had promised to his people at their election. How the law, or *tôrâh*, was to be related to this was never clearly defined, and enabled later circles in Judaism to look for some quite radical solutions to the relationship between law and eschatology, which were the two dominating themes affecting Jewish life at the close of the Old Testament period. The Qumran Community, the rise of Christianity, and the emergence of Rabbinic Judaism in the post-Old Testament era each reflects different answers arrived at in seeking to resolve the tensions between these two themes.

## 4. FROM TÔRÂH TO LAW

We have already had occasion to note at more than one point that tôrâh cannot be identified as 'law' in the strictly juridical sense, but must certainly be construed more widely. However, to translate it as 'instruction', as is sometimes advocated, is itself very inadequate, and fails to satisfy some of the important aspects of the nature of tôrâh. Since the standard English translation of the term has consistently been 'law', and since the English word 'law' has a wide variety of senses, we may settle for continuing this practice, even though it has obvious limitations. It is, in any case, already anticipated in considerable measure by the way in which the Greek (Septuagint) translation has used nomos as a counterpart for tôrâh, which is carried over into the Latin (Vulgate) version by the use of lex. In a very real measure, therefore, the modern English reader of the Old Testament is committed to seeking some understanding of the kind of 'law' with which this literature presents him.

We have already noted that the tôrâh does include a significant collection of civil case laws (the Book of the Covenant in Exod. 20.22–23.19), and a version of this undoubtedly provided a framework for the central part of the book of Deuteronomy, where the idea of an Israelite tôrâh underwent such an important change. It is primarily by reference to the theology of covenant that the role of tôrâh is clarified, and here we find that the analogy with the stipulations of political (vassal) treaties has been most helpful. The sanction which hovers over these stipulations is that the covenant relationship would be broken and all its privileges and guarantees forfeited. This is the conceptual world that applies to Israel's covenant with Yahweh, the major difference being that the analogy is applied completely to the religious sphere. There is, therefore, a legal juridical background to this understanding of tôrâh, although its closest analogy would appear to be that of international, rather than civil, law. To disobey the tôrâh-law which God had given would be to forfeit the privileges which belong to living in covenant with him. This had both a positive side in that life within this covenant entailed the blessing of living under the providential care of Yahweh, and of enjoying all those benefits of the land and nationhood which the book of Deuteronomy sets out. Conversely, there was also a negative side which threatened the loss of these privileges and the suffering of all manner of ills and disadvantages which betokened Yahweh's curse (cf. Deut. 11.16–17; 28.15–68).

In the main post-exilic period which witnessed the extensive literary expansion of *tôrâh* the most prominent of Yahweh's gifts – the land and a national identity – had already been lost to Israel. We can see, therefore, quite readily that an element of historical tension and hope came to surround the understanding of the law and its blessings. Obedience to the law had to be viewed within the particular dimension of hope and eschatological expectation which coloured Jewish existence during these years. Once again we find that the twin themes of law and eschatology did not develop in separate compartments in Judaism, but in a very tightly woven interrelationship.

It is also clear that during this period a number of factors contributed to the shaping of the understanding of the role of *tôrâh* in Judaism. Worthy of special note is the marked sense of joy and delight in the law, as the supreme expression of God's love for his people which we find in the *tôrâh*-psalms (Pss. 1 and 119). There is no hint here that the law promises anything but help and blessing for his people. The same is also true in essence in Psalm 19B (Ps. 19.7–14), which is a late addition to an older psalm of a very different character. Yet here, in what are possibly scribal additions, we detect a note of puzzlement and even frustration with the *tôrâh* (vv. 12–13). Some of the sense of human inadequacy when faced with the law begins to appear.

More striking still, however, in regard to the problems engendered by the new emphasis upon *tôrâh* was the inevitable fixity of its written form. In order to be effective it is necessary that laws should from time to time be revised and adapted to the changing needs and conditions of society. We see this when we compare the original Book of the Covenant with that part of it which appears in a revised form in Deuteronomy 12 ff. This latter is in a real sense a *mišnâh* – a second version – of the law.[14] It was inevitable, therefore, that there should have

grown up a tradition of *mišnâh* by which the law was to be
understood and applied in specific situations. Even though the
literary deposit of this does not appear until post-Old Testament times, the need for it had clearly developed earlier.
Whether too the identification of *tôrâh* with wisdom (Deut.
4.6; cf. Ecclus. 24.8–12) had the effect of injecting into the
understanding of *tôrâh* a sense of its universal and timeless
validity, is certainly worthy of consideration.

In any case the acceptance and application of the written
*tôrâh* by Jews living among Gentiles in the Diaspora posed its
own range of questions about the universal validity of the law.
How it related to Gentile laws and customs was an issue that
could not be evaded. All the more was this so once significant
numbers of Gentile proselytes and adherents began to be
associated with Judaism. The need for an effective apologetic
towards the Gentile world also created a need for considering
the universal applicability of *tôrâh*. No longer could it be
regarded simply as a covenant law applicable to Jews only, but
some awareness needed to be displayed of its relevance to all
mankind, and of its claim to be a universal expression of moral
and religious truth. A very clear example of the way in which
this need affected Jewish interpretation can be seen in the
exposition by Philo of Alexandria of the Ten Commandments.[15]

In so many respects questions concerning the 'theology' of
*tôrâh* raise issues of this nature relating to the distinction between
universal and particularist elements in the law. They reveal a
vital area in which the study of 'intertestamental' Judaism and
of its early rabbinic developments becomes an indispensable
realm of investigation for an effective theological approach to
the Old Testament material. The questions which are so
frequently raised about the unity of the New Testament with
the Old can only be seen in a truly historical and critical perspective when they are seen in the light of this background. In
a great many ways the New Testament reveals a markedly fresh
and radical approach to the problems of the theology of law.

Yet Judaism itself could only develop and maintain its sense
of continuity with the past by reaching a distinctive perspective regarding the nature and validity of the *tôrâh* as law. We
can see that in its Pentateuchal form many issues of great

importance to the interpretation and application of the written *tôrâh* were left unresolved. Two issues alone need be mentioned for the great bearing which they have upon the way in which Jewish and Christian interpretation has been forced to deal with them. The first concerns the fact that as the written *tôrâh* grew in scope and comprehensiveness, so did its wider coverage threaten to undermine its authority and applicability. The fact that no clear lines of demarcation between the greater and lesser demands of the law were set out, meant that it was inevitable that someone should ask 'Which is the greatest commandment?' (cf. Matt. 19.18). The literary form and structure of the Pentateuch does little to answer this, save in the special prominence which it accords to the Ten Commandments. In later ages both Jews and Christians came to accept, almost without question, that these commandments were laws of a greater degree of importance than others. Yet to make this judgment, a theological, as distinct from a purely literary or historical, approach has to be undertaken.

Of comparable and related complexity is the question of a distinction between those demands of *tôrâh* which referred to the cult and those which referred to personal and social matters of morality. In its own structure the *tôrâh* does not distinguish between the two. It is evident that at an early period the nascent Christian Church discarded almost entirely the laws which referred to the cult, since these no longer carried any great meaning for Christians who had separated themselves from the temple and synagogues of Judaism. In Judaism also, however, the destruction of the temple in AD 70 compelled a quite new approach to these demands, which we find increasingly subject to new interpretations of a distinctly moralising kind.[16] In time the entire ancient edifice of cultic assumptions and sensitivities withered away, and needed to be replaced by a more easily intelligible frame of reference. A theological approach to Old Testament *tôrâh*, therefore, cannot go about its task of seeking meaning and relevance in this material if it fails to pay heed to certain basic post-canonical developments. To a very considerable extent a theology of the Old Testament must be a theology of *tôrâh*, since this concept provides the literature with its most imposing principle of unity.

CHAPTER SIX

# THE OLD TESTAMENT
# AS PROMISE

If we regard the way in which Christians have in the past
found theological meaning and significance in the Old Testament, then one feature stands out above all others. This is the
conviction that the Old Testament is a book of prophetic
promise, which foretold an age of salvation that was to come.[1]
For the early Christians this age had come with the events
concerning Jesus of Nazareth, so that the age of the New
Testament and the early Church could be regarded as one of
fulfilment.

This simple scheme, that the Old Testament is a work of
'promise' and the New Testament one of 'fulfilment', provides
a basic groundwork from which a wide range of interpretations
have been developed. In Christian theology and liturgy no
other way of approaching the Old Testament has attained
anything like a comparable popularity or claim to authority.
Nor is this simply a late development, since it pervades the
New Testament in every one of its writings. Supremely this
promise is regarded as having been spoken by the prophets:

And all the prophets who have spoken, from Samuel and
those who came afterwards, also proclaimed these days (Acts
3.24).

The prophets who prophesied of the grace that was to be
yours searched and inquired about this salvation; they
inquired what person or time was indicated by the Spirit of
Christ within them when predicting the sufferings of Christ
and the subsequent glory. It was revealed to them that they
were serving not themselves but you, in the things which
have now been announced to you by those who preached the
good news to you through the Holy Spirit sent from heaven,
things into which angels long to look (1 Pet. 1.10–12).

In spite of the strength and firmness with which this 'argument from prophecy' has appeared in the Christian tradition, we find, somewhat surprisingly, that the main lines of a more modern critical evaluation of Old Testament prophecy have proceeded rather differently. The great strength of the prophets has been seen in the clarity and forthrightness with which they denounced the social and religious wrongs of their society, so that it was by this means that they became the heralds of a truly moral understanding of the kingdom of God. Where they have been seen as the forerunners of Jesus, it has usually been as a consequence of their sense of righteousness and social justice as essential to any true service of God. Alongside this has gone a great emphasis upon their exposure and condemnation of the hollowness of all worship where it has not been allied to a concern for righteousness. Perhaps here, more than in most other respects, the historical-critical attempt to present a theological assessment of prophecy has departed from the major lines of interpretation which had previously prevailed almost totally in Christian thinking. Whereas the latter has seen the prophets as the foretellers of salvation, the more critical approach has highlighted their role as the heralds of doom and judgment. How has so marked a difference of viewpoint arisen?

A number of factors have played a part, but foremost among them is the concern which has prevailed in a modern critical approach to prophecy to get back to the authentic words of the original prophet. It is particularly when we examine the earlier prophets who flourished in the eighth century that we find that the main weight of their preaching was concerned with denouncing the sins of Judah and Israel. Although in all of the canonical prophets the present text includes sayings of a hopeful nature, in some instances, especially that of Amos, serious doubt has been thrown on their authenticity. Even in the case of a prophet like Isaiah, where a considerable number of very important prophecies of coming deliverance and salvation appear, it becomes evident that not all of them are certainly to be ascribed to the original eighth-century prophet. In any case a very forceful and strongly backed warning of coming doom also appears in Isaiah's preaching.

It is not until the latter half of the sixth century, with the prophecies of Isaiah 40–55, that a clear and unbroken announcement of Israel's impending deliverance and restoration is made. In other words, it was only when the exile was almost over and the judgment could be seen to have passed that the prophets began to sound forth the hope of restoration which tradition has most closely associated with them.

A not inconsiderable disparity is evident, therefore, between the traditional Christian and Jewish lines of prophetic interpretation, and the modern critical understanding of prophecy. On the surface it would seem that the aspect of prophecy which theological interpretation in the past has found to be most significant is one which critical scholarship has come to regard as more peripheral to the prophetic canon of the Old Testament.[2]

Yet another problem appears in regard to the biblical interpretation of prophecy. The quotations already cited from the New Testament, as well as a great number of supporting instances in which actual prophecies from the Old Testament are quoted, show that by the first century AD the view was fully accepted that the prophets had referred to events that were to take place centuries after they had spoken. Their foresight was believed to reach ahead to declare events that were far beyond the horizon of normal understanding and expectation. Yet this raises serious credibility problems in regard to the nature of God's providential control of history. Even more clearly it stands at variance with what we find in much of the prophetic literature of the canon, where we see that the prophets were addressing their contemporaries about the meaning and outcome of events which were taking place at that time, or which were shortly expected to take place. The time-span which prophecy was believed to cover has evidently been stretched to a quite remarkable degree. The general impression which the discerning reader obtains is that the New Testament writers have been carried away in their enthusiasm to interpret the events which stand at the centre of the Christian faith. They have done so to such an extent that they have quite freely and arbitrarily appealed to almost any Old Testament prophecy which could, in the light of what had taken place, be regarded as a foretelling of the life, death and resurrection of Jesus. The

appearance is consequently one of a 'false' interpretation which
has arisen after the events had transpired which are interpreted
in this way.

Much of the debate which gave rise to the modern critical
understanding of prophecy took place at the beginning of the
eighteenth century, leading on to a quite new approach at the
end of that century under the stimulus of the German Romantic
philosopher J. G. Herder and the pioneer of critical scholarship
J. G. Eichhorn.[3] It is neither necessary nor practicable to
examine the course of the debate, nor the validity of the views
which have prevailed. We may note, nevertheless, that to
abandon the assumptions of the New Testament writers may
be quite in order for an Old Testament scholar, but is scarcely
very satisfactory for a student of the New. It results simply in a
growing hiatus between the critical theological approach to the
Old Testament and a critical approach to the Bible as a whole.
We have already said earlier that this is undesirable, since it is
the Bible as a whole that forms the Christian canon.

However, we may urge very strongly that the hiatus between
the traditional theological and the critical approach to the
study of the Old Testament prophets has been allowed to grow
wider than it really need have done. The loss of interest from
the Old Testament side in seeking to show how the kind of
interpretation of prophecy that prevails in the New Testament
has come about is not properly justified. We may appeal to
three features which call for careful re-appraisal. In the first
place, it is not simply New Testament authors who treat the
prophetic corpus of the Old Testament in this way. In Ecclesiasticus 49.10 the Jewish attitude to the twelve 'minor' prophets
is reflected:

> May the bones of the twelve prophets also send forth new life
> from the ground where they lie! For they put new heart into
> Jacob, and rescued the people by their confident hope.

Here all twelve prophets, including Amos, are regarded as
primarily concerned with having preached a message of hope
and of coming salvation. Nor is this in any way an isolated
example of Jewish understanding, since when we examine the
interpretation of prophecy which prevailed in the Qumran

community, we find a similar assumption that the prophets foretold the coming of days of salvation in a distant future.[4] The major difference between Christian and Jewish interpretation of prophecy does not lie in the kind of foretellings which are regarded as central, but rather in the fact that the early Christians regarded these prophecies as fulfilled. Jewish interpreters, however, still awaited their fulfilment even when, as at Qumran, they regarded this as imminent.

A second feature also enables us to gain a better grasp of the theological significance of prophecy by comparing the original texts with the ways in which the New Testament interprets them. The assumption that the original prophet knew how his prophecies would be fulfilled, and that this must be treated as the 'correct' interpretation of a prophecy is far too simple a view. The prophet himself recognised that a measure of 'openness' applied to his words, and that only God himself, expressing his will through events, would determine their ultimate meaning and 'truth'. It is in accordance with this that we find in the prophetic books of the Old Testament a very extensive range of interpretations and applications of prophecy, which critical scholarship has generally regarded as 'secondary'. A clear example is to be found in the way in which the prophecy attaching to the name Shear-jashub ( = 'a remnant shall return') is developed in the book of Isaiah (Isa. 7.3; cf. Isa. 10.20–3; 11.11, 16).[5] These interpretations are not from the original prophet, but they serve to show how later generations of scribes and interpreters applied the original name to new situations and circumstances out of the conviction that its fulfilment would be revealed by God in events. In other words, there was a genuine measure of 'openness' which allowed prophecies to be applied to more than one event, and these events would themselves serve to show how the prophecy was 'fulfilled'. What we see in the New Testament, and in a closely similar fashion in Qumran, is merely a further extension of this type of prophetic interpretation which already exists in the prophetic books. When we find therefore a distinctive interpretation of the idea of a 'remnant' in Romans 9.27 (cf. Rom. 11.5) it is simply a development of a pattern of interpretation which already exists in the Old Testament itself. It concerns the interpreter of the Old Testament, therefore, as much as that of the New.

A third feature is also relevant in this regard, and arises out of the observations already made. It has belonged in great measure to the critical study of the Old Testament prophets that it should distinguish between the authentic and inauthentic sayings of each of them. Only so can the preaching of the prophet himself be recovered. Yet the books of the prophets have displayed very little concern to preserve the biography, or teaching, of an individual prophet. Rather the attention has been focused on the prophecies themselves as messages from God, so that no hesitation has been felt in relating various prophecies to each other. We see this very clearly in Ben Sira (Ecclesiasticus), and the way in which he could lump together the twelve prophets as having all proclaimed the same basic message. Evidently the literary form of the collection has itself contributed to the way in which prophecy has been understood.[6]

This raises certain fundamental questions about the actual course of development and whether it is the literary coming together which has occasioned the attempts at an overall pattern of interpretation. To some extent this is no doubt true, but it seems probable that an underlying conviction that the prophets did all proclaim a message which showed features of a common theme and expectation has helped to fashion the literary collection into its present form. At least there were current certain basic themes and conceptions relating to prophecy which enabled a connected corpus to emerge. Nor should we assume that the form of the prophetic literature has been largely dictated by liturgical and scribal necessity. A deeper level of theological connection can be seen to be present, as is shown by the marked repetition of a number of basic themes.

We may argue, therefore, that a theological study of the theme of 'promise' in the Old Testament must seek to elucidate the way in which this theme arose as the central one in the understanding of the preaching of the prophets. Before this can be achieved, however, it is necessary that we should obtain a clearer grasp of the earliest preaching of the canonical prophets of the Old Testament.

## I. PROPHECY AND THE JUDGMENT OF ISRAEL

The earliest of the canonical prophets of the Old Testament is Amos (*c.* 760–750 BC), whose message can be conveniently summed up in his own words: 'The end has come upon my people Israel; I will never again pass by them' (Amos 8.2; cf. 5.2).

The reasons why this end must come upon Israel are spelt out in terms of the oppression of the poor, the corruption of justice, and the disregard of fundamental human rights (cf. Amos 2.6–8; 5.10–12; 6.4). In spite of attempts to show that the prophet was displaying a new depth of insight into the heinousness of these crimes, and thereby injecting a new moral emphasis into Israel's religion, there is little clear evidence that this aspect of his preaching was in any way all that novel. Rather, it was the serious consequences which he foretold as a punishment for these sins that gave to them a new priority. It is when we come to ask how these threats were fulfilled that we begin to encounter the measure of 'openness' in a prophet's preaching.

The fact that Amos, and his contemporary Hosea, both preached in the northern kingdom of Israel, shows that it is the 'end' of this kingdom which was most of all in the prophet's mind. The coupling of this judgment with the fall of the house of Jeroboam II (786–746 BC) would corroborate this (Amos 7.9; cf. Hos. 1.4–5). The central part of Amos's preaching, therefore, was a warning of the coming political downfall of the northern kingdom of Israel, which was realised through the severe onslaught upon that kingdom by the Assyrians, culminating in the fall of Samaria in 722. The presence in Amos of related warnings to Judah (Amos 2.4–5; 3.1; cf. 1.2) indicates that a comparable threat was applied to the southern kingdom. Whether this was actually spoken by Amos himself, or whether it represents a secondary application at the hands of editors, has been a matter of considerable debate. Most probably the latter is the case, but in any event it does not affect the question of the meaning of the sayings.

We find similar instances in Hosea, where threats uttered against Israel are applied to Judah in a way that appears to be secondary (cf. Hos. 1.7; 4.15; 6.11; 11.12). The primary message of both prophets, therefore, can be seen to have been a warning of military and political disaster facing the northern kingdom of Israel in the eighth century B C. The fact that in the third quarter of that century this kingdom was virtually wiped out as an identifiable political entity would appear to mark the main basis of fulfilment associated with such sayings.

The major difference between the two prophets is to be found in the reasons which each adduces to justify the coming disaster. Against the social nature of the sins which are uppermost in Amos, Hosea rebukes the people more directly for their religious abuses, including idolatry, false ritual, and the resort to abhorrent sexual practices (Hos. 4.11–14, 17–19; 6.8–10). Brief as this summary must be, it is sufficient to show the appropriateness of interpreting these prophets as preachers of doom and judgment. That there are also present in the respective books of their sayings a number of prophecies giving assurance and hope must be understood in relation to this primary basis. Whether these hopeful prophecies are to be ascribed to the same prophets, or to later editors, is really of less importance than the recognition that these words of hope do not in any case stand at the centre of their message. We can therefore deal with them separately.

We may note briefly some characteristics of a third prophet of the eighth century, Isaiah of Jerusalem, who was active rather later, in the period 740–700 B C. Two features may be singled out in respect of the book which bears his name. The first is that the original eighth-century prophet's preaching is preserved in chapters 1–39, but that here we can discern a very extensive amount of editorial development and elaboration. The second is that chapters 40 ff. stem from the sixth century and later, and are clearly to be detached from the earlier chapters.

We may sum up the outstanding features of Isaiah's prophetic message very briefly. First, we note that we find a message announcing doom and judgment from God, both on Israel and Judah, comparable to that of Amos, only this time it is the southern kingdom which stands at the centre of the threat (Isa. 3.1–5; 5.5–6; 28.14–18; 29.1–4). Furthermore, Isaiah was undoubtedly preaching in, and against, Judah, after the remnants of the northern kingdom collapsed in 722 B C. In

the case of Isaiah, as compared with Amos and Hosea, we find
that there is a rather fuller body of prophetic material promising
future salvation and deliverance (esp. Isa. 2.2–4; 11.1–9;
14.1–2; 32.1–8). Overall, therefore, the main features of the
preaching of the great prophets of the eighth century are to be
found in their preaching of doom and judgment. Such threats
provide a basis for an interpretation of history in which the
righteous will of God is seen to be at work.

If we add the name of the fourth major prophetic figure of
the eighth century, Micah, then the overall picture remains the
same. In the case of this prophet the complex development of
the text of the book has aroused considerable scholarly debate
over the question of how much can be ascribed to Micah himself. Yet the problems here are basically the same as in the other
instances, so that the main thrust of Micah's preaching must be
seen in his threats of coming judgment upon Judah. It is
doubtful whether any of the sayings of hope in the book are
from the original prophet, although the reason for this conclusion is largely the broad one that such prophecies would be
out of place alongside the threats.

There is a broad consistency, therefore, in the preaching of
the eighth-century prophets, which must be matched with the
calamitous political events of the last half of that century.
During this period both Israel and Judah suffered severely at
the hands of the Assyrians, and by the close of the century only
a tiny remnant of the kingdom of Judah remained as a surviving
part of what had once been a significant near eastern power.

When we look further ahead to the two great prophetic
figures of the last years of Judah, Jeremiah and Ezekiel, we find
many points which remind us of the preaching of their earlier
compatriots. There are strong indications that these men were
already familiar with traditions of the sayings of their prophetic
predecessors, especially Hosea. Very plainly the same sins
which had called forth the threats and denunciations of
prophets in the eighth century were still present in Judah in the
sixth, and could be adduced as the cause of God's wrath. The
view that the basic foundations of Old Testament prophecy are
to be seen in these threats of doom is clearly correct. In Jeremiah
and Ezekiel, however, we have a surer anchorage for words of

hope, which are largely to be dated after the disaster of 587 BC had taken place. Yet even so, in the case of Jeremiah, it is usually accepted that many of the hopeful sayings in the book do not derive from the original prophet, but from later editors. In any case it is certain that the 'Deuteronomistic' editors of the book have greatly expanded and developed the original message of hope.

Even here, therefore, we cannot escape the deep-seated problem which we first encounter with Amos. How can we find room in the preaching of prophets of doom for words of hope? The answer has generally been found in positing a very substantial work by editors and later scribes to whom so much of the hopeful material which is now in the books is ascribed. Not until the great prophecies of Isaiah 40–55 did the prophetic message became one in which hope took the central place. The message of hope would thereby appear to be a relatively late grafting in to the general pattern of prophetic preaching. How are we to reach a satisfactory conclusion on a question of this complexity, in which literary, theological and historical issues are all closely interrelated?

## 2. PROPHECY AND HOPE

The problem of the origin and meaning of the prophecies of hope and restoration for Israel must find answers to two main questions. The first concerns the circumstances in which it is possible for us to see that such a message would have been entirely appropriate. The second question concerns the reason why this message of hope has been added to each of the prophets, and why it takes very much the same form in each of them.

The first question has generally been answered by noting the real birth of the message of hope during the years of Babylonian exile, and regarding this as the first truly appropriate moment for it to have arisen. However, not all scholars have been convinced that no place for a message of hope existed in the eighth century BC. We may consider the problem in relation to one particular text, that of Amos 9.11–12:

'In that day I will raise up the booth of David that is fallen, and repair its breaches and raise up its ruins,

and rebuild it as in the days of old;
that they may possess the remnant of Edom
and all the nations who are called by my name,'
says the LORD who does this.

The use of the metaphor of the 'booth', or 'shelter', of David
to signify his kingdom raises a number of questions. The
reference could be to the collapse of the united kingdom of
David, which took place with the division into two kingdoms
after Solomon's death. Or it could be to the downfall of the
northern kingdom in 722, which had once been an important
part of the territory ruled by David. It could, however, also
refer to the fall of the Davidic dynasty from the throne of
Judah, which did not take place until Zedekiah's deposition in
587 BC. A large number of scholars have taken the reference in
the latter sense, so that the promise in these two verses, as well as
that which follows in Amos 9.13–15, have been ascribed to the
post-exilic age. On the other hand, G. von Rad, in arguing that
the reference is back to the disruption in the tenth century BC,
has defended the authenticity of the saying from Amos.[7]
   In itself the saying scarcely allows a very clear-cut decision
to be made. However, when we compare it with comparable
sayings in Hosea (e.g. Hos. 2.5), and Isaiah (e.g. Isa. 9.2–7;
11.1–9; 32.1–8) regarding the restoration of the united Davidic
kingdom, the picture gains a clearer perspective. The recent
recognition that a very significant and substantial editing of a
collection of Isaiah's prophecies occurred during the reign of
Josiah (640–609 BC),[8] enables us to see that a very attractive
case can be made out for recognising that the age of Josiah
witnessed a very marked resurgence of hope for the restoration
of Israel. The clearest indication of this is to be found in the
Deuteronomic movement and its ambition of re-establishing a
united Israel modelled after the old kingdom of David. Certainly by this time in the seventh century BC, there were indications of the weakening of the Assyrian grip on Judah, and substantial signs of new hope and expectation abroad in the land.
There is no reason, therefore, why all the hopeful prophecies
to be found in Amos, Hosea and Isaiah should be later than this
time. The assumption that all of them must be post-exilic is

unnecessarily rigid. In fact several scholars have concluded that, even if serious doubt remains about the presence of a clear word of hope in Amos, at least with Hosea and Isaiah these prophets looked for a restoration of Israel beyond the judgments which they foresaw.[9] There are strong reasons, therefore, why it should be fully recognised that a message of hope entered into the mainstream of Israelite-Judean prophecy no later than the seventh century BC, and probably before this time.

It remains doubtful, however, whether this message of hope can be properly called eschatological, for the simple reason that Judah had survived to become a remnant of the old kingdom of Israel. Very possibly the beginning of the 'remnant'-theology in Isaiah is to be traced back to this time, although the original prophecy had looked in a very different direction. What was anticipated was a resurgence of Israelite power and independence after the disastrous years of Assyrian oppression and suzerainty. Such a hope could take up the themes and images which belonged to a far older stage of Israel's worship and religious life. Especially here we can see an influence from the older Jerusalem traditions associated with the Davidic monarchy and the great festivals celebrated in the temple there. All of these belong to the general theme of hope, rather than with an eschatology in the full sense.

What was lacking for an eschatology was a sense that a full and complete end had overtaken the survivors of Israel, so that an entirely new beginning needed to be made. This is the new element that came with the disaster which overtook Judah in 587, with the destruction of the temple and the removal of the Davidic king. The two institutions which seemed to have achieved most in providing a sense of continuity with the greatness of Israel's past were swept away. From this time onwards the whole direction of the prophetic faith turned to look for the return of that part of the community of Judah which had been carried into Babylonian exile in 598 and 587. We find this very fully demonstrated in the way in which the book of Jeremiah has been expanded and developed. The prophet's words of hope for a renewal of normal life in Judah (cf. esp. Jer. 32.15) have been very fully and extensively elaborated by Deuteronomistic editors to show that this fulfilment could only come when the return from exile took place (Jer. 24.1–10; 29.10–14; 32.36–44). We find a similar hope of a return from the Babylonian exile at the centre of the message of Ezekiel (cf. Ezek. 36.8–15; 37.15–23; 40–8), and then coming into full flower in the preaching of the prophet of Isaiah 40–55 (Isa. 40.1–5; 43.1–7, 14–21; 45.20–3).

The prophets who followed after the time of Babylon's downfall, when the first company of returning Jews made their way back to their homeland, elaborate still further on this hope of a return. They do so, however, in language which becomes increasingly extravagant, and which displays a growing frustration with the political and social possibilities of the times. The prophetic hope of a return to the land and a restoration of Israel acquires a marked supernatural and apocalyptic character (cf. Isa. 60.1–22; 61.1–7; 66.12–16). In this way the prophetic eschatology appears to have slipped further and further away from the realities of history, and to have moved into a strange world of apocalyptic images and themes. Yet these themes and images themselves derive from the older cult and prophecy of Israel.

When we look at the canonical collection of the Latter Prophets we find that there is a certain connectedness between the different prophets, and signs that their preaching has been treated as a part of a larger whole. It is the conviction that all the prophets were speaking about the death and rebirth of Israel that has brought together prophecies which stretch across more than two centuries. Beginning with Amos and the onset of the threat from Assyria in the middle of the eighth century, and continuing until the early returns of the fifth century, Israel and Judah had suffered traumatic disasters. The specific and individual circumstances of threat and danger have been swallowed up in a wider portrayal of doom and judgment which applies to all Israel. History has become subsumed in eschatology. Yet in a comparable fashion, the message of hope that began no later than the middle of the seventh century has become an all-embracing message of Israel's restoration and future greatness. No hesitation and compunction has been felt, therefore, by the editors of the separate prophetic books in applying this message of hope to each of the books. Such a hope belonged to the prophetic 'message', even though, from a strictly literary viewpoint, it did not derive from each individual prophet. Individual prophetic hopes and promises have become part of a much greater theme of 'promise' which came to be seen as characteristic of prophecy as a whole.

### 3. THE FORMS OF PROPHETIC HOPE

The particular way in which the prophetic books have been put together, supplemented and expanded to form a large canonical collection, has clearly been the result of a very extended process. Nevertheless, within this process a number of basic concepts and themes have played a dominant role. Where the modern critical scholar is rightly desirous of listening to the differing sound of each of the prophetic voices, the editors of the collection have worked with a different aim, and have tended to obscure these different tones by the way in which they have edited the collection into a whole. The result now is that we frequently find difficulty in determining the authenticity or otherwise of particular sayings, as we have already noted especially in the case of the hope expressed by Amos and Hosea. Certainly it has not been the needs of liturgical use alone that has determined this, but rather the conviction that the prophetic message is a unity, the ultimate author of which is God himself. The theological student of the meaning of prophecy must consequently be content at times to accept some degree of uncertainty as to when a particular saying was added to a book, since to note this has not been in any way a concern of the original editors.

However, this way of treating the prophetic books, in which some consistency of pattern and ideas is evident, does enable us to see the importance of a number of recurrent themes which form the centre of their message of hope. We may now note briefly what these are. At the head of them we can undoubtedly place of the expectation of a return from exile (cf. esp. Jer. 24: 1–10; 29.10–14; Ezek. 36.8–15; Isa. 40.1ff.). The plight of those deported to Babylon has become a kind of model or symbol of the plight of all the scattered and dispossessed Jews who formed the Diaspora. The very word 'exile' comes to take on a larger significance as a description of the scattered Jews of every land.

Behind this we can also detect the importance of the consequences that arose from the Assyrian deportations from the northern kingdom in the late eighth and seventh centuries BC (cf. Jer. 31.7-9; Ezek. 36.8-15; Isa. 49.6). The return of these people too, however completely they appeared to have become lost among the nations, became a part of this hope of a return. So the return to Jerusalem and to Mount Zion became the classic image of how Israel's restoration would take place (cf. Isa. 60.1-22; Joel 3.9-17). With this is coupled a related theme that members of Gentile nations will join with them, to pay homage to them and to act as their servants (cf. Isa. 33.1-24; 35.1-10). This theme of 'return' also implies the great importance that was attached to the promise of the land. Never is there the slightest suggestion that Israel's misfortune of being scattered among the nations should be a permanent condition, or that it might re-establish its national existence in some other territory than that promised to the patriarch Abraham. This land itself becomes central to the theme of promise.

There is, however, a very deep concern in the prophetic message of hope that Israel should recover its status as a nation. In particular, the division into two separate kingdoms of Israel and Judah is viewed as an act of sin, which must not be repeated. The Israel of the future is consequently foreseen as a single united Israel under a single ruler (cf. Ezek. 37.15-23).

This brings us to the third of these basic prophetic themes of hope, which is that the new Israel is to come under a restored king of the Davidic line (Amos 9.11-12; Hos. 2.5; Isa. 9.2-7; 11.1-9; 32.1; 33.17; Jer. 33.19-26; Ezek. 37.24-8). This hope, which found a basic point of reference in the older Davidic promise tradition delivered by the prophet Nathan in 2 Samuel 7.13, became the foundation of the later 'messianic' hope. Since the restored king was to be an 'anointed' ruler (Hebrew māšíaḥ) of the Davidic family, there is some basis for speaking of a 'messianic' hope. Yet this was certainly not the full expectation of a remarkable superhuman figure such as developed in later Judaism. Rather, it was a hope of the restoration of a Davidic ruler, based on the belief that this dynasty alone had been entrusted with this privilege by God.

Two factors in particular belonged to this hope. In the first place it was important, since the renewal of the monarchy would signify for Israel the return to full political independence. In this particular form the hope was destined never to be realised, even though the possibility that it would be at one time seemed real and even imminent (Hag. 2.23). In the second place the expectation of a return of the kingship, restricted to the Davidic line, was important for the concept of the unity of Israel. It is no surprise, therefore, to discover that eager eyes must have surveyed the fortunes of the Davidic family for a long time after Zerubbabel's death (cf. 1 Chr. 3.16–24). Throughout the period when this hope was at its greatest, it is evident that the main weight of interest lay with the belief in the divine destiny of the descendants of David, rather than with any deep commitment to the monarchy as an institution on the part of Israel. In this form the hope appears gradually to have waned, only to re-appear later in a more radical form with the expectation of a messiah of more transcendant proportions, but once again descended, as prophecy foretold, from the house of David.

In relation to the messianic hope we find how the written form of prophecy lent new possibilities to the interpretations which could be placed upon it. The hope of a restoration of a Davidic kingship became transformed into a wider portrayal of the coming of a heavenly saviour figure. The prophecies on which the later hope was built, as in the Messianic Testimonia from Qumran,[10] were the earlier prophecies seen in a new context of expectation. It is in no way the special divine status of the king in ancient Israel which has aroused this pattern of interpretation, but rather the unique importance of the Davidic family in Israel's history.

A further basic theme, or model, of the prophetic hope is the belief in an ultimate glorification of Mount Zion as the centre of a great kingdom of peace. Jerusalem itself becomes a place of the greatest importance, with its rebuilt temple looked to as the place where God's 'glory' or 'presence' would appear (cf. Ezek. 48.35; Mal. 3.1). To this the nations would come as an act of pilgrimage and homage, rather in the way that their representatives had done long before in the short-lived kingdom of David (Isa. 2.2–4 = Mic. 4.1–5; cf. Isa. 60.14; 61.5).

It becomes evident on examination that all of these images of what the restoration of Israel would bring have been drawn in one way or another from the tradition of Israel's past history as a nation. The central role of Israel as the people of God is everywhere assumed and used as a basis for depicting the future. Yet this is not in any way out of a conviction that history is cyclic in its nature, and that an inevitable 'return to the past' would take place as future years unrolled. In general such a deterministic view of history appears to have been almost completely alien to the Israelite tradition of thought. It is instead the belief that Israel's election must mean something, both for Israel itself and for the nations which would be blessed through it, that lies at the heart of these convictions. In calling Abraham, God had begun a task which he had not completed. Indeed the intransigence of the old Israel and its resort to idolatry were regarded as having frustrated this purpose. Yet the purpose itself had not, and could not, be abandoned. God would bring to fruition that which he had begun. By an understandable human reaction, the very frustrations and disappointments of the post-exilic age appear to have intensified the strength and firmness of the conviction that the final goal of God's purpose – the eschatological age of salvation – would certainly come.

It is difficult, to the point of impossibility, to speak of this element of 'promise' and eschatological hope in the Old Testament in terms of a 'doctrine', or of a rounded theology. Its literary form is primarily that of prophecy, and its ideas are expressed through images and thematic models, and not through firm doctrines or fixed schemes in which the sequence of events could be determined. The very flexibility of the literary and verbal expression of such hopes and images meant that there could be no single form of interpretation which could be heralded as self-evidently correct.

It is against this background that we must understand the rise of certain key-words and sometimes bizarre images in Jewish hope. In some circles this gradually developed into a new literary form, which we can call apocalyptic, of which the book of Daniel is the only full example in the Old Testament.[11] This new type of literature, however, which for a period flourished extravagantly in Judaism, arose out of earlier prophecy, and carried its images and themes to strange extremes. For this to have happened one essential prerequisite was necessary, and this was that prophecy should already have become an accepted part of a canonical literature. The new 'prophecy' was essentially the ability to discover the further messages that were believed to lie hidden in the old (cf. Dan. 9.2).

With the arrival of apocalyptic the concept of God's promise to Israel acquired a new medium of expression. Yet already we find an abundance of indications that it was a medium with genuine antecedents in the way in which earlier prophecy had been studied, interpreted and re-applied by the editors of the prophetic books themselves. There is no clear and broadly acceptable definition by which the passage from prophecy to apocalyptic can be readily traced. The strange images and symbols of the latter have their antecedents in the poetry and conventional descriptions of divine activity which we find in the former. With this new literary form there went a clear pattern of interpretation which could treat all prophecy as a kind of apocalyptic, with hidden meanings contained in every word, and names and numbers used as ciphers. Hence it is no surprise to discover from the way in which the prophetic books of Nahum and Habbakuk were interpreted at Qumran that they could be regarded as though they were a form of apocalyptic.[12] All prophecy had come to be seen as a veiled form of revelation, the fundamental message of which was the judgment that still awaited the sinners of the earth and the salvation that was to come for Israel.

Already, therefore, we discover that the particular assumptions about Old Testament prophecy that we find in the New Testament are firmly anticipated in the Old. If we are to seek some defence of the early Christian claim that the prophetic message of the Old Testament had been fulfilled in the events concerning Jesus of Nazareth, then we must begin to trace critically and historically the way in which prophecy itself developed from the preached utterances of inspired individuals to become a written series of texts, collected together and edited to form great books. These were then subsequently interpreted as a vast repository of hidden truths and revelations which the

skilful interpreter and the discerning student of events could
use to discover the will of God.

## 4. THE PROMISE IN THE LAW AND THE WRITINGS

So far we have looked at the theme of promise in the Old
Testament in relation to the books of the prophets. Attempts
that have been made from time to time to trace the ultimate
origin of this concept of promise further back than the prophets,
to discover its roots either in an ancient mythology or a particular tradition of the cult, must be rejected. It is the way in
which the prophets gave new hope to Israel and Judah, after
the ruination of the old kingdoms had occurred in the eighth
to the sixth centuries BC, that has given rise to this fundamental
theme of promise.

Yet when we turn to the New Testament for some guidance
upon the way in which the promise was being interpreted in
the first century AD we find that passages from the Pentateuch
and the Writings could be interpreted as though they were
prophecy. This is most notable in the way in which royal
psalms are interpreted as foretellings of the coming of the
messiah in early Christian preaching, so that the text of the
psalm, which was certainly originally composed and intended
for liturgical use, is treated exactly as though it were prophecy.
The divine declaration of Psalm 2.1–2 is interpreted in Acts
4.25–6, as a prophetic foretelling of the sufferings of Jesus, in
precisely the same way as though it had been preserved in a
book of prophecy:

> Why did the Gentiles rage,
>     and the peoples imagine vain things?
> The kings of the earth set themselves in array,
>     and the rulers were gathered together,
>     against the Lord and against his Anointed.

Even in the case of a psalm which carries in itself no special
indication that it was a royal psalm (Ps. 118), we find that it
could be treated as containing a prophecy of the rejection of the
messiah by God's people in Acts 4.11. Evidently what has taken
place is that the category of prophecy, and the assumptions and

methods of interpretation that were believed to belong to it, have been carried over to other parts of the Old Testament. This recognition is of great importance in the modern critical attempt to uncover the origins of the messianic hope in ancient Israel. It also matters greatly in connection with attempts to claim a far greater number of the psalms as being concerned with the kingship of Israel than any explicit statement in the text warrants. So attempts have been carried through in which the institution of kingship itself, and the distinctive high ideology associated with this, have been regarded as the real basis of Israel's 'messianic' hope.[13] Yet this can be true only by reaching a very extended understanding of what such a hope truly entails.

We have already seen that, so far as the main essential of the 'messianic' hope was concerned, this derived from the expectation of the restoration of the Davidic family to the kingship of a renewed Israel after the Babylonian exile. The distinctive elements of the old royal ideology as such, difficult as this is to define on account of its highly symbolic language, came to be caught up in this, but was not its main stimulus. The prophetic interpretation of specific psalms has not arisen because these psalms were originally thought to be prophetic in their nature, but rather as a consequence of the trends and developments which were taking place in the formation of a collection of canonical texts.

This raises a very deeply rooted issue in relation to the hope of a messiah as it is expressed in the Old Testament. We find that not one of the texts which the New Testament appeals to in support of such a hope can, from a strictly historical-critical point of view, be held originally to have been intended in the way in which it was later taken. Nor is this an exclusively Christian phenomenon, since we find a comparable situation with regard to the collection of Messianic Testimonia at Qumran.[14] Yet, in spite of this certainty about their original meaning, it is precisely these texts which have formed the seed-bed of the messianic hope. We are faced here with the phenomenon that old texts were being read with new eyes, and in the context of a broader hope which prophecy as a whole was felt to have warranted. When this began to happen is almost impossible to determine, though the evidence from Qumran indicates that it was towards the very end of the Old Testament period. The existence of a sacred canon of prophetic writings provided a platform on which a number of very powerful and influential images of the meaning of 'promise' could be built. From the point of view of the messianic interpretation of certain psalms, it appears most probable that the same stimulus towards a new dimension of interpretation had been felt. It is in fact possible that those editors who incorporated into the Psalter the texts of royal psalms, which must have appeared obsolete at a time when Judah had no king, did so out of a genuine hope that Israel would again need them. In this case a dimension of hope was present in the act of retaining compositions which the contemporary political scene made inapplicable in their original sense. The formation of the canon, therefore, must have had its own part to play in projecting the ideas and images associated with the kingship into the future. If this is so, then the more specifically 'messianic' interpretation of these and other psalms which we find in the New Testament marks a further step along a path that had already been begun in the Old Testament period itself.

To the general reader of the Bible it is no doubt more than a little bewildering to find that the assumption that each passage or text can have only one original and 'correct' meaning is not adhered to in the Bible itself. With prophecy in particular certain sayings and phrases came to be the subject of a very extended process of 'exegesis' in which a whole series of meanings could be uncovered.[15] Difficult as it is for historical criticism to trace these developments, we must recognise the importance of such a process to the Bible as a whole. Two factors must be borne in mind. It was in significant measure the belief that prophetic texts had a further meaning which was yet to be disclosed in the future which contributed to their being retained in a sacred canon. At the same time this very process of fashioning a permanent written collection, which could be read and pondered on in ages long after their original deliverance, encouraged the further search for such new and hidden meanings. Important key names and themes, such as those of 'the remnant' (Shear-jashub) and of 'God with us' (Immanuel), had already acquired a substantial history of interpretation within the Old Testament itself. It belongs to the understanding of the theme of promise in this literature that this remarkable dimension of historical depth in its patterns of interpretation should be followed through and understood. Perhaps most of all is it regrettable that even where there has been a desire to note the unity of the Bible as a whole, this major feature of the Bible's own expression of unity should be neglected.

This same type of 'prophetic' interpretation of the Old Testament can also be seen to have affected the Pentateuch. When Paul interprets the promise to Abraham (Gen. 12.1–3), it is noteworthy that it is taken in such a way as to show that it was still believed to refer to the future: 'The promise to Abraham and his descendants, that they should inherit the world . . .' (Rom. 4.13).

This particular interpretation is striking since it reflects directly on the entire understanding of 'the land' and of its relationship to Judaism. Accepting the ambiguity in the Hebrew word 'land/earth' (Hebrew *'ereṣ*), the narrower reference has been discarded. The original text of the promise almost certainly belongs to one of the oldest written strata of the Pentateuch (J), which must surely have proceeded originally to narrate how this promise was fulfilled in the conquest by Abraham's descendants of the land of Canaan. This 'fulfilment' is now replaced by that given in the book of Joshua, which, however, falls in the Former Prophets and not in the Pentateuch itself. Something of a break has been made between the affirmation of the promise and the account of its fulfilment, suggesting, as Paul takes it up, that the promise exceeded the fulfilment that had been given.[16] In this way the editorial formation and shaping of the Pentateuch has contributed its own measure of interpretative context, so that the old text could take on a new level of meaning. To contrast the 'original' meaning of the text with the revised and extended meaning which we find in Paul's epistle would be to ignore the considerable history of reflection and re-application which had taken place between them. In this process the canonical form of the Old Testament has evidently had a part to play.

To some extent it must be argued that the formation of a

canon of sacred writings is not only a function of religious life, but itself constitutes a measure of interpretation. By placing scripture alongside scripture a whole new range of interpretations became possible. Through comparison, association, and sequential ordering, a basis for exegesis could be established which far exceeded that which existed for the original independent document, in so far as critical scholarship has been capable of defining and outlining this. Hence, the association of certain psalms with prophecy has allowed these psalms to be treated as prophecy. Similarly, the importance of eschatological promise in prophecy has allowed the ideas and themes proper to this expectation to be read across into the assertions and promises of the Pentateuch. While it is attractive and convenient from a hypothetical standpoint to treat 'text' and 'interpretation' as two separately identifiable stages of investigation, we quickly find from a practical position that the two merge into one another. The canon itself establishes a context of its own which must be considered in understanding each of its parts.

From this perspective we can see that the early Christian claim that the whole Old Testament is a book of prophetic promise cannot be regarded as something imposed on the literature from outside. Rather it reflects an understanding which exists within the Old Testament canon itself. We find, therefore, that the Old Testament is presented to us with two major themes governing its form and establishing a basis of understanding from which all its writings are to be interpreted. It is a book of *tôrâh* – of the 'law' of the covenant between God and Israel. Yet it is also a book of promise, for it recognises the tensions that have arisen within this covenant relationship and the fact that Israel stands poised between the election of God, with all the promises that this entails of land, national life, and the task of bringing blessing to the nations, and its fulfilment. The law itself is both a gift and a goal. While we can see that historically the theme of 'law' belongs primarily to the Pentateuch and that of 'promise' to the Prophets, in practice all parts of the literature could be interpreted from the perspective of both themes. However, their mutual interrelationships, and the questions of priority between them, do not appear with any rigid fixity. In their own ways, both Judaism and Christianity saw the relationships differently as they built upon the Old Testament and established their own priorities in interpreting its demands upon the continuing 'Israel of God'.

# CHAPTER SEVEN

# THE OLD TESTAMENT AND THE HISTORY OF RELIGION

We have argued in discussing earlier the problems of method associated with an Old Testament theology that this literature can more adequately be regarded as reflecting 'religion', rather than 'theology' proper in a narrower sense. All the varied institutions of ancient Israel's life, its cultic rites and sanctuaries, its personalities and historical fortunes, are reflected in its different writings. Certainly it may be regarded as a more easily definable undertaking to attempt a history of Israelite religion than to recount the particular theology that this religion gave rise to. If theology is understood as the handmaid of religion, then we can see that only in a very different way from that which now pertains can the religion of ancient Israel be said to have possessed a rounded body of theology. Instead we have argued that an Old Testament theology must more openly recognise that its function is to elucidate the role and authority of the Old Testament in those religions which use it as a sacred canon and regard it as a fundamental part of their heritage.

This points us to the role of the Old Testament in fashioning the theological thought of Judaism and Christianity, and also in a more derivative fashion, that of Islam. The three great 'Abrahamic' religions all find in the Old Testament a source of authority and revelation for their own beliefs and practices. That the institutions and *realia* of ancient Israel's religion no longer exist must be fully taken into account in our seeking to understand how the inner theological 'truth' of this religion can still be an authoritative reality for us. There should therefore be a fruitful interplay between an understanding of the way in which the Old Testament has been read and interpreted in the religions that derive from it, and the results of a scientifically critical investigation into the nature and background of the religion, from which it has itself come.

There is, we may believe, a real measure of continuity between the religion of Israel in the Old Testament and the religions that have derived from it. However, the claim that this is so, and the attempts to present some theological demonstration of the reality of this continuity, raise a wide variety of questions about the nature of religion and the ways in which a continuity of tradition within it can be felt. We may note the facility with which extreme positions can be, and sometimes have been, adopted. On the one hand, it may be argued that all religions are in some degree continuous with each other, since behind each of them the same divine Reality must be manifesting himself to mankind. Against this can be set the opposite position in which the particularism of one religion can be so fervently held as to deny any reality at all to other religious traditions, and the radical discontinuity evident in the one tradition maintained. It is not difficult to find evidence in Christian theological thinking of the adoption of this latter position.

However, the claim that there is a radical discontinuity between Christianity and Judaism, as has not infrequently been held in some streams of Christian thinking, raises questions about the relationship of Christianity to the Old Testament. To assert, as has sometimes been done, that Christianity is the legitimate heir of the Old Testament, but that it is to be sharply distinguished from Judaism, raises questions of a complex kind.[1] Alternatively, it has, much less frequently and satisfactorily, been held that Judaism is the natural heir to the Old Testament, which represents an imperfect revelation, and that Christianity is to be distinguished sharply from this as well as from Judaism. The claim that has been defended, that the Old Testament represents a religion of 'failure', would appear to belong in this category.[2]

It is not difficult to recognise that other possibilities of understanding present themselves, and that various positions can be asserted, but much less easily defended convincingly. What constitutes continuity and discontinuity in religion, and how is it to be measured? Clearly identity of doctrine, or of ritual, or of institutions, can all play some part, but it is of the very nature of religious life that each of these undergoes periods of change and adaptation. The thousand years of Israelite-Jewish history which are reflected in the Old Testament reveal an immense number of such changes. It may be argued here that it is part of the immense theological worth of the Old Testament that it raises these issues and compels us to deal with them. Furthermore, it may also be contended that it has been the frequent neglect of the Old Testament that has led to the adoption of more narrowly assertive positions in Christian and Jewish theology than the study of the Old Testament itself properly warrants. Undoubtedly the Christian attitude to Judaism has been very different when the Christian commitment to the Old Testament has been fully grasped.

Similarly, the indifference to the theological value of a proper study of the history of religion might have been averted, had the resources of the Jewish-Christian tradition in the Old Testament been more fully appreciated. Not least, it may be argued, a number of features which modern discovery has revealed about the Bible and its background would have appeared less disturbing to some traditional assumptions with regard to it than has in fact been the case. Not only is the Old Testament an important guidebook for an understanding of the historical roots of the three great monotheistic religions of the world, but it is also an open window upon the immense riches and insights of the great religious traditions of the ancient orient.

## 1. THE OLD TESTAMENT AND THE RELIGIONS OF THE ANCIENT EAST

In 1876 the distinguished orientalist George Smith published a translation of a Babylonian cuneiform text, which he entitled *The Chaldean Account of Genesis*.[3] In commenting upon this text, he, and other scholars who have followed after him, noted the close similarities between the Babylonian text and the biblical account in Genesis 1, and argued that the former had influenced the latter. It is not necessary to recount the vast list of further discoveries which have followed in the wake of Smith's publication and of the remarkable range of Babylonian, Assyrian, Egyptian and other texts which have now come to light and which have been used to elucidate the pages of the Old Testament. Close or distant parallels of one kind or another in a very wide range of literature, extending at times to whole sections, at others to words and phrases, and at other times to the type, or general idiom of a story, have been revealed. It would be foolish and rash in the extreme to suppose now that an adequate understanding of the Old Testament can be undertaken without reference to the rich treasures of this comparative literary material.

However, underlying literature there are concepts, ideas, rituals and a range of mythological images, all of which are reflected in the content of the writings. It is, in retrospect, not altogether difficult to understand that the initial surprise at these discoveries should have led to a movement in which the dependence of the Old Testament on the more readily discoverable sources of Mesopotamian religion and culture, namely that of Babylon, should have led to extreme assertions of biblical dependence. Hence the pan-Babylonists, as they became known, and the 'history-of-religion school', to which they were related, pursued a kind of reductionism in which a large part of the biblical tradition came to be traced back to antecedent stages of Mesopotamian religion.[4] Everywhere parallels were noted, but differences ignored.

So, too, the belief that a common culture pattern reveals itself across the ancient orient, including the biblical world of Israel, has found its advocates, particularly in the so-called 'myth and ritual school'.[5] Properly and understandably, reactionary and defensive positions have been taken up, and the unsatisfactoriness of such extreme assertions about the dependence of the biblical tradition exposed. Especially has this been so in the presentation of an Old Testament theology, where the uniqueness of the Israelite religious tradition has been vigorously defended. Consequently, the task of presenting an Old Testament theology has become an increasingly complex one, since some knowledge of its religious background has become indispensable.

The problems that are raised by the availability of a considerable wealth of literature, with a much enhanced knowledge of the world from which this literature came, are themselves substantial. We may simply note a few of them, and the bearing which they have upon the Old Testament and its theology. At a literary level it is undeniably clear that the Old Testament rests on the compositions and achievements of an ancient oriental tradition which can be traced back to the Sumerians. In mythology and law particularly, the great history of these literary traditions is evident. However, in psalmody also Mesopotamian and Canaanite forms can be traced beneath the surface of the Old Testament psalms, and in proverb, fable and anecdote a great range of oriental parallels have been noted.

Yet even here to speak of 'dependence' raises questions at a literary level which are not easy to answer. What does similarity denote in such a context, and how close does a parallel have to be in order to claim that one text is dependent upon another? Furthermore, it is evident from a religious point of view that a psalm becomes a very different composition if the God to whom it is addressed is changed. So also if texts, particularly mythological texts, are transferred from a polytheistic to a monotheistic frame of reference they are altered to a very substantial degree. Yet in almost every case it is evident that we are faced with differences and modifications of a more substantial character than this when we note the similarities of Old Testament passages to comparable written sources of the ancient Near East. It cautions us to proceed in the most careful way in speaking of 'literary dependence' in trying to describe and understand the literary connections of the Old Testament with the literatures of the peoples which formed its background.

The question of literary connections, and the attempt to evaluate these in determining direct, or indirect, dependence of one tradition upon another, is however, less difficult than related issues concerning religious dependence. Nevertheless, the raising of the literary question enables us to see that there are inevitable similarities between the problems raised by comparative studies of literature and those concerned with religion. When we examine the history of Israel's religion in the light of all the evidence that is now available to us from the Canaanite and Mesopotamian spheres we are presented with a surprising number of undoubted connections. The Old Testament itself is fully aware of this, although it offers little information about the particular sources, or origins, of rites and institutions. Nevertheless, the sanctuaries of ancient Israel were certainly very like the Canaanite sanctuaries which they displaced, and the Jerusalem temple was built with the aid of Phoenician craftsmen (1 Kgs. 5.1–12; 7.13–14). In many instances the physical appearance and furnishings of a particular shrine can scarcely have been altered when it passed from Canaanite to Israelite hands. Similarly, in artefacts, rites and symbolism there were innumerable connections between the religion of Israel and the older religious traditions of Canaan which preceded them. For many worshippers it must have been very difficult at times to detect obvious physical signs of the change of religious occupation. It is unnecessary to list examples of all the parallels that have been discovered because they are so many that any survey of the Canaanite and Babylonian religions quickly brings them to light.

Yet if this element of continuity between the religion of Israel and the older religions of Canaan and Mesopotamia is everywhere evident, so also is evidence of change and discontinuity. No doubt the most obvious and inescapable change was that the new religion was devoted to Yahweh, the God of Israel, and that this in itself carried with it a unique tradition. In particular it is noteworthy that the Israelite tradition was blatantly and almost self-consciously, aware of its separate identity, and of the dangers of confusing one tradition with another. The very insistent demand that Yahweh alone should be worshipped points us in this direction. Other features of the religion serve to support such an assessment. It is easy, therefore, to make assertions that all the practices, sanctuaries and ideas that it 'borrowed', Israel also transformed. Myths were re-interpreted, ideas were subtly adapted and modified, new concepts added and older, cruder, ideas pruned away. Always the old tradition was being reminted and refashioned so that it became more truly expressive of the Israelite tradition.

Yet we must remember that Israel possessed no consultative committee, or doctrinal commission, which could meet to decide such issues. Changes usually had to be fought for, and to make their way by force of conviction in the light of the traditions that already existed. Continuity was not something that could be determined by vote, or by reference to an agreed set of principles. It had to be felt and accepted as experience was combined with tradition. In this sense there must have been a kind of nascent 'canonical tradition' long before the written canon of the Old Testament came into existence. In many ways the needs and changes which made a sacred canonical text an appropriate way of guiding the development of the religion were simply the continuing reflection of needs which had existed since the days of Moses. In such a context it becomes a very unsatisfactory proceeding to speak exclusively in terms of either 'borrowing', or of 'radical separation'. To a very real extent both phenomena are to be found, and in some respects they represent the same developments looked at from different points of view. An example of this may be cited in the case of rites of sacrifice, where substantial agreement exists among scholars that most, if not all, the types of sacrifice that became current in Israel were already extant in Canaan before the rise of Israel.[6] Some may have been taken over from further afield and instituted in Israel along with other aspects of the royal cultus of Jerusalem at the time when the temple was built there. The precise occasion and source of Israel's adoption of such rites is of less consequence than the certain assumption that the rites themselves were not new when they were introduced into Israel. Nevertheless, the act of adopting such rites established them in a new context of tradition and religious life which immediately began to change and modify the way in which they were understood and used. Hence we find that eventually Israelite-Jewish faith arrived at a unique conception of the meaning and significance of sacrifice which has left a profound legacy of ideas and spirituality long after the original rituals have ceased to be practised.

A not dissimilar development faces us when we consider the building of the temple of Jerusalem, which, in design and concept, marked one of the most radical steps in a 'syncretistic' direction that Israel's religion adopted (cf. Acts 7.47–50). Yet out of this institution a whole new range of thought and understanding about the presence of God among men was engendered (cf. 1 Kgs. 8.27–53), so that the importance of the temple to

post-exilic Judaism is readily intelligible. From being a questionable institution, which many must have regarded as a symbol of pagan infiltration, the Jerusalem temple became for Judaism the bastion of orthodoxy and the guardian of tradition.[7]
In this respect the use of such terminology as 'syncretism' and 'uniqueness' in describing religious changes needs the most careful examination. A number of scholars have pointed to the age of David and Solomon as one in which a powerful 'syncretistic' movement took place in Israel, with the adoption of a wide range of institutions, ideas and mythological traditions which subsequently played a considerable part in Israel's life.[8] Conversely the age of Nehemiah in the fifth century BC has been regarded as one of vigorous exclusivism and even of religious intolerance. It has been believed to mark a strong 'anti-syncretistic' tendency in Israelite-Jewish life.

There are clearly good reasons why such terminology should be used, but it remains questionable whether they do adequate justice to the complex nature of religious development. At a deeper level, which is the level to which theological investigation must probe, these developments are not altogether unrelated expressions of the same consciousness of a unique religious tradition. The great difference between the developments of the two periods lies in the markedly different political and cultural circumstances which prevailed at the different times. At the time when the Israelite empire was founded under David a whole new territory and culture had to be claimed for Yahweh. The buoyant optimism and confidence of the period reflects itself in the confident freedom in which the Yahwistic tradition felt able to mould and absorb all that it retained and re-established of the older Canaanite tradition. It was an age in which the religion and cult of Yahweh was creating its own forms and patterns, and therefore it was inevitable that these should have drawn upon the traditions and institutions which were already to hand.

When we compare this with the age of Nehemiah the historical contrast is immense. This was an age of recovery, when some return to the past and its glories was essential if Judaism was to be reborn on the ruins of the old Jewish state. The needs of religion pointed in a very different direction. To call one 'syncretism' and the other 'exclusivism' is to see only the surface of the situation. The differing circumstances of the time required that the consciousness of preserving and developing a distinctive religious tradition should manifest itself in different ways. Nor is this simply a question of the history of particular religious rites and institutions, although it is somewhat easier to trace the way in which the development moved in regard to these. In the conception of God we find that the same complex interaction between Israel's own nascent tradition concerning Yahweh and older strata of religious worship manifests itself. The most clear-cut example of this is to be found in the way in which the identification of Yahweh with El, the high-god of Canaan, whose worship can be traced still further back into the Mesopotamian sphere, is freely accepted by the Old Testament.[9] Conversely, any attempt at identifying Yahweh with Baal appears to have encountered resistance, so much so that the final form of the Old Testament tradition openly rejects such identification. Baal becomes a name of shame and abhorrence.[10]

The fact that these developments have occurred has become commonplace to historians of Israel's religion, and they have been illuminated by the availability of the resources of ancient Near Eastern texts from Ras Shamra and elsewhere. What is more difficult from a theological point of view is to identify the reasons why the development took place in the way it did. The common assumptions that the sexual elements of the Baal cult are sufficient explanation of this leave too much in doubt. For one thing it is clear from certain of the Ras Shamra texts that a prominent sexual element also prevailed in connection with El, and the supposition that certain deities were uniquely 'fertility gods' is almost certainly overdrawn. The giving of life and fertility was an aspect of deity in many forms, and elements of sexual imagery and ritual are to be found in an immense area of ancient religious life as comparative studies show. Furthermore, it is seldom clear why particular aspects of deity tended to polarise around the names of particular gods. There were almost certainly features of tradition and ritual associated with El which were unacceptable to the early Israelite religion, and which had to be dropped, or more actively repressed, by the mainstream of that religion. Even as late as rabbinic times, we find that practices of an orgiastic and sexual nature continued to survive, or re-appear, in Jewish worship at the temple itself, even though every effort was made to suppress them. The ways in which a particular religious tradition develops are many and varied, and it becomes impossible to bring them all under one or two labels, such as 'syncretistic' or 'exclusivist'. Nor can these issues be relegated to the more abstract and theoretical worlds of the study of the history of religion. They carry with them the most profound theological implications.

When we come to consider a question which must ever lie in the background of any serious study of Old Testament theology, namely, the reasons why Christianity diverged and separated from Judaism, so that it could no longer be regarded as an unorthodox Jewish 'sect' but had to be regarded as another 'religion', we are presented with issues of this kind. From a Jewish viewpoint the early Christian movement must have appeared dangerously 'syncretistic' and rash in the way in which it dealt with, and interpreted, the inherited tradition of *tôrâh*. Yet from the other side, it is equally clear that the early Christian advocates and apologists regarded Jewish developments, especially in the wake of the destruction of the temple in AD 70, as falsely 'exclusivist'. We can see that each was able to appeal to recognisable traits and characteristics of religious life which the Old Testament reveals to us. The study of the nature of religion in the Old Testament, therefore, and of the signs of continuity and discontinuity with older ancient Near Eastern religious life is itself a task of great theological consequence.

All of this points us in the direction of a fresh need to examine the nature of religious polemic in the Old Testament and for some attempt to trace the ways in which Israelite tradition itself developed and moulded theological thought. As we have already claimed, the emergence of a written canon of *tôrâh* was certainly preceded by a kind of unwritten, semi-official 'canonical tradition'. In this the various kinds of religious authority in ancient Israel all had their part to play; royal, priestly, and prophetic voices all contributed to the establishing of norms and patterns of religious life. The role of tradition, developing ultimately into a canon of *tôrâh*, thereby becomes a subject of great consequence to an Old Testament theology.

## 2. RELIGIOUS POLEMIC IN THE OLD TESTAMENT

The foundation of all religious polemic in the Old Testament is to be found in the first of the Ten Commandments: 'You shall have no other gods before me' (Exod. 20.3).

The words 'before me' (Hebrew *ʿal-pānāy*) could more easily be translated 'alongside me', and would appear to have had most direct relevance to a cultic situation in which it was usual for more than one god to be worshipped at a sanctuary. However, it certainly came to imply that no other god was to be worshipped in preference to Yahweh, or instead of him.[11] The firmness and rigidity of this tradition clearly betokens the strength that it had obtained in Israelite religion, and the deep roots that it had there. Certainly at a later stage, when monotheism had come to be fully accepted within Israel, this demand could be understood in conformity with the belief that to acknowledge any god other than Yahweh would have been to turn to a false god who had no real existence. This demand, and the prominent position which it holds in the Old Testament, must be seen as the basis of all other forms of religious polemic in the Israelite tradition and as central to the unique way in which Israel's religion developed. It asserts that there is an unbridgeable gulf between the worship of Yahweh and all other religions which involve the worship of 'other' gods. Yet decisive as this distinction becomes, the demand inherent in this commandment leaves a great deal unclear and indefinite. The more we study the tradition the more this becomes evident. For one thing it leaves undefined what exactly is meant by 'having' another god, and what degree of recognition might be accorded to such. This issue clearly became important in the political sphere where the acceptance of a treaty might well involve some limited recognition of the existence and authority of other gods. The sharp antagonism that appears in certain prophets to the making of such treaties, especially Isaiah (cf. Isa. 28.18; 30.1–5), has usually been associated with an interpretation of the commandment in this way.

The commandment also leaves open what it is precisely that constitutes the religion of Yahweh. In cases where the worship of other gods involved the recognition and use of images, it is clear that the second commandment would have precluded this. However, we find that the religion did not proceed in easily predictable ways. As we have noted earlier, the Israelite found little difficulty in identifying Yahweh with El, so that the old El-shrines where Israel's ancestors had worshipped could be freely adopted into Yahwism. In some cases there are reasons for believing that even the cult-images of the older tradition were adopted in this way, as appears to have happened at Bethel (cf. 1 Kgs. 12.28). That this came eventually to be firmly rejected reveals to us something of the way in which a growing stringency appears in the manner in which the demand was interpreted.

It is certainly in regard to the widespread use of images in religion in the ancient east that the strongest form of Old Testament religious polemic emerges. 'Idolatry' becomes the term *par excellence* by which to describe all forms of religion unacceptable to Yahweh. Eventually this came to apply to virtually every form of visual and iconographic symbolism, so that the religions of Judaism and Islam have become strongly iconoclastic as a result of it. Even where such symbolism had at one time been fully accepted within the Israelite Yahwistic tradition (cf. 2 Kgs. 18.41; cf. also 1 Kgs. 15.12–13) it came eventually to be rejected. Not only were images of gods rejected, but images of all kinds. The original cult-polemic progressed more and more into a form of theological evaluation which regarded all visual symbolism as illicit and objectionable. Such a viewpoint was capable of becoming profoundly theological when understood as based on a doctrine of the incorporeality of God, and his transcendent nature, which reflects itself in the later Jewish view that all images were gods 'made with hands' (cf. Mark 14.58; Acts 17.24). Eventually such a polemic came to be directed at the temple itself, as falling under this category of symbolism (cf. Acts 7.48). The primary reasons which have moulded the religious polemic of the Old Testament, therefore, are seldom overtly expressed, and were evidently capable of a good deal of flexibility in their interpretation.

We must also recognise the very important level of political motivation which has affected the lines of religious polemic which are to be found in the Old Testament. This comes most markedly into the forefront in regard to Assyria, where the prophet Isaiah could argue that the actions of the Assyrian king had impugned the sovereignty of Yahweh (Isa. 10.5 ff.; cf. Isa. 37.23). It is therefore possible that some of the polemic to be found in the books of 1 and 2 Kings against the 'high-places' of the land (cf. 2 Kgs. 17.9–12; 18.4; 21.3–5; 23.4–14), contained an element of hostility against forms of Assyrian practice which had become established in Judah. Certainly it is hard to avoid the conclusion that much of the sharp polemic directed against the cults of the northern kingdom, which resulted as a consequence of the division into two kingdoms, was politically motivated (so esp. 1 Kgs. 12.25–33; 2 Kgs. 23.15–20). The same would also appear partly to explain the sharpness of the polemic against idolatry in Isaiah 40–55, where the condemnation of images almost certainly refers to images of Babylonian deities (Isa. 40.18–20; 41.7; 44.9–20). Yet here we see how specifically religious, and more obviously political, reasons became intertwined, so that it is no longer possible to insist that one is uppermost. This also appears to be the case later, when we consider the sharpness of the antagonism that arose between Jews and Samaritans (cf. Ecclus. 50.25–6).

Yet a third type of religious polemic in the Old Testament is firmly based on ethical convictions and the recognition that the worship of particular gods carried with it participation in immoral sexual rituals. We have already mentioned this in connection with the cult of Baal, where a strong ethical condemnation appears, as is shown by the story of the cult of Baal-Peor (Num. 25.1–13). Although sexual immorality gains the greatest notoriety in such ethical polemic against what was regarded as alien to the true Yahwistic tradition, we also find more subtle ways in which opprobrium could be heaped on what was offensive. An instructive example is to be seen in the story of the unsavoury origins of the image and cult of the Danites (Judg. 17–18). This is all the more interesting on account of the connection that this cult had with the family of Moses (Judg. 18.30). In the Old Testament the very emphatic attention to the righteousness of Yahweh suggests a familiarity with forms of religion in which a marked indifference to moral issues could be tolerated and even encouraged. We unfortunately lack sufficient evidence to make a detailed comparison between the ethical patterns of Israelite religion and those of Canaan, but there is no serious reason to doubt the validity of the assessments that the Old Testament makes (cf. Deut. 9.4–5). It is in every way likely that many of the cults and traditions that Israel found in the land did not link the idea of God directly with moral behaviour.

It is in this area of ethical polemic that we encounter the great changes that occurred in the Israelite conception of holiness. This cultic concept was associated with various related beliefs about the 'taboo' qualities of holiness and the special dangers that attached to the 'profaneness' (Hebrew *ḥōl*) of those places and artefacts which belonged to other gods (cf. Isa. 52.1, 11). The special demands of warfare also came to be linked with this (cf. Josh. 7.10–21). Yet gradually all became moralised, and the reasons that were looked for in explanation of the unacceptability of what was 'profane' came to be seen as predominantly moral (cf. Mark 7.14–23). Just as *tôrâh* became a wide-ranging body of instructions and regulations dealing with religious, political and moral life, so also the polemic which was directed against other religions, and those features of these religions which were felt to threaten Yahweh, became a mixture of religious, political and moral issues. Whereas the Old Testament suggests to us a situation in which a clearly rounded datum of religious truth was given by Moses, and needed only to be preserved, we find upon historical-critical investigation, that the hammering out of this Yahwistic tradition was itself the result of a prolonged development.

When we turn to the Persian period of Israelite-Jewish religious development we encounter yet new forms of polemic and new measures to maintain the authority and strength of the old Israelite tradition. Most marked here is the growth of arguments based on the claim that alien ethnic groups had entered into Israel as a consequence of Assyrian deportations (cf. Ezra 4.2–3). Behind such assertions many scholars have seen the beginning of the Samaritan schism, since such polemic came to play a significant part in this. Furthermore, the concern to maintain the purity and currency of Hebrew as the language of Judaism gave rise to measures designed to remove the risk that this might be abandoned (cf. Neh. 13.23–7). How far this concern was motivated by cultic interests, and how far it reveals that language had become an important badge of community identity, is now not entirely clear. In post-exilic Judaism ethnic purity became a desirable goal in itself, once the political and social instability of the Jewish community in Judah and Jerusalem came to imperil the continuity of what was felt to be essential to the Israelite-Jewish tradition.

Even more forcibly we find a polemical antagonism appearing in Judaism in Hellenistic times, once certain basic institutions of Jewish life were threatened. These were particularly those of circumcision and the purity of worship in the Jerusalem temple, as the Maccabean rising attests. By this time, however, the main lines of Jewish polemical argument had become so well established that it was sufficient to insist that these evils had befallen Jews as a result of pagan idolatry (cf. esp. Ezek. 20.8, 24, 32). In apocalyptic imagery it was possible, not only to ridicule the evils of idolatry (cf. Dan. 3.1–30), but also to argue that great supernatural powers of evil were manifesting themselves through it (cf. Dan. 11.36–9).

From a historical perspective it is not difficult to see that religious polemic plays a very powerful and positive role in establishing the identity of a particular religious tradition. Certainly this was so in Israel, where issues came clearly to the surface, and the distinctive identity of the religion manifested itself, in opposition to the religious traditions of its environment. What was 'pagan', 'profane', or 'idolatrous' came to be defined in terms of actual realities of practice and artefact which Israel encountered in its religious environment. It is impossible to suppose that the Old Testament would be what it is, or that Israel's religion would have developed in the way it did, if it had not grown up against the historical background of the ancient Near East. Egypt, Canaan, Assyria, Babylon, Persia and Greece have all left their mark upon the Old Testament and have affected in different degrees the kind of religious thought and practice which we find there. They have therefore 'influenced' this religion; but to interpret this to mean that such influence was always of one kind, or moving in the same direction, would be totally false. At times such influence was positive and at others negative, and only the most careful comparative studies can bring to light the full measure of its effect upon Israelite-Jewish thought.


### 3. AUTHORITY IN ISRAELITE RELIGION

If the different forms of religious polemic which are to be found in the Old Testament disclose to us what was felt to be opposed to the Israelite religious outlook, then its own conception of authority should enable us to see what distinctively belonged to it. That which had been 'revealed' to Israel was that which belonged uniquely to its faith, and which had to be defended. Supremely the Old Testament expresses this conception of authority through its assertions and traditions about the origins of its faith and practice. That which God had given to Moses, or even earlier to Abraham, or even earlier still to all mankind (cf. Gen. 9.1–7), was that which was authorised as valid and authoritative.

It is in this area that historical studies of Israel's religion, comparative religious studies and biblical criticism have appeared to challenge basic assertions of the Bible. Here, too, we find that the conceptions of the Old Testament canon, which represents the end product of more than a millennium of religious development and literary growth, seem to stand in tension with its own assertions about the origins of its traditions. The Pentateuch covers the 'Mosaic' period of Israel's origins, when the covenant was established and the birth of Israel as a nation affirmed. Yet, from a literary point of view, we know, as a result of historical literary criticism, that the final shape of the Pentateuch was not arrived at until the fifth, or fourth, century BC. The final form of the Prophets and Writings was reached later still. The assertions, therefore, in the Pentateuch that 'God said to Moses', or that 'God spoke (through Moses)', are evidently a shorthand way of affirming the Mosaic authority of traditions that had established themselves over a long period of time. What is more, this intervening period of growth in the tradition is very fully reflected in the way in which the final 'authorised' form of the tradition has been preserved. For the Old Testament, therefore, the figure of Moses, and the occasion of the making of Israel's covenant with Yahweh, have become key themes, or models by which the authority of what had shown itself to belong to the Israelite religion could be asserted and maintained. We see this particularly in the way in which the great wealth of cultic legislation in the Pentateuch, which is ascribed to revelation through Moses, in reality records and reflects so much of the history of Israel's worship in the Jerusalem temple. What might, superficially, appear to be a mistaken ascription to Mosaic origin, is in fact a most important feature of the Old Testament understanding and interpretation of religious authority. That which belongs to the tradition became that which was ascribed to Moses.[12]

It is in consequence of this developing sense of authority that we find that the interpretation of the work of Moses has been greatly enlarged and enhanced in the course of the building up of the Old Testament literature. From initially being a historical leader of the escaping slaves of Egypt, Moses has come to be viewed as prophet, priest, and even in some measure a kingly figure. In the finished form of the Old Testament Moses is the 'founder' of the religion of Israel and the figure whose mediation was felt to be essential to provide adequate authority for what was to be believed and practised by Jews. To this extent the growth in the concept of a canon, and the building of this around the names and work of a few great individuals, was an important aspect of the development of a concept of authority in the religion of Judaism. Moses, David and Solomon become names by which a special authority was accorded to the traditions of various aspects of Jewish life and faith.

It is in this area particularly that a peculiarly complex range of historical, literary and theological issues begin to show themselves. The concept of a canon was itself not a given datum of the earliest forms of Israelite religion, but rather one which increasingly obtruded itself as the effective way in which religious authority was to be asserted. By it the various streams of tradition were united and woven together into a fixed whole. It would be quite wrong, in consequence, for us to accept the canon uncritically as a given basis of revelation and authority which precluded our looking behind it to the circumstances and literature out of which it arose. Equally, however, it would be wrong to neglect this 'finished' form of Israelite-Jewish tradition as though it represented only an accidental deposit of tradition from a particular age. As we have already claimed, there was a nascent 'canonical tradition' long before the written form of the canon began to appear with Josiah's 'book of *tôrâh*'.

The distinctive way in which Israelite religious authority came to manifest itself in the canonical Old Testament is itself of great interest. Basically we can discern that, as in other religions, various kinds of authority were effective in ancient Israel. The role of the king is the most obvious, and we find throughout the entire monarchic period of Israelite history that the kings of Israel and Judah acted with sovereign freedom in the way in which they determined the shape of Israel's cult. From David's installation of his sons as priests (2 Sam. 8.18), to Solomon's building of the temple (1 Kgs. 6.1–38), and the innumerable ways in which each of the kings is praised or blamed for the way in which he controlled the cult (cf. 1 Kgs. 15.11–15; 22.52–3; 2 Kgs. 10.18–31; 12.4–16, etc.), we find that the king's authority in religion was recognised and accepted. Yet Josiah's acceptance and encouragement of the great reform (2 Kgs. 22.11–23.27) was both a reflection of this royal privilege and the acknowledgment of a greater authority (cf. Deut. 17.18–20). With the demise of the monarchy as an ongoing institution after 587, the acceptance of a *tôrâh* of unique authority to the religion became of the greatest importance.

As in many religions we find that the various local priestly dynasties also exercised a considerable authority in ancient Israel. The sharp contention between particular priestly groups (cf. Num. 16.1–50), and the obvious effect of the restriction of priestly service to the single sanctuary of Jerusalem (cf. Deut. 12.2–14), all reflect an awareness that priestly duties were specially authorised by God (cf. Exod. 28.1–43). Nevertheless, we find in the Old Testament that there appear always to have been certain limitations upon the degree of authority which priestly families exercised in Israel. Against the king they were powerless, even when a long tradition and popular regard gave to them a special position (cf. 1 Kgs. 2.26–7). In the longer term we find that the emergence of a written *tôrâh*, addressed to, and interpreted by, lay persons, progressively eroded away the distinctive authority of Judah's priestly families. The many controversies which underly this are only partially known, although it eventually led to a way of Jewish life which required no priests.

It is in regard to prophecy that we find the most striking and influential development of the concept of authority in the Old Testament. The ability of the prophet to speak as the mouthpiece of God himself, and so to declare directly the divine will, was of great significance. The form of Israel's kingship (cf. 2 Sam. 7.1–17), and the building of the temple in Jerusalem (cf. 2 Sam. 7.13; 24.1ff.), were both developments in the religion which found authorisation through prophets. Even more, the role of Moses, as the unique founder of Israel's religion, could be interpreted as that of a prophet (Hos. 12.13; Deut. 18.15; cf. Num. 12.6–8). However, the whole canonical corpus of prophecy shows us further that the resurgence of Jewish life and religion after 587 was very largely guided and encouraged by the work of particular prophets.

Not least we may claim too that the special emphasis upon individual personalities, and the way in which the entire canonical tradition has been moulded around the names of a few great *epigoni*, or 'leaders', of the religion reflect the experience and unique regard for prophetic authority. This did not, of course, solve all problems, since we encounter the phenomenon of false prophecy (cf. Deut. 13.1–5; 18.20–2; Mic. 3.5–8; Jer. 6.13–15; 28.1–17), and there was evidently a need for an established tradition by which prophecy could itself be tested. Yet overall, and even exceeding that of the king (cf. 2 Sam. 12.1–15; 1 Kgs. 21.1–24), the authority of the prophet would appear to have had a profound influence upon the way in which a uniquely given 'word of God' came to be enshrined in a sacred canon of writings.

A conception of authority is undoubtedly of the essence of religion, since it affirms the particular value of traditions and practices, as well as enabling religions to meet and deal with change. The immense upheavals that took place in Israel's

history, involving the almost total collapse of its major religious
and political institutions, reveal how deeply a sense of authority was embedded in the religion. It was sufficient, both in
its strength and flexibility, to enable Israel to overcome these
setbacks, and to create new forms sufficient to deal with them.

In a number of respects we may argue that the problems of
continuity in religion and of authority are closely intertwined.
They are, in their respective ways, simply the same phenomena
looked at from different methodological and historical points of
view. When we ask why religions survive and maintain a sense
of continuity, we are looking, from a neutral historical position,
at a phenomenon of social and religious life. Change is accepted
and new forms and institutions welcomed, because they are
regarded as necessary for a continuity with the past. Yet from
the 'inner' theological perspective of the religion itself, the
possibility of continuity, and the acceptability of new institutions, are decided by assumptions and beliefs about authority.
That which is 'authorised' is that which is necessary for maintaining continuity. Not only do we find in the Old Testament
most instructive illustrations of the way in which the role of
authority in maintaining a sense of religious continuity operated
in ancient Israel, but we also find in it important guidelines for
recognising the connections which Jews and Christians have
found between their own faith and life and that of the Old
Testament. The question of the authority which the Old
Testament should have within Judaism and Christianity must
be considered in the light of the way in which authority itself
came to be considered in the religion of ancient Israel.

#### 4. THE OLD TESTAMENT IN RELIGION

From the general perspective of world religions the legacy of the
Old Testament is very distinctively marked. It has given rise to
three great 'book' religions: Judaism, Christianity and Islam,
although the connection with the latter is somewhat different
from that in the other two.[13] The authority of the 'book', the
canonical literature, has been so highly regarded that the main
patterns of life and worship have been moulded around it. Most
obviously has this been so in Judaism where the basic forms of

worship are built up around the sacred scriptures. So also the various features of Jewish life, and almost every aspect of conduct and custom, have required to be authorised by the book. In order for this to come about a vast literature in the Mishnah and the Talmud has become necessary, which provides an indispensable part of the interpretative approach to the contents of the Old Testament. On the one hand this has given rise to what one Jewish scholar has described as 'the burden of the Book',[14] yet on the other it has assisted in the maintenance of a sense of continuity with the Old Testament. This continuity has seldom been allowed to slip into being a mere veneration for an ancient and sacred text. Rather, its ethical and theological content has been explored, considered and re-applied in an ongoing process of intellectual discussion. The many shades of Jewish life and religious opinion have all found themselves compelled to relate themselves to the preserved text of the scriptures without which Judaism would not be what it is. The nature of this Jewish appeal to, and involvement with, the Old Testament, may be looked at briefly after we have noted the main patterns of Christian concern with this literature.

It is from within the Christian tradition, as we noted in the opening chapter, that the primary search for an 'Old Testament Theology' has developed. Only on the fringes of the major Christian theological traditions has it been contended that the Old Testament should be abandoned, and even where this has occurred, there has been little consistency in the reasons advocated for doing so. We may, however, return to the point that the Old Testament does not by itself constitute the Christian canon, but has existed alongside the New Testament. It is here that we encounter the greater theological dilemma. The New Testament accepts and interprets the Old Testament by appeals and arguments which are very different in method from those of historical criticism. Simply to repeat, or to elaborate upon, the appeals of the New Testament to the Old by a system of typology has found only limited support among modern Christian scholars. Rather, it has seemed preferable to look for broader ways in which the necessity of the Old Testament to the Christian tradition has been maintained. Ideas of 'progressive revelation' and of 'preparation' have frequently been used. So, even in a modern critical theology of the Old Testament, it has appeared necessary to assert the rightness of reading the Old Testament through 'Christian' eyes: 'A theology of the Old Testament which is founded not on isolated verses, but on the Old Testament as a whole, can only be a Christology, for what was revealed under the old covenant, through a long and varied history, in events, persons and institutions, is, in Christ, gathered together and brought to perfection'.[15]

In a similar vein it may be claimed that the unity of the Old Testament within itself is entirely consonant with the unity of the Bible as a whole: 'Unless it is based upon the principle of the unity of the two Testaments, and *a fortiori* on the internal unity of the Old Testament itself, it is not possible to speak of a theology of the Old Testament'.[16]

Neither of these positions can properly be regarded as self-explanatory, nor particularly convincing without a great deal of modification. It is clearly right that a Christian should approach the Old Testament through the New, and with a clear consciousness of his commitment to Christ as the 'goal' of the Old Testament. At the same time it is also essential that this commitment should be examined critically, by tracing the ways in which the particular assertions that Jesus represents the 'fulfilment' of the Old Testament have arisen. Similarly, in regard to the unity of the Bible, it is obviously important that the Christian should be aware of other ways of tracing this than those which the New Testament alone adumbrates.[17] The 'unity' of the Old Testament can appear very differently when looked at through Jewish, rather than Christian, eyes. Nor should such a consciousness of the Jewish approach to the Old Testament hinder the Christian from recognising his own commitment to it. We have argued earlier that the various patterns of Christian, New Testament, interpretation of the Old, have important antecedents in the Old Testament itself and the way in which it has been put together.

However, it is most noticeable in regard to the attitude to *tôrâh* that the Christian approach to the Old Testament has differed from that of Judaism. The belief that Jesus has authorised a new freedom towards the *tôrâh* (cf. Matt. 5.17–48), has enabled Christians to approach the Old Testament with considerable detachment in so far as it concerns the obligation to obey each rule laid down in that literature. The principle that 'the written code kills, but the Spirit gives life' (2 Cor. 3.6) has encouraged a confidence in regarding the *tôrôth* of the Old Testament as no more than a compendious illustration of certain basic religious and ethical principles. Within the mainstream of Christian tradition these basic principles have been seen as outlined in the Decalogue (Exod. 20.2–17), but even this has been brought into briefer summary (cf. Luke 10.25–8). As a consequence of this approach to *tôrâh* no particular problem has been found in an almost total disregard by Christians of the cultic legislation of the Old Testament. This has been treated as an obsolete 'ceremonial' law, the greatest exegetical use of which has been in the number of typological applications to which it has been put (cf. Heb. 4.14; 5.10; 7.1–28, etc.).

However, alongside this relatively limited concern with the practical implications of the *tôrâh* of the Old Testament, Christian tradition has continued to find a profound theological significance in it. Its comprehensive divine demand has been felt as a necessary summons which must lead Christians to the central core of the New Testament message of salvation, with its doctrines of atonement and forgiveness.[18] Looked at from the viewpoint of these very rudimentary summaries, it is evident that the Christian and Jewish approaches to the Old Testament have differed very widely. Even where closely related conclusions about the nature of the divine demand in *tôrâh* have been arrived at, the exegetical routes that have been followed have differed considerably.

If we look at the role of the Old Testament in Islam we find that yet another, widely divergent, approach reveals itself. Throughout the Qur'an the assumption of a fundamental revelation to Abraham is accepted, to which the life and work of Muhammad can be related. Furthermore, the centrality of the most basic Old Testament theological demands in monotheistic doctrine and the rejection of idolatry are profoundly in evidence. So too are many of the Old Testament's central ethical demands. It is noteworthy in connection with Muhammad's role as a prophet that this overall category for the interpretation of his life and work continues and develops one of the most prominent forms of the Old Testament's understanding of divine revelation and authority. Neither Judaism nor Christianity has developed an understanding of the prophetic office to anything like the extent that this has taken place in Islam. There are therefore grounds for recognising that, in this, Islam has preserved and made use of an aspect of the Old Testament which neither of the other two 'Abrahamic' religions has been able to do.

These outlines of the way in which the Old Testament has left a legacy in three great modern world religions are necessarily brief and elementary. Yet they are sufficient to show that the realities of this legacy are not difficult to find and to trace, and that they project an important role for the study of an Old Testament theology. That the 'message' of the Old Testament can be reduced to any simple formula, or brief outline of ideas which are to be found within its writings, is clearly a very inadequate theological approach. If theology is to serve as a handmaid of religion, then it must endeavour to trace and understand the particular way in which the Old Testament has moulded and fashioned theological thought in the modern world. No simple reductionist approach can possibly suffice, but only the most careful scrutiny of the way in which the ideas and concepts of the Old Testament have been taken up, developed and used historically. Such an approach must surely have an important part to play in establishing some bridges between the traditional lines of theological study and the more recently developed concern for an adequate historical and comparative study of religion. In a very real way the theological legacy of the Old Testament provides such a bridge which spans the religions of Judaism, Christianity and Islam.

# CHAPTER EIGHT

# THE OLD TESTAMENT AND THE STUDY OF THEOLOGY

Any study of the subject of Old Testament theology ought to be concerned, not only with the way in which the Old Testament may, historically, be held to have given rise to theological ideas, but how the continued pursuit of such a subject may stimulate theological thought. Both on account of its own antiquity, and also as a result of the predominantly historical approach to the main subject areas concerned with the Old Testament, the discipline appears to be more a historical, than a truly theological, one. Certainly the study of the history of ancient Israel, and of the history of its religion and literature, creates an impression that the prevailing methodology is historical rather than theological. To an extent this must be inevitable within the nature of the subject matter, but it must also be questioned whether the trend in this direction has not gone too far.

Can we not now develop a more self-evidently theological approach to the study of the Old Testament which will extend its relevance beyond what is currently customary? A number of factors suggest that this can and should be done. Perhaps most of all in this regard we should note the way in which questions of methodology have come increasingly to occupy the foreground of attention in relation to Old Testament studies, so that a substantial part of any curriculum concerned with it must pay attention to this. As it is, the particular methodological problems of literary and historical criticism have tended to occupy almost the entire field of study, to the unintentional neglect of other aspects of the subject which might well have deserved more consideration.

A further factor arises at the present time which makes a re-examination of the aims and presuppositions of the study of the Old Testament within a theological curriculum particularly appropriate. Both on account of the extensive range of possible subjects that come within the purview of theology and religious studies, and also as a consequence of changes of motivation towards such study, a far greater degree of choice has become commonplace in the make-up of any particular theological course. How a useful theological course should be planned, and what subject areas and methods it should focus most attention on, have become questions that are immensely relevant to the continuance of theology as an academic discipline. Yet it is very difficult to find more than very brief and elementary discussion of these issues in relation to what theology itself is considered to be, and what entitlement it has to be classed among the major intellectual disciplines of the modern world.

Not least it has become apparent, from a number of sides, that the whole question of what constitutes theological thought has been subjected to extensive re-examination, and that, what have in the past been accepted starting-points for theological enquiry, have in many cases been abandoned. More direct and immediate starting-points have been sought in religion itself, and in the ways in which people interpret their religious experiences, rather than in the historically given data of Bible and creeds. All of this has a prominent bearing upon the Old Testament, because it has encouraged the assumption that this literature is only peripherally related to the religious life of the modern world, and that it might more appropriately be dealt with in a department of ancient history, or of oriental studies, rather than one of theology. The consequence has been that Old Testament theology, and Old Testament studies generally, have appeared more amenable to becoming optional, rather than essential, parts of a normal theological course.

It would be inappropriate to indulge in any form of special pleading on behalf of the Old Testament, but it is at least worthwhile to consider what advantages may be thought to accrue from the theological study of it. Furthermore, it is certainly in order to examine ways in which aspects of the study of the Old Testament, other than those which currently predominate, might be explored and developed. In this way it may also be possible to single out those features of its study which have in the past been felt to contribute essentially to theological discipline and understanding to see how they might be more adequately furthered. Certainly it would appear to be desirable that even within Old Testament studies some greater range and flexibility should be introduced so that a wider choice can be established as to which subjects and methods are to be most fully explored. At present it is inescapably clear that the major disciplines of the subject – the history of Israel and of its literature and religion – are based upon methodological assumptions which were laid down more than a century ago. While it would be rash, and certainly mistaken, to suppose that they are no longer relevant, it is also evident that their continued dominance leaves other areas and approaches neglected. No doubt it may be claimed in defence that this situation has contributed effectively in the past, but it can scarcely any longer be held to be entirely desirable in the present.

A further point may be made in respect of the study of the Old Testament as an aspect of modern theological enquiry. From within the Christian tradition the value and relevance of the Church's commitment to the Old Testament have been subjected in recent decades to more serious and searching enquiry than at almost any other time in the history of the Church since its first break with Judaism. It is not a little disconcerting to find that, when such major issues that concern the Old Testament are being raised in Christian theological debate, the main areas of the study of it do little to relate to them or to prepare for them. From within the Christian tradition it is increasingly commonplace that little use is made of the Old Testament, or that such use as is made, is based upon liturgical and aesthetic considerations which pay little attention to modern theological discussion. There is undoubtedly present a measure of divorce between what is being used liturgically and what can be defended theologically.

We can discern a need, therefore, for the Church to bring out into the open, more fully than hitherto, its own understanding of its commitment to the Old Testament and for this to be more adequately integrated into the common basis of theological study. As it is at present, it is not at all uncommon to find that a large mass of historical and literary information about the Old Testament is presented as a groundwork for a theological understanding of it. What is to be done with this information, how it is to be used theologically, and even how it relates to the kind of use made of the Old Testament in past ages of the Christian Church are dealt with only marginally, or not at all. To look more widely than this, and to ask how the Old Testament is understood in Judaism, and how this relates to its use in Christianity, are issues that are almost entirely neglected, save in relation to specialised courses in the study of Judaism. There are clearly areas, therefore, in which a considerable range of studies concerned with the Old Testament can be integrated into modern theological thought with probable advantage to the understanding of theology as a whole. In many cases it may be considered best that these should supplement, rather than supplant, the disciplines that are at present followed. In other cases it may be felt that a wider choice may be established so that the student can decide for himself which areas are best likely to serve his own needs.

### I. THE OLD TESTAMENT AND BIBLICAL STUDY

Since the Old Testament is a constituent part of the Christian Bible, it may appear at first glance somewhat strange that the issue of how it should be studied as a part of this Bible should be raised separately. Yet there are several points that may be held to arise from issues dealt with in earlier chapters. The first of these concerns the predominantly 'historicist' approach to the study of the literature of the Old Testament. The major disciplines of study tend predominantly to be concerned with historical dimensions of interpretation and with the criteria and critiques of historical investigation. Since any special subject area of ancient Israelite life, be it political institutions, religious thought, or political and social history generally, are all dependent on the literary-historical criticism of the Old Testament, there is a measure of overlap. In fact, it may be argued that the 'history of Israel' as a major subject-area has obtained the widest popularity, and contributed most usefully to the understanding of the Old Testament, only when its remit has been drawn unusually widely. It is questionable, for example, whether the study of the major Old Testament prophets should be dealt with at all in a political history of ancient Israel, and it is very clear that for some periods the gaps in knowledge are so large as to raise major problems of understanding.

Even more strikingly, it must become apparent that the very emphasis upon a discipline that is primarily a 'history', tends to elevate the question of 'historicity' in the biblical narratives to an unusually high degree. This has been doubly unfortunate in regard to the Pentateuch, for example, and particularly in respect of the patriarchal narratives. What they are as narratives, whatever terminology is chosen to describe them either as legend or saga, must be understood first, which does not necessarily mean that we must simply concern ourselves with what history lies behind them. This is not at all to suggest that the question of historicity is not important, or should not be raised, but simply to insist that it is not the only aspect of the material that matters to us from a religious and theological point of view. As it is, a negative evaluation on the question of historicity, has tended to become confused with a negative evaluation about the value of the literature.

Primarily it would appear that a major significance of the raising of questions of historicity in regard to the oldest narratives of the Old Testament is an apologetic one. Yet this must often lie at the edge of the literary and theological study of a narrative. This is clearly so in regard to the life and work of Moses, where it must be insisted that there are overwhelming arguments of a broad and general nature which point to his historical reality.[1] He is all but indispensable to our acceptance of the fact of Israelite religion. Yet it is also true that the tradition of his achievements has become so central a part of the Israelite heritage that it is virtually impossible now to uncover the flesh and blood personality that lies buried beneath them. Moses is lost beneath his own greatness, so that by a strange historical paradox the strength of the record that leads us to recognise his historical reality also veils him from us.

In another area, too, we must note how the very achievements of modern research make the more familiar subject-areas of the history of Israel and its religion increasingly difficult to undertake. This is through the archaeological investigation of the Holy Land and its neighbouring territories. The wealth of relevant material that is now available, the range of sites that have been explored, and the store of information that has been accrued, make it almost impossible for the non-specialist to keep abreast of it all. Yet it is of great importance to the student of the Old Testament that he should acquire some knowledge of the techniques and limitations of archaeology so that he may gain some broad impression of where it fits in. The dangers of either exaggerating or minimising its contribution can then be avoided.

These considerations suggest that the time may well be ripe for some re-appraisal of the way in which the historical-critical approach to the literature of the Old Testament should be undertaken. The traditional disciplines are already so large as to be scarcely manageable if they are to be tackled in depth. Yet they represent only one dimension of the way in which the Old Testament as a whole can be held to contribute to the study of theology. What we have advocated in the preceding chapters has in part been directed towards widening the area of study that is associated with the Old Testament. This would suggest that some reasoned narrowing of the specifically historical aspect of its study must be accepted. If so, then it would appear practicable to combine together the particular fields of the study of the history of Israel and its literature and religion with a special emphasis upon the methodology of historical criticism generally. Clearly this would apply first to the literary criticism of the Old Testament, where questions of method require to be assessed and evaluated before we can achieve the 'results' that past generations have so easily presumed to be 'assured'. In any case, it must be insisted that there is a considerable measure of overlap between literary and historical criticism, since so much that is important within the criteria of literary criticism depends upon questions about the development of religion in ancient Israel. Similarly, it is almost impossible at times to make firm distinctions between the history of 'Israel' and of its 'religion', as the case of the prophets testifies. It may also not pass unremarked that a volume covering the history of Israel, which has become one of the most widely used of all theological textbooks in the English-speaking world, takes an extremely wide remit of its subject.[2] A great deal that belongs to the field of literary criticism and the history of religion is to be found within it. There would appear to be no reason, therefore, why this process should not be more fully carried forward, and already some particularly useful and successful volumes of this kind have appeared.[3]

It may be suggested in the light of this that the distinctively historical-critical side of Old Testament studies could be brought into a more compact compass in order that other aspects of the subject should be given more adequate attention. Certainly in this respect it would appear to be of the greatest importance to the Christian study of the Old Testament that very full and careful attention should be devoted to the manner, method and presuppositions of the interpretation of the Old Testament in the New. From the theological point of view this is the very groundwork of the commitment of the Christian to the Old Testament. That this is so has been noted on more than one occasion in volumes on Old Testament theology, but with next to no attention being devoted to its details.

It may be felt in rejoinder to this that this particularly is the responsibility of the New Testament scholar, which is undoubtedly partially true. However, we have had occasion to point out the marked separation that has grown up between New and Old Testament approaches to such a basic subject as 'the message of prophecy'. To the average student the impression is created, with some genuine justification, that the New Testament writers simply misunderstood the Old Testament and made of it whatever they wished. The whole study of the interpretation of scripture, which begins in the Old Testament itself, is seldom pursued as a major aspect of biblical study generally.

From the very foundations, therefore, the understanding of the Christian commitment to the Old Testament is set under a peculiar cloud. It is made to appear a consequence of the ephemeral fads and fancies of the age of the New Testament, and to have little or no valid connection with what the Old Testament actually says. To some extent this situation has resulted from the complexity of the problems that are involved in studying the development of a tradition of biblical exegesis in Judaism. Yet it is also a reflection of the sharpness of the separation that has tended to result from the division of biblical studies between the Old and New Testaments. There are obviously some areas where the separation is advantageous, but there are also some features in which it has acted as a stimulus to separation and, sometimes, divorce. By more careful defining of the problems, and by a proper degree of co-operation between specialists in the two Testaments, a more satisfactory basis of study could be built up in which the contributions from both sides could be examined. Certainly, it must be held to be mistaken to suppose that the way in which the New Testament interprets the Old is only primarily of concern to students of the former. It reflects very directly upon the latter as well, since the reasons why the Christian has, in the past, been committed to the Old Testament are first found there.

This particular issue also concerns the question of the unity of the Bible, which obviously has quite far-reaching importance for any approach to the use of the Bible in theological research at all. From a historical-critical point of view it is plainly unsatisfactory to express such a unity simply by imposing patterns of thought upon the whole.[4] Rather, we must examine fully and critically those key themes by which the unity is set out in the Bible itself. We have already suggested that the starting-point for doing this must lie in a study of those key concepts of 'law' and 'promise', by which such a unity has been discerned within the Old Testament.

## 2. THE OLD TESTAMENT AND THE STUDY OF THEOLOGY

The extent to which use has been made of the Old Testament by the great theological giants of Christendom has varied considerably, but it has seldom been entirely absent. Certainly within the Reformed tradition the impact of Luther's and Calvin's handling of the Old Testament, with their own great differences, have tended to mould the approach to the Old Testament in preaching, liturgy and hymnology for a vast number of Christians.[5] Yet it is unusual to find any consistent concern to study this impact as a facet of understanding the Old Testament and its theological meaning. Rather, the tendency has been to consider it appropriate almost exclusively within the general area of research of the particular theologian in question. Hence Luther's use and understanding of the Old Testament has been thought to reflect upon Luther, but scarcely upon the Old Testament. This is plainly wrong, and has undoubtedly contributed to the general impression that Old Testament theology is unrelated to any other branch of theology and is free to develop its own methods and to pursue its own goals. This is not the case, and the way in which this literature has been used and interpreted by theologians must be held to provide a significant datum of what Old Testament theology is about. As it is at present, the general tendency to leave aside such questions, as outside the orbit of Old Testament studies proper, has meant that the serious academic study of this literature has become isolated from the questions of what we are to do with it once we have studied it. Certainly this must be held to have contributed to the situation in which the liturgical and theological approaches to the Old Testament have parted company.

No doubt much of the reasoning that lies behind the assumption that the study of how the major theologians of Christendom or the philosophers of Judaism have interpreted the Old Testament does not belong to the subject of Old Testament theology, arises from certain convictions about the nature of theological truth. We have endeavoured to argue in the preceding pages that summaries of the religious ideas that are to be found, either directly or indirectly, reflected in the Old Testament, should not by themselves be called a 'theology'. Some basis of 'system' or 'unity' is necessary in order to provide a context and a frame of reference by which such ideas can be brought into an inner theological harmony as an expression of truth about God and the world. This is what the theologian or philosopher does, and it is important for an understanding of the religious significance of the Old Testament that the way in which this is done should be examined critically.

There is therefore a great deal of relevance for the appreciation of the Old Testament as a collection of theological writings in a critical examination of the way in which major theologians have dealt with it. At the outset we suggested that this concern has come increasingly to dominate the discussion about Old Testament theology. Basic questions of methodology and ordering of the material have come to provide the more essential 'theological' dimension of enquiry about the religion of the Old Testament. Since this is so, it would appear highly desirable that the way in which the Old Testament has been understood and interpreted by one or two of the greatest thinkers of Christendom should normally have a place in the study of it as a theological work. Such would not simply reflect upon the theologian himself, but upon the material he handles. For the modern Protestant, it is evident that such figures as Luther and Calvin would have to be considered as major candidates for such a task.

To some extent we must note the lack of readily accessible books dealing with Old Testament theology from this point of view, and the fact that the greatest work in this field has long since become lamentably out of date.[6] The temptation is all too readily at hand to deal with such a subject as a history of Old Testament interpretation. Yet this is not what is required, and simply reflects the modern temptation to see all subjects from a distinctively historicist point of view. The enormity of the task of dealing with anything like an adequate history of the interpretation of the Old Testament in Christianity, let alone noting developments in Judaism as well, rules out any fully comprehensive course of study in this area. Yet what is needed is the ability to appreciate the particular problems of the theologian, so that the singling out of one or two major figures could undoubtedly serve admirably to reveal the distinctive problems of a theological frame of reference.

It cannot then escape our notice that it was in many ways the difficulties which revealed themselves between the different approaches, with their separate assumptions, varying from one theologian to another, that prompted the search for a more adequate historical and critical examination of the theological ideas of the Bible. Does it not then appear as if the new theological enquiry about the Old Testament is simply reversing this process and choosing to ignore the results of historical criticism? The answer must certainly be in the negative, for it would be a sad failure of nerve were we to allow the achievements of two centuries of critical research to be discounted. What we have advocated is the bringing together of the results of historical criticism and theological research into a more fruitful period of cross-questioning and confrontation. All too readily the situation has come into being, as a result of the division of subject matter, in which neither historical criticism nor theological explanation have much to say to each other. Certainly this is so in respect of the Old Testament. It is not misplaced to suggest, therefore, that 'Old Testament theology' has scarcely been a branch of theology at all, but rather a subordinate area of the history of the religion of ancient Israel.

By bringing more fully into the open the way in which theologians of the past and present have viewed the Old Testament it may be hoped that a new stimulus can be given towards re-opening a dialogue that has all too often appeared to be closed. The reader will quickly recognise in this a re-opening of the debate about the role and function of biblical criticism within theological research. Perhaps more than any other single facet of modern Christian theology the fact of a critical knowledge of the make-up and origins of the Bible has forced theology to seek new directions. For this reason a new phase of interest into the aims and origins of modern biblical criticism has taken place, turning attention back from the theological aims of the nineteenth century to those of the eighteenth. Nor has Judaism escaped the effects of this enquiry so far as the Old Testament is concerned, even though it tended to maintain a greater aloofness at first to the major claims of literary and historical criticism. Consequently both Christianity and Judaism have come to see the Old Testament in a different light from that which prevailed almost unquestioned for many centuries. We now see very clearly that it is an ancient literature, which belongs to a relatively distant past, and must be understood accordingly.

It is perhaps not altogether surprising that in the first flush of excitement at this realisation there should have been an extreme tendency to regard the Old Testament as a 'primitive' literature, and even at one time to question whether writing was at all commonplace in the age of its founding heroes. This extreme misconception must now happily be abandoned.

At the same time, alongside this sense of the antiquity of the Old Testament, there has been an accompanying awareness that it is a human literature and that it has a human origin. The doctrine of divine inspiration and the belief that the Old Testament is a gift of divine revelation had both, at one time, tended to hide the fact that the Old Testament was given to the world through men. That behind the human writers we can discern the Spirit of God, and that behind their thoughts we learn the truth of God, cannot any longer lead us to suppose that the Old Testament may be treated as a collection of books that fell from heaven. The men and women of Israel who were the heroes, authors and preservers of these writings are themselves a part of this work of inspiration and revelation. In fact it is very hard to see how there can be any satisfactory belief in the inspiration of the Old Testament which is not very closely connected to the belief in the divine election of Israel. The Old Testament itself is so clearly and unmistakably a product of this belief in God's electing will.

All of these factors point us to a deeper involvement in the work of biblical criticism than simply to learn its main results and conclusions. As a substantial aspect of theological method it has a significance in its own right, which suggests that its theological implications ought to be given careful consideration. It is undoubtedly when the work of 'pre-critical' interpreters is set against the modern critical approach that very marked differences in the understanding of the Old Testament begin to emerge.

Yet it must not be supposed that this has always been exclusively to the advantage of the critical approach. All too readily this has appeared restricted and barren because it has been unable to deal adequately with some of the wider theological issues that are raised. As an example of this we may note again the questions raised by the prohibition of images in the Old Testament. The original historical reasons for making this restriction are not known to us, and are never clearly and decisively set out in the Old Testament. Nor indeed can we obtain more than a partial view of the way in which it was interpreted in relation to different kinds of ancient religious iconography and visual symbolism. Nevertheless, from a theological point of view, it has had a very lasting effect upon the understanding of God in the religions deriving from the Old Testament. It has been especially linked with a doctrine of divine incorporeality, and with ideas of God's uncreated and transcendent nature. There would, therefore, appear to be more to be said about it from a theological, than from a more narrowly historical, point of view. In any case, it is the theological ideas that have been related to it that have made it so profoundly important in religion, rather than the original motivating reason which had long since been forgotten even within the period of the Old Testament's growth. This would firmly point us in the direction of accepting that the bringing together of historical and theological questions about such basic issues can only be of benefit to Old Testament studies.

What we are advocating through the comments made above, and more broadly in the argument that the time has come for a fresh approach to the study of Old Testament theology, is that a different and much wider starting-point for this subject must be accepted. Instead of treating it as a subordinate branch of the historical criticism of the Old Testament, it should be regarded properly as a branch of theology. Without the contribution that the theologian can provide in bringing system, structure and some evaluation of priorities into the organisation of the material, the task of writing an Old Testament theology would appear to be an impossible one. It would simply record a phenomenology of the religious ideas of ancient Israel.

### 3. THE OLD TESTAMENT AND THE STUDY OF RELIGION

We have already had more than one occasion to point out in the preceding pages the value of the Old Testament for the study of religion. This arises first and foremost as a result of the fact that it forms a major part of the Christian Bible, and the whole of the Bible of Judaism. It has also greatly influenced Islam. In a remarkable way, therefore, it establishes a bridge across three religions, which challenges the common assumption that they can each be treated and understood quite independently of each other. Yet, having made this claim, it must also be fully admitted that the distinctive way in which the Old Testament has usually been studied has meant that this ambivalence in its religious significance has seldom been explored.

At times it has not been uncommon for Christian teaching concerning the Old Testament to remain totally indifferent to the aims and assumptions of Jewish interpreters of this literature. Jewish-Christian dialogue has been regarded as a specialised field in its own right which is scarcely felt to be part of the province of Old Testament study. However, as soon as any serious attempt to put together an Old Testament theology is made, it raises questions which inevitably impinge upon the way in which Jewish interpreters of the Old Testament have gone about their task. This becomes especially noticeable once any concern is expressed for the unity of the Bible as a whole from the Christian point of view.

At a somewhat conflicting opposite extreme, the advocates of a radical discontinuity between the Old Testament and the New have held that it is the negative aspects of the former which have survived in Judaism. It is presented as a religion of 'Law' in contrast with the Christian religion of 'Grace'.[7] Surprisingly, therefore, a rather ambiguous attitude towards the Old Testament has emerged in modern Christianity which has tended to read the Old Testament through the eyes of St Paul. On the one hand it has been accepted as an inherited and necessary part of the Christian Bible, and on the other its very 'Jewishness' has frequently been looked upon as a part of its imperfection. Undoubtedly one major step which, it may be hoped, could lead to some crossing over of these traditional boundaries of attitude would be for a more adequate understanding from a Christian perspective of the way in which Judaism has understood and used the Old Testament.

Since the scale of such a task, and the complexities of historical and linguistic expertise which it requires, cannot be said to be less than those that are necessary for a history of the Christian interpretation of the Bible, it is clearly impossible for any overall comprehensive coverage to be attempted. Yet once again, we must not allow the impossibility of achieving an extensive coverage to discourage us from exploring some basic resources. What is important from the point of view of Christian theology, as well as from that of the history of religion, is the realisation that a major realm of cultural and academic achievement lies to be discovered in the way in which Jews have interpreted their sacred scriptures. It must surely be of greater value to the average theological student to obtain some elementary knowledge of the great Jewish interpreters of the Old Testament, and of the way in which they have carried through their task, than to extend into greater detail the amassed results of historical criticism. From the point of view of orientation and general perspective it may be held that this basic knowledge would in itself contribute significantly to the general awareness of the value of the Old Testament for the history of religion. Once again this is not to advocate the ignoring of the historical-critical approach, but rather to attempt to set it in a better perspective. By allowing it to be set against the conclusions of the older philosophers and commentators of Judaism, as well as of Christianity, its own special use and contribution can the more clearly be seen.

It must certainly also be claimed that the attempt to look at the Old Testament from within a Jewish, as well as a Christian, standpoint, brings to the forefront some of the most valuable discoveries from the side of religious understanding. Constantly we are made to recognise that the hearing of the word of God in the Old Testament, which must be an essential part of the task of finding within it a theology, is a task which implies a context and a tradition of understanding. We cannot read this literature in a vacuum, but only within the assumptions and preconceptions that are provided for us by the homiletical and theological traditions of Judaism and Christianity in which we stand. It must be held to be one of the major aims of a genuinely historical-critical approach that it can begin to discover what these assumptions and preconceptions are, and to learn how they have arisen. In this it is primarily the discovery of finding that they are challenged, and sometimes, rejected, by a different tradition that establishes the starting-point for a truly theological self-criticism.

It is very important, therefore, for the study of the New Testament, and of the history of Christian theology more generally, to examine what constitutes the 'Jewishness' of the Old Testament and how this relates to the origin and development of Jewish faith. Clearly, one aim of such an elementary introduction to Jewish interpretations of the Old Testament would be to provide a more informed basis for dialogue between these two sister religions. Yet the assumption that this is the sole aim of such a study must be rejected. It matters as much to an understanding of the nature of religion itself.

From a social and intellectual perspective it may be argued that the role of the sacred text in the great 'book' religions of the world is itself a subject of considerable interest and value. Basic problems of textual transmission, semantic development and history, and of the whole culture-relatedness of ancient texts and ideas begin to reveal themselves. Few exercises are more salutary in examining apparently clear and unambiguous ancient writings than to discover the extraordinary variety of ways in which they have been understood. How these changes of understanding occur, and the intellectual, social and cultural pressures that give rise to them, are an essential part of the study of the remarkable phenomenon of religion itself. In the modern world, in which sensitivity to features of historical change and the common acceptance of beliefs in progress and development are present almost universally, the role of the sacred text in religion needs fuller appreciation and examination than ever before.

Undoubtedly, one eminently useful and conveniently accessible introduction to these theological problems is provided by the study of the very different paths which Christian and Jewish interpretations of the Old Testament have followed. At times they have proceeded independently, and at other times they have exercised a powerful mutual interaction upon each other. If the Reformation of Christianity in the sixteenth century can be seen to owe much to the stimulus of the new Jewish and Hebrew learning about the Old Testament, so in the nineteenth and twentieth centuries can Judaism be seen to have been greatly affected by the historical-critical approach to the Old Testament, the main aims and methods of which were fashioned in Christianity. Perhaps also it is not altogether out of place to suggest that the very difficulty, and perhaps near impossibility, of understanding fully a sacred text such as the Old Testament from within another religious tradition, is reason enough why it should be attempted.

If there are evident advantages for the Christian in obtaining some elementary knowledge of the way in which Jewish interpretation of the Old Testament has proceeded, so also must there be some gain in recognising the legacy of the Old Testament in Islam. The difficulties here are immense, and the available literature lamentably small for the Christian to use. However, the discovery that the subject exists and is capable of useful exploration is itself a further pointer to the way in which the Old Testament can contribute to the study of religion.

We may also note another feature of the study of religion to which the Old Testament may be regarded as a very convenient introduction. Since the eighteenth century an increasing interest has been drawn to 'the natural history' of religion, with its particular concern with the forms of growth evident within it. Out of it there have grown up the important branches of study dealing with the sociological and anthropological aspects of religion, as well as attempts to trace patterns of evolution in religious ideology. There now exists, through the past century of discovery about the ancient Near East, a vast wealth of comparative literature to the Bible from ancient Mesopotamia and Egypt. The various forms of religion, with its mythological texts, its sacred rites, and its vast temples and images, which these discoveries have brought to light form an indispensable background to the Old Testament. The resources now exist, therefore, for a critical and balanced appreciation of the history of religion in the ancient East, which are closely related to the Old Testament. It would in no way be a reflection on the distinctive genius and achievements of ancient Israel, to argue that through this literature an even larger legacy than that contributed by Moses has been bequeathed to the modern world.

It is not at all uncommon to find even today that the sheer antiquity of the Old Testament, and the remarkably fresh world that it uncovers for us, which is so unlike our own, are barely noted by many who read it. Yet this dimension also is one which can be obtained by the study of the Old Testament as a branch of modern theological discipline. It can serve to challenge the prevalent myth of modernity, and the falseness of many assumptions about what is 'relevant' in religion, by forcing us to think afresh about such claims. Its very ability to reveal to us the practice of religion in a culture different from our own, may be held to be among one of the great assets of the study of the Old Testament.

## 4. THE OLD TESTAMENT AND MANKIND

Different periods of human history have been felt by philosophers and educationists to have their own worth as expressive of certain fundamental human values. Most of all in this regard we are familiar with the importance that has been attached to the great ages of classical Greece and Rome. It is interesting to find that attempts have been made in recent years to suggest that ancient Israel belongs along with the study of these great ancient civilisations. Perhaps this is so, but it would be hard to defend the inclusion of this extra candidate without considering the claims of others too, especially ancient Babylonia and Egypt. There are no criteria to which all would agree which can be employed in such a competition.

We may none the less seek to note some of the important features which have been discerned within the Old Testament, and which may be held to have a special value for mankind as a whole. Several years ago it was suggested that a distinctive feature of Israel's faith was that it attained a great vision of humanity as a reality in and for itself.[8] Probably the perspective here was more than a little overdrawn, with a measure of undervaluing of the more uniquely 'Israelite' characteristics of the Old Testament. Nevertheless there is a vision of this kind, and the immense potency of the image of the pilgrimage of the nations to Mount Zion (Isa. 2.2–4 = Mic. 4.1–5) and of a great kingdom of peace with its centre at Jerusalem (Pss. 46, 48, 76) undoubtedly point us in this direction. The emphasis upon the special role of Israel's election, and of the inclusion of nationalistic sentiments in the Old Testament, ought not to be allowed to obscure this wider humanitarian vision. However imperfectly it was grasped at various periods in Israelite-Jewish history, there is present in the Old Testament a vision of all mankind attaining the peace and prosperity that the 'goodness' of creation foreshadows (cf. Isa. 11.1–9).

Along with this we must certainly also place a marked sensitivity in its pages to the plight of all who are oppressed or disadvantaged in one way or another. The cry of the prophets for righteousness, and their merciless exposure of injustice, corruption and the abuse of power and wealth, reveal a universal dimension of human social existence. The insistence that there can be no true religion and no knowledge of God without righteousness, has given to the legacy of the Old Testament a measure of perennial vitality and relevance. So, too, the belief in a God who brought his followers 'out of the house of bondage' has given to the conception of divine providence and care a more than 'nationalistic' dimension. He has come to be seen directly as the God of all who are oppressed, so that the cry of all who are suffering as the result of injustice and violence is interpreted as a prayer to him. Because morality itself knows no national boundaries so inevitably such a conception of God has broadened out into an awareness of his concern for all humanity.

This has also led to a particular attractiveness of the presentation of religion and its duties in the Old Testament. This is concerned with its world-affirming nature, and what has, for want of a more adequate term, been called its 'worldliness'.[9] The concerns of God are the concerns of man in his real world, so that 'sin' is not another realm of behaviour which relates to a separate area of cultic activity. Rather, it belongs to daily life itself and to the obligations which man encounters in his family, social and political existence. In this regard one of the most striking and memorable facets of the Old Testament lies in its portrayal of righteousness as a claim that is laid upon all, and which none can manipulate to their own advantage, or escape from. The narratives of the prophetic exposure of David's sin against Uriah and Bathsheba (2 Sam. 12.1–23) and of Elijah's condemnation of Ahab for his abuse of the law (1 Kgs. 21.1–24) stand as classic expressions of the belief that 'right' stands above every human institution, even that of the monarchy. The former narrative is particularly instructive on account of its great antiquity, combined with its exposure of 'murderous intention' as the basis of a royal crime.

As early Jewish interpreters like Philo, or the Christian Tertullian, saw clearly, the Ten Commandments have a significance and importance which stretches far across the frontiers of those who can trace their descent to Moses and those who came with him out of Egypt. With very little adaptation they become a brilliant summary of fundamental moral demand. Questions of the date of origin of the Decalogue become of relatively minor significance when compared to the extraordinary comprehensiveness of its moral awareness. It has given to religion itself a foundation of morality, which has enabled those religions which derive from the Old Testament to find in it a continued challenge and standard by which to test their own, more complex teachings.

We ought not to omit in regard to the Old Testament a brief comment upon its value as literature. The artistry of story-telling, the skill of coining witty and clever sayings, the freshness of poetic image and metaphor, all combine to make the Old Testament an especially rich literature.[10] It is unfortunate to find that the search for accuracy and precision of translation has, in recent years, tended to forgo the attempt to capture the special nuances of style and poetic imagination which grace so much of the Old Testament. Few tales have been recounted with more feeling and pathos than the story of David's receipt of the news of Absalom's death (2 Sam. 18.31–3), and yet this is accomplished with an incredible economy of words, and with no employment at all of any distinctively 'psychological' vocabulary. If the Israelite iconoclastic rejection of images, and so much that belongs to the visual and plastic arts as a sphere of religious aspiration, has led at times to a devaluing of many aspects of visual beauty as an approach to the divine, yet it is at least partly compensated for by the wealth of literary artistry that the Old Testament contains. Seldom has writing of great theological worth been expressed more beautifully than in its pages. The study of it, therefore, cannot be thought to slump into a dull and barren experience.

It may also be worthy of comment that the Old Testament, precisely because of the rich variety of its literary forms of expression, has frequently been abused by an irrational fringe of misinterpretation. Failure to appreciate the complexity that belongs to the proper understanding of an ancient text with an inability to appreciate its different stylistic and formal characteristics have given rise to a curious 'underground' of biblical misappropriation. Instead of poetry, metaphor, and a very complex tradition of symbolic imagery and expression, a continued stream of misapplication has survived. Nor has this remained outside the mainstreams of Jewish and Christian life. The oddities of Kabbala, the absurd assumptions of astrology, the political eccentricities of pseudo-interpreters of apocalyptic, and the high-handed claims of those who would find in the Old Testament evidence of the visits of ancient space-men, have all contributed to a bizarre underworld of biblical 'follies'. All of them are, in their separate ways, the result of a curious combination of literary insensitivity and religious, or pseudo-scientific, imagination. Their existence is more prevalent than the claims for the rational and scientific nature of our age would lead us to expect. They are also witnesses to the dangers of neglect, so that their very vitality in our times is a testimony to the ignorance of the basic realities of the Bible among a people who have not forgotten the centuries of Jewish and Christian insistence upon its authority and unique character. The average minister is far more likely to find himself faced with questions which arise from these popular misconceptions than he is from enquirers who have been perplexed by the writings of a serious Old Testament theologian. In their own strange way they characterise the curious puzzles and uncertainties that beset an age in which religious education has moved further and further away from a serious reading and exposition of the Old Testament.

We may, in closing, note again the very important values and perspectives which may be held to derive from a continued concern by modern man with his own more distant past. The Old Testament remains an ancient literature, even though it has now been antedated considerably by the recovery of so many writings from Sumeria and ancient Egypt. Nevertheless, it is not a collection that has been recently recovered by the skill of archaeologists, but one that has been preserved, and in this way, willed to survive. The reason for this clearly lies in the belief held by so many in its divine origin and inspiration. It has thereby maintained for many a constant sense of continuity with their own past. It has, in fact, become a bridge between the past and the present. In it men have expected to find something more than a history, valuable as this in itself is, and to see lasting and unique expressions of truth. Such a truth has not simply been about the past, or about the conditions and achievements of human existence in the past. Rather, such truth has been about man himself, and his eternal and inescapable confrontation with God. Its very humanity has mirrored more than human values, and affirmed a belief that wherever he goes man is faced with decisions about himself and his world which lead him to recognise the presence of the Spirit of God:

> Whither shall I go from thy Spirit?
>   Or whither shall I flee from thy presence?
> If I ascend to heaven, thou art there!
>   If I make my bed in Sheol, thou art there!
> If I take the wings of the morning
>   and dwell in the uttermost parts of the sea,
> even there thy hand shall lead me,
>   and thy right hand shall hold me.
> If I say, 'Let only darkness cover me,
>   and the light about me be night,'
> even the darkness is not dark to thee,
>   the night is bright as the day;
>   for darkness is as light with thee. (Ps. 139.7–12)

# NOTES

CHAPTER 1 (pp. 1–25)

1. Attention may be drawn to the following recent volumes: G. F. Hasel, *Old Testament Theology. Basic Issues in the Current Debate* (1972; ²1976); R. B. Laurin (ed.), *Contemporary Old Testament Theologians* (1970); and B. W. Anderson (ed.), *The Old Testament and Christian Faith. A Theological Discussion* (1969).

2. E. Jacob, *Theology of the Old Testament* (Eng. Tr., A. W. Heathcote and P. J. Allcock, 1958), p. 11.

3. The origin and history of the discipline are conveniently summarised by H. J. Kraus, *Die biblische Theologie. Ihre Geschichte und Problematik* (1970).

4. Cf. esp. M. Hengel, *The Son of God* (Eng. Tr., John Bowden, 1976).

5. G. L. Bauer, *Theologie des Alten Testaments* (1796). Cf. H. J. Kraus, op. cit., pp. 88–91.

6. J. S. Semler, *Abhandlung von freier Untersuchung des Kanon* (4 Vols, Halle, 1771).

7. G. Hornig, *Die Anfänge der historisch-kritischen Theologie (Forschungen zur systematischen Theologie und Religionsphilosophie* 8) (Lund/Göttingen, 1961), p. 75.

8. Cf. B. S. Childs, *Biblical Theology in Crisis* (1970); J. A. Sanders, *Torah and Canon* (1973); and D. A. Knight (ed.), *Tradition and Theology in the Old Testament* (1977), pp. 259–326.

9. For the New Testament's interpretation of the Old, cf. F. F. Bruce, *This is That. The New Testament Development of Some Old Testament Themes* (1976); R. Longenecker, *Biblical Exegesis in the Apostolic Period* (1975); and A. T. Hanson, *Jesus Christ in the Old Testament* (1965).

CHAPTER 2 (pp. 26–52)

1. The general picture of the growth of the Old Testament from smaller to larger literary units is usefully described by K. Koch, *The Growth of the Biblical Tradition. The Form-Critical Method* (Eng. Tr., S. M. Cupitt, 1969).

2. One of the strongest attempts to do this is to be found in R. Kittel, *Great Men and Movements in Israel* (Eng. Tr., C. A. Knoch and C. D. Wright, 1925). The work by Fleming James, *Personalities of the Old Testament* (1939) follows very closely that by Kittel.

3. B. Duhm, *Die Theologie der Propheten* (Bonn, 1875).

4. The different approaches appear very markedly between the theologies of G. von Rad and W. Eichrodt. Cf. D. G. Spriggs, *Two Old Testament Theologies (SBT* Second Series 30) (1974).

5. The theory is closely associated with the name of G. von Rad. Cf. his *Old Testament Theology* (Eng. Tr., D. M. G. Stalker, 1962), Vol. I, pp. 121–8. Criticisms are expressed by L. Rost, 'Das kleine geschichtliche

Credo', in *Das kleine Credo und andere Studien zum Alten Testament* (Heidelberg, 1965), pp. 11–25; and N. Lohfink, 'Zum "kleinen geschichtlichen Credo". Dtn. 26, 5–9', *Theologie und Philosophie* 46 (1971), pp. 19–39.

6. For the main ideas and institutions associated with the presence of God in the Old Testament, see my book *God and Temple* (1965).

7. The main features of Israelite worship are described in H. H. Rowley, *Worship in Ancient Israel. Its Form and Meaning* (1967); and H. J. Kraus, *Worship in Israel. A Cultic History of the Old Testament* (Eng. Tr., G. Buswell, 1966).

8. For such terminology, cf. the articles in E. Jenni and C. Westermann (eds), *Theologische Handwörterbuch zum Alten Testament*, (2 Vols, Stuttgart/Zürich, 1971, 1976).

9. Cf. esp. L. Lévy-Bruhl, *Primitive Mentality* (Eng. Tr., L. A. Clare, 1923).

10. J. Pedersen, *Israel. Its Life and Culture* (Vols I–II, 1926); (Vols III–IV, 1940).

11. For myth, cf. G. S. Kirk, *Myth. Its Meaning and Functions in Ancient and Other Cultures* (1970); and E. Cassirer, *Language and Myth* (Eng. Tr., S. K. Langer, 1946).

12. Cf. J. W. Rogerson, *Myth in the Old Testament* (*BZAW* 134), (Berlin, 1974).

CHAPTER 3 (pp. 53–78)

1. The question is dealt with very helpfully by S. Herrmann, *Israel in Egypt*, (Eng. Tr., M. Kohl), *SBT* Second Series 27 (1973).

2. Cf. H. H. Rowley, *The Faith of Israel* (1956), pp. 72, 180 ff.

3. For the ideas of God in the Old Testament, cf. R. C. Dentan, *The Knowledge of God in Ancient Israel* (1968), esp. pp. 125–96.

4. For the understanding of holiness, especially in its cultic aspects, cf. J. Pedersen, *Israel. Its Life and Culture* (Vols III–IV), pp. 198–263; and N. H. Snaith, *Distinctive Ideas of the Old Testament* (1944), pp. 21–50; cf. also O. R. Jones, *The Concept of Holiness* (1961).

5. For this name and its interpretation in Judaism and Christianity, cf. G. H. Parke-Taylor, *Yahweh: The Divine Name in the Bible* (1975).

6. For a summary of the main possibilities regarding its origin, cf. J. P. Hyatt, *Exodus* (1971), pp. 75–8.

7. For this problem, see F. M. Cross, *Canaanite Myth and Hebrew Epic* (1973), pp. 1–75; and W. F. Albright, *Yahweh and the Gods of Canaan* (1968), pp. 47 ff.

8 H. H. Rowley, *The Faith of Israel*, p. 48.

9. Cf. J. Abelson, *The Immanence of God in Rabbinical Literature* (1912).

10. See esp. A. Weiser, *The Psalms* (Eng. Tr., H. Hartwell, 1962); cf. also Jörg Jeremias, *Theophanie. Die Geschichte einer alttestamentlichen Gattung* (*WMANT* 10) (Neukirchen-Vluyn, 1965).

11. For this aspect of the understanding of God, see esp. C. J. Labuschagne, *The Incomparability of Yahweh in the Old Testament* (*Pretoria Oriental Series* V, 1966).

12. For the emergence of monotheism, see H. H. Rowley, 'Moses and Monotheism', in *From Moses to Qumran. Studies in the Old Testament* (1953), pp. 35–63.

CHAPTER 4 (pp. 79–103)

1. The dominant theory has been that of an amphictyony in which the twelve tribes participated in worship at a central sanctuary. Cf. M. Noth, *Das System der Zwölf Stämme Israels (BWANT IV:1)* (Stuttgart, 1930). Criticisms of this view are expressed by A. D. Mayes, *Israel in the Period of the Judges (SBT Second Series 29)* (1974); and C. H. J. De Geus, *The Tribes of Israel* (Assen/Amsterdam, 1976).

2. G. Bucellati, *Cities and Nations of Ancient Syria (Studia Semitica 26)* (Rome, 1967).

3. See note 1 above. Reference may also be made to M. Noth, *A History of Israel* (Eng. Tr., P. R. Ackroyd, rev. ed., 1960).

4. Cf. H. G. M. Williamson, *Israel in the Books of Chronicles* (1977).

5. For this theology of election, cf. H. H. Rowley, *The Biblical Doctrine of Election* (1951).

6. In this respect considerable modification is now required of the position advocated in my book *God and Temple* (1965), pp. 40 ff.

7. For the concept of the land, see W. D. Davies, *The Gospel and the Land. Early Christianity and Jewish Territorial Doctrine* (1974); and W. Brueggemann, *The Land* (1974).

8. Cf. R. Martin-Achard, *A Light to the Nations* (Eng. Tr., J. Penney Smith, 1962).

9. A very extensive literature now exists dealing with the vocabulary and concept of covenant. See esp. D. R. Hillers, *Covenant. The History of a Biblical Idea* (1969); D. J. McCarthy, *Old Testament Covenant. A Survey of Current Opinions* (1972); E. Kutsch, *Verheissung und Gesetz. Untersuchungen zum sogenannten 'Bund' im Alten Testament (BZAW 131),* (Berlin/New York, 1973); L. Perlitt, *Die Bundestheologie im Alten Testament, (WMANT 36)* (Neukirchen/Vluyn, 1969); and P. Buis, *La notion de l'alliance dans l'Ancien Testament* (Paris, 1976).

10. For the background and theology of the book of Deuteronomy, see my book *God's Chosen People* (1968).

11. This development is studied in detail in the work by L. Perlitt, *Die Bundestheologie im Alten Testament* (1969).

12. This aspect of Israel's covenant tradition is dealt with in my book *Abraham and David. Genesis XV and its Meaning for Israelite Tradition (SBT Second Series 5)* (1968).

13. J. Begrich, 'Berit. Ein Beitrag zur Erfassung einer alttestamentlichen Denkform', *ZAW* 60 (1944), pp. 1–11 = *Gesammelte Studien zum Alten Testament,* ed. W. Zimmerli *(Th.B.*21) (Munich, 1964), pp. 55–66.

14. E. Kutsch, *Verheissung ind Gesetz,* pp. 6–27.

15. G. E. Mendenhall, 'Covenant', in *The Interpreter's Dictionary of the Bible* (1962), Vol. I.

16. An attempt to trace the earlier development of this is made by J. Halbe, *Das Privilegrecht Jahwes. Ex. 34, 10–26 (FRLANT* 114) (Göttingen, 1975).

17. J. Halbe, op. cit., finds evidence of such earlier usage in Exod. 34.10, 27, but the validity of this is contested.

18. For the tension between the conditioned/unconditioned features of Israel's covenant theology in its relation to prophecy, see J. Bright, *Covenant and Promise. The Future in the Preaching of the Pre-exilic Prophets* (1977).

19. Cf. my book *Abraham and David*, pp. 79 ff.

CHAPTER 5 (pp. 104–130)

1. For the understanding of the Old Testament as law, see P. Grelot, *Le sens chrétien de l'Ancien Testament (Bibliotheque de Théologie* Vol. 3) (Tournai, 1962), pp. 167–208.

2. Cf. J. A. Sanders, *Torah and Canon* (1973).

3. The question of the meaning and use of *tôrâh* is discussed extensively by G. A. Ostborn, *Torah in the Old Testament. A Semantic Study* (Lund, 1945).

4. Cf. J. A. Sanders, *Torah and Canon*, pp. 36 ff.

5. Cf. my book *God's Chosen People*, pp. 89–105.

6. See esp. R. Rendtorff, *Das überlieferungsgeschichtliche Problem des Pentateuch (BZAW* 147) (Berlin/New York, 1977).

7. This is most evident in the work of G. von Rad, *Old Testament Theology* (Eng. Tr., D. M. G. Stalker, Vol. 1, 1962; Vol. 2, 1965).

8. Cf. W. Eichrodt, *Theology of the Old Testament* (Eng. Tr., J. A. Baker), Vol. I (1961), pp. 36 ff.

9. Cf. my article 'Covenant and Canon in the Old Testament', in *Creation, Christ and Culture. Studies in Honour of T. F. Torrance* (ed. R. W. A. McKinney, 1976), pp. 1–12.

10. For this theme a useful brief study is given by W. Zimmerli, *The Law and the Prophets* (Eng. Tr., R. E. Clements, 1965); cf. also R. V. Bergren, *The Prophets and the Law (Monographs of the Hebrew Union College* IV, 1974).

11. Cf. my book *Prophecy and Tradition* (1975), pp. 8–23, and the literature cited there.

12. Cf. esp. R. V. Bergren, *The Prophets and the Law*, pp. 181 ff.

13. Cf. my *Prophecy and Tradition*, pp. 8 ff.

14. Cf. J. Weingreen, *From Bible to Mishna* (1976).

15. Philo, *De Decalogo; De Specialibus Legibus* (Loeb Edition, Eng. Tr., F. H. Colson, 1937).

16. Cf. J. Neusner, *The Idea of Purity in Ancient Judaism (Studies in Judaism in Late Antiquity* I, Leiden, 1973), esp. pp. 72 ff.

CHAPTER 6 (pp. 131–154)

1. Cf. P. Grelot, *Sens chrétien de l'Ancien Testament*, pp. 327–403.

2. For the significance of this in regard to the interpretation of prophecy, see my article 'Patterns in the Prophetic Canon', in *Canon and Authority.*

*Essays in Old Testament Religion and Theology* (ed. G. W. Coats and B. O. Long, 1977), pp. 42–55.

3. Cf. J. G. Herder, *The Spirit of Hebrew Poetry* (Eng. Tr., J. Marsh, 2 Vols, Burlington, Vt., 1833; reprinted in one vol. Naperville, 1971). See also E. Sehmsdorf, *Die Prophetenauslegung bei J. G. Eichhorn* (Göttingen, 1971).

4. Cf. F. F. Bruce, *Biblical Exegesis in the Qumran Texts* (1960).

5. For the conception of the Remnant in the Old Testament and interpretation of these passages, see G. F. Hasel, *The Remnant. The History and Theology of the Remnant Idea from Genesis to Isaiah* (*Andrews University Monographs. Studies in Religion* Vol. V, Berrien Springs, 1974).

6. Cf. my essay 'Patterns in the Prophetic Canon', passim.

7. G. von Rad, *Old Testament Theology*, Vol. II, p. 138.

8. H. Barth, *Israel und das Assyrerreich in den Nichtjesajanischen Texten des Protojesajabuches* (Diss. Hamburg, 1974).

9. Cf. J. Bright, *Covenant and Promise*, pp. 92 ff.

10. Cf. G. Vermes, *The Dead Sea Scrolls in English* (1962), p. 245.

11. For the origin of apocalyptic and its relation to prophecy, see P. D. Hanson, *The Dawn of Apocalyptic. The Historical and Sociological Roots of Jewish Apocalyptic Eschatology* (1975).

12. Cf. G. Vermes, *The Dead Sea Scrolls in English*, pp. 230–40.

13. Cf. A. Bentzen, *King and Messiah* (ed. G. W. Anderson, ²1970); and T. N. D. Mettinger, *King and Messiah. The Civil and Social Legitimation of the Israelite Kings* (*Coniectanea Biblica. Old Testament Series* 8, Lund, 1976).

14. See above, note 10.

15. For this process of scriptural interpretation in Judaism, see the study by G. Vermes, *Scripture and Tradition in Judaism* (Leiden, 1961).

16. Cf. G. von Rad, *Old Testament Theology*, Vol. II, pp. 357 ff.

CHAPTER 7 (pp.155–178)

1. Cf. for this position, H. H. Rowley, *The Unity of the Bible* (1953), pp. 90 ff.

2. Cf. R. Bultmann, 'The Significance of the Old Testament for the Christian Faith', in *The Old Testament and Christian Faith* (ed. B. W. Anderson, 1963), pp. 8–35.

3. George Smith, *The Chaldean Account of Genesis* (1876).

4. For this movement, see esp. A. Jeremias, *The Old Testament in the Light of the Ancient East. Manual of Biblical Archaeology* (Eng. Tr., C. L. Beaumont, 2 Vols, 1911). See also A. Jeremias, *Die Panbabylonisten. Der Alte Orient und die aegyptische Religion* (*Im Kampfe um den Alten Orient* I, Leipzig, 1907).

5. See esp. S. H. Hooke (ed.), *Myth and Ritual* (1933); *idem* (ed.), *The Labyrinth* (1935); *idem* (ed.), *Myth, Ritual and Kingship* (1958). For a criticism of these positions, cf. H. Frankfort, *Kingship and the Gods* (1948); *idem, The Problem of Similarity in Ancient Near Eastern Religions* (1951). A mediating perspective is to be found in H. Ringgren, 'The Impact of the Ancient Near East on Israelite Tradition', in *Tradition and Theology in the Old Testament* (ed. D. A. Knight, 1977), pp. 31–46.

6. Cf. R. de Vaux, *Studies in Old Testament Sacrifice* (1964); H. Ringgren, *Sacrifice in the Bible* (*World Christian Books* 42) (London, 1962).

7. Cf. my *God and Temple*, pp. 40 ff.

8. H. J. Kraus, *Worship in Israel* (Eng. Tr., G. Buswell, 1965), pp. 201 ff.

9. Cf. F. M. Cross, *Canaanite Myth and Hebrew Epic* (1973), pp. 44 ff.

10. Cf. W. F. Albright, *Yahweh and the Gods of Canaan* (1968), pp. 47 ff.

11. For the interpretation of this commandment, see J. J. Stamm and M. E. Andrew, *The Ten Commandments in Recent Research* (*SBT* Second Series 2) (1967), pp. 81 ff.

12. For the differing portrayals of Moses in the Old Testament, see G. von Rad, *Moses* (*World Christian Books* 32) (1960).

13. Cf. I. Maybaum, *Trialogue between Jew, Christian and Muslim* (1973); H. P. Smith, *The Bible and Islam* (1897); A. Geiger, *Judaism and Islam* (Eng. Tr. F. M. Young, 1898; rep. New York, 1970).

14. C. G. Montefiore, *The Old Testament and After* (1923), p. 299.

15. E. Jacob, *Theology of the Old Testament*, p. 12.

16. ibid., pp. 12–13.

17. Cf. Montefiore, op. cit. pp. 292 ff.

18. Cf. G. Wingren, *Creation and Law* (Eng. Tr., R. Mackenzie, 1961).

CHAPTER 8 (pp. 179–200)

1. The question of the historical figure of Moses in modern research is dealt with by E. Osswald, *Das Bild des Moses in der kritischen alttestamentlichen Wissenschaft seit Julius Wellhausen* (*Theologische Arbeiten* XVIII, Berlin, 1956); a conservative presentation of his work is to be found in D. M. Beegle, *Moses. The Servant of Yahweh* (1972).

2. I am thinking here especially of J. Bright, *A History of Israel* (1958, [2]1974).

3. Cf. N. K. Gottwald, *A Light to the Nations, An Introduction to the Old Testament* (1959); and B. W. Anderson, *The Living World of the Old Testament* ([2]1975).

4. See esp. F. F. Bruce, *This is That. The New Testament Development of Some Old Testament Themes* (1976).

5. For Luther, see esp. H. Bornkamm, *Luther and the Old Testament* (Eng. Tr., E. W. and R. C. Gritsch, 1969); for Calvin, see A. J. Baumgartner, *Calvin Hébraïsant et interprete de l'Ancien Testament* (Paris, 1889).

6. This is the immensely valuable work by L. Diestel, *Geschichte des Alten Testaments in der christlichen Kirche* (Jena, 1869).

7. Cf. F. Hesse, *Das Alte Testament als Buch der Kirche* (Gütersloh, 1966), pp. 90 ff.

8. A. Causse, *Israel et la vision de l'humanité* (Paris/Strasbourg, 1924).

9. Cf. W. Zimmerli, *The Old Testament and the World* (Eng. Tr., J. J. Scullion, 1976).

10. Cf. T. R. Henn, *The Bible as Literature* (London, 1970).

# SELECT BIBLIOGRAPHY

WORKS ON OLD TESTAMENT THEOLOGY

Barr, J., *Old and New in Interpretation. A Study of the Two Testaments* (SCM, London, 1966)

Childs, B. S., *Biblical Theology in Crisis* (Westminster Press, Philadelphia, 1970)

Dentan, R. C., *The Knowledge of God in Ancient Israel* (Seabury Press, New York, 1968)

Eichrodt, W., *Theology of the Old Testament* (Eng. Tr., J. A. Baker, SCM, London, Vol. I, 1961; Vol. II, 1967)

Fohrer, G., *Theologische Grundstrukturen des Alten Testaments* (De Gruyter, Berlin/New York, 1972)

Frei, H. W., *The Eclipse of Biblical Narrative. A Study in Eighteenth and Nineteenth Century Hermeneutics* (Yale University Press, New Haven/London, 1974)

Hasel, G. F., *Old Testament Theology. Basic Issues in the Current Debate* (Eerdmans, Grand Rapids, 1972, ²1976)

Knight, D. A. (ed.), *Tradition and Theology in the Old Testament* (London, 1977)

Kraus, H. J., *Geschichte der historisch-kritischen Erforschung des Alten Testaments von der Reformation bis zur Gegenwart* (Neukirchen Verlag/Neukirchen Vluyn, 1956)

Kraus, H. J., *Die biblische Theologie. Ihre Geschichte und Problematik,* (Neukirchen Verlag/Neukirchen Vluyn, 1970)

Mowinckel, S., *He That Cometh. The Messiah Concept in the Old Testament and Late Judaism* (Eng. Tr., G. W. Anderson, Blackwell, Oxford, 1956)

Rad, G. von, *Old Testament Theology* (Eng. Tr., D. M. G. Stalker, Oliver and Boyd, Edinburgh/London, Vol. I, 1962; Vol. II, 1965)

Rowley, H. H., *The Faith of Israel. Aspects of Old Testament Thought* (SCM, London, 1956)

Vriezen, Th. C., *An Outline of Old Testament Theology* (Eng. Tr., S. Neuijen, Blackwell, Oxford, 1958)

Wolff, H. W. (ed.), *Probleme biblischer Theologie. G. von Rad zum 70. Geburtstag* (Chr. Kaiser Verlag, Munich, 1971)

Wolff, H. W., *Anthropology of the Old Testament* (Eng. Tr., M. Kohl, SCM, London, 1974)

Wright, G. Ernest, *The Old Testament and Theology* (Harper and Row, New York, 1969)

Zimmerli, W., *Grundriss der alttestamentlichen Theologie* (W. Kohlhammer, Stuttgart, 1972)

WORKS ON OLD TESTAMENT LITERATURE

Driver, S. R., *An Introduction to the Literature of the Old Testament* (T. & T. Clark, Edinburgh, ⁹1913)

Eissfeldt, O., *The Old Testament. An Introduction* (Eng. Tr., P. R. Ackroyd, Blackwell, Oxford, 1965)

Fohrer, G., *Introduction to the Old Testament* (Eng. Tr., D. Green, SPCK, London, 1970)

Gottwald, N. K., *A Light to the Nations. An Introduction to the Old Testament* (Harper and Row, New York/Evanston/London, 1959)

Habel, N. *Literary Criticism of the Old Testament* (Fortress Press, Philadelphia, 1971)

Kaiser, O. *Introduction to the Old Testament. A Presentation of its Results and Problems* (Eng. Tr., J. Sturdy, Blackwell, Oxford, 1975)

Koch, K., *The Growth of the Biblical Tradition. The Form-Critical Method* (Eng. Tr., S. M. Cupitt, A. & C. Black, London, 1969)

Miller, M., *The Old Testament and the Historian* (Fortress Press, Philadelphia, 1975)

Noth, M., *A History of Pentateuchal Traditions* (Eng. Tr., B. W. Anderson, Prentice-Hall, Englewood Cliffs, 1972)

Rendtorff. R., *Das uberlieferungsgeschichtliche Problem des Pentateuch* (*BZAW* 147, De Gruyter, Berlin/New York, 1977)

Soggin, J. A., *Introduction to the Old Testament; from its Origins to the Closing of the Alexandrian Canon* (Eng. Tr., J. Bowden, SCM, London, 1976)

Tucker, G. M., *Form Criticism of the Old Testament* (Fortress Press, Philadelphia, 1971)

WORKS ON ISRAELITE RELIGION AND ITS BACKGROUND

Albright, W. F., *Yahweh and the Gods of Canaan* (University of London, Athlone Press, London, 1968)

Alt, A., *Essays on Old Testament History and Religion* (Eng. Tr., R. A. Wilson, Blackwell, Oxford, 1966)

Clements, R. E., *God and Temple. The Idea of the Divine Presence in Ancient Israel* (Blackwell, Oxford, 1965)

Clifford, R. J., *The Cosmic Mountain in Canaan and the Old Testament* (Harvard University Press, Cambridge, Mass., 1972)

Cross, F. M., *Canaanite Myth and Hebrew Epic. Essays in the History of the Religion of Israel* (Harvard Univ. Press, Cambridge, Mass., 1973)

Fohrer, G., *History of Israelite Religion* (Eng. Tr., D. Green, SPCK, London, 1973)

Frankfort, H., *Kingship and the Gods* (Chicago Univ. Press, Chicago/London, 1948)

Hooke, S. H., *Babylonian and Assyrian Religion* (Blackwell, Oxford, 1962)

Kuntz, J. K., *The Self-Revelation of God* (Westminster Press, Philadelphia, 1967)

Mendenhall, G. E., *The Tenth Generation. The Origins of the Biblical Tradition* (Johns Hopkins Univ. Press, Baltimore/London, 1973)

Preuss, H. D., *Verspottung fremder Religionen im Alten Testament* (*BWANT* V:12, 92, W. Kohlhammer, Stuttgart, 1971)

Pritchard, J. B., *Archaeology and the Old Testament* (Princeton Univ. Press, Princeton, 1958)

Ringgren, H., *Israelite Religion* (Eng. Tr., D. Green; London, 1966)
Ringgren, H., *Religions of the Ancient Near East* (Eng. Tr., J. Sturdy, SPCK, London, 1973)
Thomas, D. Winton (ed.), *Archaeology and Old Testament Study* (Clarendon Press, Oxford, 1967)
Thomas, D. Winton (ed.), *Documents from Old Testament Times* (Nelson, London, 1958)
Vaux, R. de, *Ancient Israel. Its Life and Institutions* (Eng. Tr., J. McHugh, Darton, Longmann and Todd, London, 1961)
Vriezen, Th. C., *The Religion of Ancient Israel* (Eng. Tr., H. Hoskins, Lutterworth Press, London, 1963)

WORKS ON THE OLD TESTAMENT IN CHRISTIANITY, JUDAISM AND ISLAM

Anderson, B. W. (ed.), *The Old Testament and Christian Faith* (SCM Press, London, 1963)
Baeck, L., *Judaism and Christianity* (Eng. Tr., W. Kaufmann, Philadelphia, 1958)
Baker, D. L., *Two Testaments. One Bible* (IVP, London, 1976)
Bornkamm, H., *Luther and the Old Testament* (Eng. Tr., E. W. and R. C. Gritsch, Fortress Press, Philadelphia, 1969)
Bruce, F. F., *This is That. The New Testament Development of Some Old Testament Themes* (Paternoster Press, Exeter, 1976)
Bruce, F. F., *Biblical Exegesis in the Qumran Texts* (Tyndale Press, London, 1960)
Davies, W. D., *The Gospel and the Land. Early Christianity and Jewish Territorial Doctrine* (University of California Press, Berkeley/Los Angeles/London, 1974)
Dodd, C. H., *According to the Scriptures* (Nisbet, London, 1952)
Efird, J. M. (ed.), *The Use of the Old Testament in the New and Other Essays* (*Studies in Honor of W. F. Stinespring*) (Duke University Press, Durham, N.C., 1972)
Geiger, A., *Judaism and Islam*, (Eng. Tr., F. M. Young, 1898, rep. Ktav Publishing House, New York, 1970)
Grelot, P., *Sens chrétien de l'ancien Testament* (*Bibliotheque de Theologie*, Vol. 3, Tournai, 1962)
Hanson, A. T., *Jesus Christ in the Old Testament* (SPCK, London, 1965)
Jacobs, L., *A Jewish Theology* (Darton, Longman and Todd, London, 1973) 1973)
Kelsey, D. H., *The Uses of Scripture in Recent Theology* (SCM, London 1975)
Longenecker, R., *Biblical Exegesis in the Apostolic Period* (Eerdmans, Grand Rapids, 1975)
McKelvey, R. J., *The New Temple. The Church in the New Testament* (Oxford Univ. Press, London 1969)
Nineham, D., *The Use and Abuse of the Bible* (Macmillan, London, 1976)
Rowley, H. H., *The Unity of the Bible* (London, 1953)

# GENERAL INDEX

Abraham, 14, 34, 37, 53, 88, 95, 98f., 103, 145, 147, 152, 170, 177f.
amphictyony, 85
anthropomorphism, 35, 38, 58f.
apocalyptic, 31, 143, 147ff., 199
archaeology, 183f.
ark, 68, 91
authority, 15f., 24f., 29, 33, 40f., 51, 104, 110f., 130f., 155, 170ff.
canon, 8ff., 13ff., 27, 30, 37, 53, 59f., 64, 72, 74, 100ff., 104ff., 133f., 143f., 150ff., 161f., 164f., 171ff.
cherubim, 68
Church, 4, 6, 8, 25, 47, 81f., 131
covenant, 14f., 82, 96ff., 109ff., 118ff., 153
creation, 66, 75f.
cult, 5, 20ff., 31, 33f., 38ff., 49, 54f., 59, 61ff., 67f., 91f., 107f., 112, 130, 138, 143, 149, 160, 165, 167, 172
David, 141f., 145ff., 150, 162f., 171, 197f.
Deuteronomy, 17, 31, 88f., 93f., 96ff., 107ff., 121, 127, 141f.
Diaspora, 43, 54, 129, 144
election, 34, 82, 86ff., 109, 118, 126, 153
eschatology, 71, 92, 94, 126, 128, 140ff., 147ff.
exile, 85, 90, 94, 103, 113, 133, 140ff.
exodus, 63, 66, 84
faith, 13, 26f., 19f., 32, 38, 55
Hebrew, 47
Hellenism, 59
history, 31, 33ff., 39, 46, 50, 55, 87f., 114ff., 121, 133, 143, 183
holiness, 5, 42, 45, 61, 70, 89, 105, 107, 168
idolatry, 65, 69, 76

image, 43, 59f., 65, 69, 75f., 166f., 198
inspiration, 14
Islam, 174f., 194f.
Israel, 9, 13, 18, 25, 30, 34, 36ff., 42ff., 48, 54ff., 65f., 72ff., 79ff., 96ff., 107ff., 132ff., 168, 173
Jerusalem, 14, 20, 40ff., 45, 54, 62, 91f., 142f., 145f., 162f., 169, 196
Jesus, 8, 21, 42, 57, 121, 131ff., 148
justice, 60, 132, 137
kingdom of God, 21, 132, 141
kingship, 33, 35f., 83, 85, 89f., 106, 111f., 122, 145f., 150ff., 172
land, 34, 92ff., 128, 143, 145, 152
law, 16ff., 24, 30, 62, 101f., 104ff., 168, 177
liturgy, 6, 10, 15, 18f., 24, 27f., 33, 131, 144
love, 61, 108f., 128
magic, 51f.
messiah, 11, 21, 90, 94, 145f., 149ff.
Mishnah, 22, 105
monotheism, 73
Moses, 21, 29, 34, 37, 53, 62, 107, 111f., 119, 122, 124ff., 161, 168, 170ff.
myth, 35, 49f., 77, 96, 149, 157f., 160
Old Testament Theology, and New Testament, 1, 7f., 11ff., 18, 129, 175, 182ff.
  history of discipline, 5ff.
  in Christian faith, 1ff., 15, 18ff., 24, 31, 41, 54, 57, 87, 104f., 130ff., 153f., 156f., 174ff., 181
  in Jewish faith, 1, 4, 6, 9f., 15, 18ff., 24f., 57, 76, 87, 104f., 130, 156f., 174ff., 182, 192ff.

methodology, 1ff., 15, 27, 39, 46ff., 104, 155, 176, 179ff.
  subject matter, 1f., 45f., 179ff., 187ff.
patriarchs, 13, 92ff.
peace, 14f.
Pentateuch, 14, 16f., 28, 30f., 33f., 44, 110ff., 113f., 123, 130, 149, 152ff.
phenomenology, 20
priesthood, 20f., 40f., 43, 55, 106f., 111f.
progress, 37ff., 46
promise, 14, 24, 34, 37, 106, 120f., 131ff.
prophecy, 11f., 14, 16ff., 28ff., 35, 43, 48, 51, 59, 75, 105, 111f., 114ff., 120ff., 131ff., 165, 167, 173f., 185
providence, 34f.
Psalms, 26f., 31f., 43, 48, 68, 71, 121, 149ff., 153, 159
Qumran, 134f., 146, 148, 150f.
remnant, 135, 142ff., 151
revelation, 21, 38, 41, 43, 53, 148
righteousness, 60, 168
sacrifice, 20f., 33, 40, 44f., 112, 161
salvation, 14f., 119, 126, 131ff., 139ff., 147f.
Shekinah, 70
sin, 34, 197
Sinai, 14, 34, 37, 41, 82f., 98, 103
Solomon, 33, 68, 84, 91
Son of God, 5, 49
spirit, 42, 44, 58, 69f., 200
symbolism, 23, 31, 40, 45, 48f., 67ff., 76, 92, 96, 148, 160, 166, 190
syncretism, 54, 161ff.
tabernacle, 68
Talmud, 22, 105
temple, 20, 40, 42, 68ff., 91ff., 113, 130, 142, 146, 161f., 164, 166, 173

Ten Commandments, 54f., 101, 119f., 123f., 130, 165f., 177, 198

theophany, 71

tradition, 14f., 26, 29

truth, 60

unity of Bible, 2f., 8ff., 12, 19ff., 21ff., 104ff., 130

universalism, 23, 38, 42, 47, 54, 57, 64, 76ff., 82, 89, 95f., 118, 129

wisdom, 70

# INDEX OF AUTHORS

Abelson, J., 202
Albright, W. F., 202, 206
Anderson, B. W., 201, 206
Andrew, M. E., 206
Barth, H., 205
Bauer, G. L., 7, 10, 201
Baumgartner, A. J., 206
Beegle, D. M., 206
Begrich, J., 98, 203
Bentzen, A., 205
Bergren, R. V., 204
Bornkamm, H., 206
Bright, J., 204, 206
Bruce, F. F., 201, 205f.
Brueggemann, W., 203
Bucellati, G., 203
Buis, P., 203
Bultmann, R., 205
Cassirer, E., 202
Causse, A., 206
Childs, B. S., 201
Clements, R. E., 203ff.
Cross, F. M., 202, 206
Davies, W. D., 203
De Geus, C. H. J., 203
Dentan, R. C., 202
Diestel, L., 206
Duhm, B., 29, 201
Eichhorn, J. G., 5
Eichrodt, W., 118, 201, 204
Frankfort, H., 206
Gabler, J. P., 5, 7
Geiger, A., 206
Gottwald, N. K., 206

Grelot, P., 204f.
Halbe, J., 204
Hanson, A. T., 201
Hanson, P. D., 205
Hasel, G. F., 201
Hengel, M., 201
Henn, T. R., 206
Herder, J. G., 205
Herrmann, S., 202
Hesse, F., 206
Hillers, D. R., 203
Hooke, S. H., 205
Hornig, G., 201
Hyatt, J. P., 202
Jacob, E., 2, 201
Janes, F., 201
Jenni, E., 202
Jeremias, A., 205
Jeremias, J., 203
Jones, O. R., 202
Kirk, G. S., 202
Kittel, R., 201
Knight, D. A., 201
Koch, K., 201
Kraus, H. J., 201f., 206
Kutsch, E., 99, 203f.
Labuschagne, C. J., 203
Laurin, R. B., 201
Lévy-Bruhl, L., 47f., 202
Lohfink, N., 202
Longenecker, R., 201
Martin-Achard, R., 203
Maybaum, I., 206
Mayes, A. D. H., 203
McCarthy, D. J., 203

Mendenhall, G. E., 99, 204
Mettinger, T. N. D., 205
Montefiore, C. G., 206
Neusner, J., 204
Noth, M., 203
Osswald, E., 206
Östborn, G., 204
Parke-Taylor, G. H., 202
Pedersen, J., 48f., 202
Perlitt, L., 203
Philo, 204
Rad, G. von, 104f., 141, 201f.
Rendtorff, R., 204
Ringgren, H., 206
Rogerson, J. W., 202
Rost, L., 202
Rowley, H. H., 67, 202f., 205
Sanders, J. A., 201, 204
Semler, J. S., 5, 13f., 201
Smith, G., 205
Smith, H. P., 206
Snaith, N. H., 202
Spriggs, D. G., 201
Stamm, J. J., 206
Vaux, R. de, 206
Vermes, G., 205
Weingreen, J., 204
Weiser, A., 202
Westermann, C., 202
Williamson, H. G. M., 203
Wingren, G., 206
Zimmerli, W., 204, 206

## OLD TESTAMENT

**GENESIS**
| | |
|---|---|
| 1–11 | 50, 77 |
| 1.1–2.4a | 76 |
| 2.4b–3.24 | 76 |
| 3.8 | 58 |
| 3.9 | 34 |
| 3.24 | 68 |
| 4.26 | 63 |
| 6.1–4 | 49 |
| 6.3 | 35 |
| 6.5 | 34 |
| 9.1–7 | 170 |
| 11.1–9 | 50 |
| 12–50 | 88 |
| 12.1–3 | 13, 34, 88, 92, 152 |
| 12.2 | 95 |
| 14.17–24 | 33 |
| 14.18 | 64 |
| 15.1–6 | 13 |
| 15.18 | 98, 101 |
| 15.18–21 | 93 |
| 17.1 | 64 |
| 18.2ff. | 34 |
| 19.1 | 34 |
| 19.1–29 | 34 |
| 22.1–14 | 33 |
| 22.14 | 64 |
| 22.15–19 | 34 |
| 28.11–19 | 33, 67 |
| 28.12 | 34 |
| 28.20–2 | 67 |
| 32.24 | 35 |
| 32.28 | 35 |
| 35.22–6 | 79 |

**EXODUS**
| | |
|---|---|
| 1.7–8 | 83 |
| 3.13 | 64 |
| 3.14 | 62 |
| 3.16 | 64 |
| 4.22–3 | 96 |
| 7.11 | 66 |
| 7.22 | 66 |
| 8.7 | 66 |
| 15.8 | 58 |
| 19–40 | 34, 41 |
| 19.4 | 60 |
| 19.5 | 98 |
| 19.5–6 | 82, 98, 101 |
| 19.18 | 58 |
| 20.2–17 | 41, 72, 101, 119, 177 |
| 20.22–23.19 | 97, 115, 127 |
| 22.21 | 56 |
| 23.14 | 40 |
| 23.15 | 40 |
| 23.19 | 40 |

| | |
|---|---|
| 24.15 | 69 |
| 24.18 | 69 |
| 26.1–37 | 68 |
| 28.1–43 | 172 |
| 29.42 | 71 |
| 30.6 | 71 |
| 33.7–11 | 68 |
| 33.20 | 34 |
| 34.1–28 | 120 |
| 34.6, 7 | 61 |
| 34.23 | 40 |
| 34.29–35 | 34 |
| 40.34 | 69 |
| 40.34–8 | 44 |

**LEVITICUS**
| | |
|---|---|
| 1–7 | 40 |
| 16.2 | 71 |

**NUMBERS**
| | |
|---|---|
| 10.35 | 68 |
| 12.6–8 | 173 |
| 16.1–50 | 172 |
| 23.19 | 58 |
| 25.1–13 | 167 |
| 25.1–17 | 65 |

**DEUTERONOMY**
| | |
|---|---|
| 4.6 | 129 |
| 4.13 | 101 |
| 4.13–14 | 101 |
| 4.15–18 | 75 |
| 4.16–18 | 60 |
| 4.25–6 | 93 |
| 4.25–8 | 89 |
| 4.32 | 58 |
| 4.36 | 58 |
| 4.44 | 101 |
| 4.44ff. | 101 |
| 4.45–6 | 107f. |
| 5.1–21 | 97 |
| 5.6–21 | 101, 119 |
| 5.16 | 94 |
| 6.5 | 109 |
| 6.7 | 108 |
| 6.21–3 | 33 |
| 7.6–8 | 88 |
| 8.10 | 93 |
| 8.11ff. | 94 |
| 9.4–5 | 109, 168 |
| 9.6 | 93 |
| 10.1–3 | 68 |
| 11.12 | 58 |
| 11.16–17 | 128 |
| 11.18 | 108 |
| 11.19 | 108 |
| 11.26–32 | 94 |
| 12ff. | 128 |
| 12–26 | 101 |
| 12.1–14 | 112 |

| | |
|---|---|
| 12.2–14 | 172 |
| 12.5 | 44 |
| 12.5ff. | 68 |
| 13.1–5 | 111, 173 |
| 13.8–11 | 109 |
| 15.7–11 | 108 |
| 15.15 | 56 |
| 16.1–17 | 108 |
| 16.3 | 71 |
| 17.18–20 | 111, 172 |
| 18.15 | 173 |
| 18.15–22 | 111 |
| 18.18 | 111 |
| 18.20–2 | 173 |
| 19.14–21 | 108 |
| 20.1–20 | 109 |
| 21.10–17 | 109 |
| 22.6–7 | 109 |
| 23.12–14 | 109 |
| 26.5 | 83 |
| 26.5b–9 | 33 |
| 26.5–11 | 94 |
| 26.10 | 94 |
| 28.15–68 | 94, 128 |
| 31.24–9 | 111 |
| 32.8–9 | 73 |

**JOSHUA**
| | |
|---|---|
| 1.7–8 | 122 |
| 7.10–21 | 168 |
| 24.2–13 | 33 |

**JUDGES**
| | |
|---|---|
| 11.24 | 73 |
| 17–18 | 167 |
| 18.30 | 167 |

**1 SAMUEL**
| | |
|---|---|
| 8–12 | 89 |
| 8.7 | 91 |
| 8.11–18 | 90 |
| 8.21 | 58 |
| 12.14 | 90 |
| 12.15 | 89, 91 |
| 12.17 | 91 |
| 12.25 | 89, 91 |
| 21.1–6 | 105 |

**2 SAMUEL**
| | |
|---|---|
| 2.10 | 64 |
| 5.20 | 64 |
| 6.1–15 | 91 |
| 7.1–17 | 173 |
| 7.13 | 145, 173 |
| 7.18–19 | 89 |
| 8.1–15 | 93 |
| 8.18 | 172 |
| 9.6ff. | 64 |
| 12.1–15 | 173 |

| | |
|---|---|
| 12.1–23 | 197 |
| 18.31–3 | 198 |
| 23.5 | 90, 101, 198 |
| 24.1ff. | 173 |
| 24.2 | 93 |

**1 KINGS**
| | |
|---|---|
| 2.3 | 122 |
| 2.26–7 | 172 |
| 5.1–12 | 160 |
| 6.1–38 | 68, 91, 172 |
| 6.19 | 91 |
| 7.13–14 | 160 |
| 7.15–51 | 91 |
| 8.22–53 | 69 |
| 8.27 | 44 |
| 8.27–53 | 161 |
| 11.7–13 | 90 |
| 11.11 | 122 |
| 11.32 | 90 |
| 12.26–33 | 90 |
| 12.28 | 166 |
| 15.11–15 | 172 |
| 15.12–13 | 166 |
| 21.1–24 | 173, 197 |
| 22.52–3 | 172 |

**2 KINGS**
| | |
|---|---|
| 9.1–37 | 35 |
| 10.18–31 | 172 |
| 12.4–16 | 172 |
| 17.9–12 | 167 |
| 17.13–18 | 125ff. |
| 17.15 | 101 |
| 17.16f. | 59 |
| 18.4 | 167 |
| 18.41 | 166 |
| 19.34 | 90 |
| 21.3–5 | 167 |
| 22–3 | 97f., 110, 122 |
| 22.3ff. | 112 |
| 22.9 | 112 |
| 22.11–23.27 | 172 |
| 22.14–20 | 112 |
| 23.4–14 | 167 |
| 23.9 | 112 |
| 25.9 | 91 |
| 25.13–17 | 91 |

**1 CHRONICLES**
| | |
|---|---|
| 3.16–24 | 146 |

**EZRA**
| | |
|---|---|
| 3.8–13 | 91 |
| 4.2–3 | 168 |
| 6.13–22 | 91 |

**NEHEMIAH**
| | |
|---|---|
| 13.23–7 | 168 |

**PSALMS**
| | |
|---|---|
| 1 | 128 |
| 2.1–2 | 149 |
| 2.4 | 58 |
| 2.7 | 90 |
| 5.4–5 | 61 |
| 7.11 | 60 |
| 7.19 | 60 |
| 9.4 | 60 |
| 9.11 | 40 |
| 11.4 | 60 |
| 11.7 | 60 |
| 14.7 | 40 |
| 15 | 61 |
| 18.6 | 40 |
| 18.10–11 | 50 |
| 19.7–14 | 128 |
| 19.12–13 | 128 |
| 24.4–6 | 61 |
| 25.5 | 60 |
| 25.10 | 60 |
| 33.5 | 60 |
| 36.6 | 60 |
| 44.21 | 60 |
| 46 | 196 |
| 48 | 196 |
| 64.1–9 | 60 |
| 72.8–11 | 95 |
| 72.17 | 95 |
| 76 | 196 |
| 82.6 | 104 |
| 84.5–7 | 91 |
| 87.1–3 | 91 |
| 92.12–15 | 92 |
| 96.13 | 71 |
| 104.2 | 58 |
| 110.4 | 90 |
| 118 | 149 |
| 119 | 128 |
| 132.12 | 90 |
| 132.13–14 | 91 |
| 139.7 | 70f. |
| 139.7–12 | 200 |

**PROVERBS**
| | |
|---|---|
| 3.1 | 106 |
| 4.2 | 106 |

**ISAIAH**
| | |
|---|---|
| 2.2–4 | 95, 139, 146, 196 |
| 2.3 | 106 |
| 2.3–4 | 92 |
| 3.1–5 | 138 |
| 5.5–6 | 138 |
| 7.3 | 135 |
| 7.14 | 11f. |
| 8.8–10 | 12 |
| 8.16 | 106 |
| 9.2–7 | 141, 145 |
| 10.5 | 167 |
| 10.5ff. | 75 |
| 10.20–3 | 135 |
| 11.1–9 | 139, 141, 165, 197 |
| 11.11 | 135 |
| 11.16 | 135 |
| 13–23 | 77 |
| 14.1–2 | 139 |
| 28.14–18 | 138 |
| 28.18 | 165 |
| 29.1–4 | 138 |
| 30.1–5 | 165 |
| 32.1 | 145 |
| 32.1–8 | 139, 141 |
| 33.1–24 | 145 |
| 33.17 | 145 |
| 35.1–10 | 145 |
| 37.23 | 167 |
| 40–55 | 66, 73, 95, 133, 140, 167 |
| 40.1–5 | 143 |
| 40.9 | 92 |
| 40.12–14 | 66 |
| 40.14 | 144 |
| 40.18 | 73 |
| 40.18–20 | 66, 75, 167 |
| 40.25 | 73 |
| 40.28 | 77 |
| 41.2–4 | 75 |
| 41.7 | 167 |
| 41.21–4 | 66, 73 |
| 42.1–4 | 95 |
| 42.5 | 77 |
| 42.14 | 58 |
| 43.1–7 | 143 |
| 43.11 | 73 |
| 43.14–21 | 143 |
| 44.6–8 | 73 |
| 44.9–20 | 75, 167 |
| 45.1–5 | 75 |
| 45.14–17 | 95, 203 |
| 45.18 | 77 |
| 45.22 | 77 |
| 49.1–6 | 95 |
| 49.6 | 95, 145 |
| 49.7 | 95 |
| 50.4–9 | 95 |
| 51.3 | 92 |
| 52.1 | 168 |
| 52.11 | 168 |
| 52.13–53.12 | 95 |
| 55.3 | 90 |
| 60.1–9 | 95 |
| 60.1–14 | 92 |
| 60.1–22 | 143, 145 |
| 60.14 | 146 |
| 61.1–7 | 143 |
| 61.5 | 146 |
| 61.5–7 | 95 |
| 62.1–12 | 91 |
| 65.17–25 | 94 |
| 66.12–16 | 143 |

**JEREMIAH**
| | |
|---|---|
| 2.1–3 | 60 |
| 2.2–3 | 96 |
| 2.27 | 76 |
| 3.17 | 91 |
| 6.13–15 | 173 |
| 11.1–8 | 98 |
| 11.6 | 102 |
| 11.8 | 102 |
| 18.18 | 106 |
| 24.1–10 | 94, 143, 144 |
| 28.1–17 | 173 |
| 29.10–14 | 94, 143f. |
| 31.2–9 | 102 |
| 31.7–9 | 145 |
| 31.20 | 60, 96, 102 |
| 31.31–4 | 103 |
| 31.33 | 103 |
| 32.1–15 | 102 |
| 32.15 | 102, 142 |
| 32.36–44 | 143 |
| 33.14–26 | 90 |
| 33.19 | 90 |
| 33.19–26 | 145 |
| 33.22 | 90 |
| 36.8–15 | 143 |
| 37.15–23 | 143 |
| 37.40–8 | 143 |
| 46–52 | 77 |

**LAMENTATIONS**
| | |
|---|---|
| 4.20 | 90 |

**EZEKIEL**
| | |
|---|---|
| 1.27 | 58 |
| 1.28 | 58 |
| 16.15ff. | 59 |
| 16.17 | 59 |
| 20.7 | 76 |
| 20.8 | 169 |
| 20.18 | 76 |
| 20.24 | 169 |
| 20.32 | 169 |
| 25–32 | 77 |
| 33.23–9 | 94 |
| 36.8–15 | 144f. |
| 36.26–7 | 103 |
| 37.15–23 | 145 |
| 37.22 | 87 |
| 37.24–5 | 90 |
| 37.24–8 | 145 |
| 40–48 | 94 |
| 47.7–12 | 92 |
| 48.35 | 146 |

**DANIEL**
| | |
|---|---|
| 3.1–30 | 169 |
| 9.2 | 148 |
| 11.36–9 | 169 |

**HOSEA**
| | |
|---|---|
| 1.4–5 | 35, 137 |
| 1.7 | 137 |
| 2.2 | 60 |
| 2.5 | 141, 145 |
| 4.11–14 | 138 |
| 4.13–14 | 65 |
| 4.15 | 137 |
| 4.17–19 | 138 |
| 6.8–10 | 138 |
| 6.11 | 137 |
| 11.1–9 | 60, 96 |
| 11.12 | 137 |
| 12.13 | 173 |

**JOEL**
| | |
|---|---|
| 3.9–17 | 145 |

**AMOS**
| | |
|---|---|
| 1–2 | 77 |
| 1.2 | 137 |
| 2.1 | 61 |
| 2.4–5 | 137 |
| 2.6–8 | 137 |
| 3.1 | 137 |
| 5.2 | 137 |
| 5.10–12 | 137 |
| 6.4 | 137 |
| 7.9 | 137 |
| 8.2 | 137 |
| 9.11–12 | 140f., 145 |
| 9.13–15 | 141 |

**MICAH**
| | |
|---|---|
| 3.5–8 | 173 |
| 4.1–5 | 95, 146, 196 |
| 5.3 | 12 |
| 6.6–8 | 78 |

**HAGGAI**
| | |
|---|---|
| 2.4–5 | 70 |
| 2.5 | 58 |
| 2.23 | 146 |

**ZECHARIAH**
| | |
|---|---|
| 4.6 | 58, 70 |
| 14.16–21 | 92 |

**MALACHI**
| | |
|---|---|
| 3.1 | 146 |

**ECCLESIASTICUS**
| | |
|---|---|
| 24.8–12 | 129 |
| 49.10 | 134 |

## NEW TESTAMENT

| MATTHEW | | JOHN | | ROMANS | | HEBREWS | |
|---|---|---|---|---|---|---|---|
| 1.23 | 11f. | 4.20 | 41f. | 4.13 | 152 | 4.14 | 177 |
| 5.17–48 | 177 | 4.24 | 42 | 9.6–8 | 80 | 5.10 | 177 |
| 11.13 | 18 | 10.34 | 104 | 9.27 | 135 | 7.1–28 | 177 |
| 19.18 | 130 | | | 11.5 | 38, 135 | | |
| | | | | | | 1 PETER | |
| MARK | | ACTS | | GALATIANS | | 1.10–12 | 131 |
| 2.23–8 | 18 | 2.25–8 | 18 | 6.15 | 57 | | |
| 2.25–6 | 105 | 3.24 | 131 | | | | |
| 7.14–23 | 168 | 4.11 | 149 | COLOSSIANS | | REVELATION | |
| 14.58 | 166 | 4.25–6 | 149 | 3.5 | 65 | 12.2 | 92 |
| | | 7.47–50 | 161 | | | | |
| LUKE | | 7.48 | 166 | | | | |
| 1.30–2 | 86 | 7.51–3 | 38 | | | | |
| 10.25–8 | 177 | 17.24 | 166 | | | | |